WOMEN AND TRADE

THE ROLE OF TRADE IN PROMOTING GENDER *EQUALITY*

1818 H Street NW, Washington, DC 20433
Telephone: 202-473-1000; Internet: www.worldbank.org

1 2 3 4 23 22 21 20

ISBN (paper): 978-1-4648-1541-6
ISBN (electronic): 978-1-4648-1556-0
DOI: 10.1596/978-1-4648-1541-6

Cover art: © Nadezda Grapes. Used with the permission of Nadezda Grapes; further permission required for reuse.
Cover and interior design: Rizoma, Bogotá, Colombia.

The Library of Congress Control Number has been requested.

Contents

Boxes

Figures

Maps

Tables

Foreword

Trade has improved the living standards of billions of individuals, many of whom are women. Ample empirical evidence shows that trade has led to higher productivity, greater competition, lower prices, higher incomes, and improved welfare. As the COVID-19 pandemic has revealed, however, trade can be seriously disrupted. There is a risk that some of the economic gains women have reaped through trade could be reversed by the COVID-19 crisis. Cooperation is therefore essential to preserve the conditions for a fast recovery and to create those for more inclusive and sustainable trade in the future.

Women and Trade aims to shed light on an area of trade policy that has received relatively little attention—trade and its impact on women as workers, consumers, and family members. On its surface, trade policy is gender-neutral. No country imposes tariffs or nontariff measures by gender. But a closer look at the gender dimension of trade policies reveals important differences in how trade policies affect women and men—and even in how those policies affect different groups of women.

Although the research in this report was conducted prior to the global pandemic, the report's conclusions are more relevant than ever. In the garment sector, for example, lockdown measures have led to a large number of order cancellations and many factory shutdowns in Bangladesh, Cambodia, and Vietnam. Women hold a disproportionate number of jobs in the clothing sector and make most clothing purchases as family members. But tariffs on garments remain stubbornly high compared to tariffs on other manufactured goods. This disparity amounts to a "pink tariff"—hurting women consumers across the world and keeping women workers in developing countries from broader export opportunities and better jobs.

One challenge in analyzing the links between trade and gender is the lack of relevant sex-disaggregated data. This report offers a starting point for research into how trade affects gender by establishing—for the first time—a unique dataset that disaggregates labor data by gender at the industry level for a large number of countries. The resulting analysis shows the promise that trade holds for women.

Businesses involved in international trade employ more women. In developing countries, women make up 33 percent of the workforce in firms that engage in trade, compared with just 24 percent in nonexporting firms. Trade also creates better jobs for women. Workers in both developed and emerging economies are almost 50 percent more likely to be employed in formal jobs if they work in sectors that trade more or that are more integrated into global value chains. Countries that are more open to trade, as measured by the ratio of trade to gross domestic product, have higher levels of gender equality.

Gaining a better understanding of how women are affected by trade will be essential as countries develop and the global economy recovers from the pandemic. This report points to several trends that women can take advantage of—the rise in services, the spread of global value chains, and the expansion of the digital economy. In all three of these areas, women have the opportunity to increase their share of the labor force, increase their own skills and wages, and find ways to achieve better work-life balance.

Countries that harness these opportunities will be rewarded with an expanded, more highly skilled workforce that can increase productivity and incomes. To maximize the benefits for women, however, trade policies should be evaluated to account for their different impacts on women—and to eliminate "pink tariffs" and other implicit biases. Opening up to trade in key sectors, such as services, can further create powerful opportunities for women to reap the benefits of trade. Even simple interventions to facilitate trade can make a big impact for small-scale traders. Investments in lighting and border security, for example, have been found to dramatically lower harassment against women in Sub-Saharan Africa.

The report also shows that women have an important opportunity to move into higher-skill work through trade. But these opportunities depend on putting in place complementary policies that increase investment in human capital, particularly in the areas of education and health. Such investments, which have become even more relevant in the post-COVID-19 recovery, would enable women to participate fully in the economy and reap the benefits of digital technologies. Complementary policies should include improved access to finance, including trade finance, and the elimination of legal barriers that women still face in many countries.

Trade alone is not a panacea to close the gender gap. But this report reveals the opportunities that can be seized by making trade more inclusive. It highlights how governments, international organizations, and the private sector can collectively—through complementary initiatives—create the conditions to ensure that women benefit from trade instead of being left behind.

Mari E. Pangestu
Managing Director
World Bank

Roberto Azevêdo
Director-General
World Trade Organization

Acknowledgments

Women and Trade: The Role of Trade in Promoting Gender Equality is a joint report by the World Bank and the World Trade Organization (WTO). Maria Liungman and Nadia Rocha from the World Bank and José-Antonio Monteiro and Roberta Piermartini from the WTO coordinated the report. The team is grateful for the guidance and support of our World Bank colleagues—Caroline Freund, Global Director, Trade, Investment and Competitiveness; William Maloney, Chief Economist for Equitable Growth, Finance and Institutions; the World Bank gender group under the leadership of Caren Grown, Global Director Gender; and Antonio Nucifora, Practice Manager Trade and Regional Integration Unit—and our WTO colleagues Aegyoung Jung, Chief Legal Advisor to the Director-General; and Robert Koopman, Chief Economist and Director of the Economic Research and Statistics Division.

The lead authors of the report are Erik Churchill and Deborah Winkler from the World Bank and José-Antonio Monteiro and Victor Stolzenburg from the WTO. Other authors of the report include Julia Braunmiller, Paul Brenton, Alvaro Espitia, Michael Ferrantino, Tazeen Hasan, Claire Hollweg, and Pierre Sauvé from the World Bank; and Marc Auboin, Marc Bacchetta, Anoush der Boghossian, Lee-Ann Jackson, Gabrielle Marceau, Stela Rubinova, and Ankai Xu from the WTO.

Valuable research support and background papers were provided by colleagues internal and external to the World Bank and the WTO: Erhan Artuc, Penny Bamber, Floriana Borino, Vicky Chemutai, Christina Constantinescu, Erwin Corong, Vivian Couto, Nicolas Depetris-Chauvin, Karina Fernandez-Stark, Isis Gaddis, Anusha Goyal, Danny Hamrick, Justine Lan, Eunhee Lee, Kevin Lefebre, Maryla Maliszewska, Maria Masood, Ermira Mehmetaj, Dominique van der Mensbrugghe, Enrico Nano, Anne Ong Lopez, Israel Osorio-Rodart, Guido Porto, Bob Rijkers, Samidh Shrestha, Marie Sicat, Andrew Silva, Carmine Soprano, Louise Twinning Ward, Miguel Uribe, and Huanjun Zhang.

All background papers, data, and blogs have been posted on the World Bank website, available at https://www.worldbank.org/en/topic/trade/brief/trade-and-gender.

The coordinators thank the following colleagues, internal and external to the World Bank and WTO, for useful comments and guidance during various stages of preparation of the report: Kathleen Beegle, Bénédicte de la Brière, Antonia Carzaniga, Aileen Duong Yang, Ana Margarida Fernandez, Marzia Fontana, William Gain, Ejaz Ghani, June Ghimire, Noa Gimelli, Marcus Goldstein, Caren Grown, Lee-Ann Jackson, Kare Johard, Gabrielle Marceau, Guido Porto, Michele Ruta, Heidi Stensland, and Kilara Suit.

Publication production of the report was led by Stephen Pazdan and Patricia Katayama (World Bank) and Anthony Martin (WTO). Mayya Revzina (World Bank) provided support on rights during the publication process. The team is grateful to Stuart Grudgings and Nora Mara (World Bank) for their editorial services. The graphic concept, design, and layout were carried out by Maria Andrea Santos at Rizoma. Joseph Rebello, Erin Scronce, and Torie Smith (World Bank) offered guidance, services, and support on communication and dissemination.

The World Bank team gratefully acknowledges the financial support from the Umbrella Facility for Trade (UF), the Department for International Development of the United Kingdom (DFID), the State Secretariat for Economic Affairs of Switzerland (SECO), the Ministry of Foreign Affairs of Norway, the Ministry of Foreign Affairs of the Netherlands, and the Swedish International Development Cooperation Agency (Sida).

Abbreviations

AfCTA	African Continental Free Trade Area
AGOA	African Growth Opportunity Act
EAC	East African Community
FDI	foreign direct investment
GATT	General Agreement on Tariffs and Trade
GDP	gross domestic product
GSP	Generalized System of Preferences
GVC	global value chain
ICT	information and communications technology
IT	information technology
ITC	International Trade Centre
LDC	least-developed country
MFN	most favored nation
MOOC	massive open online course
MSMEs	micro, small, and medium enterprises
NAFTA	North American Free Trade Agreement
NTM	nontariff measure
OECD	Organisation for Economic Co-operation and Development
PTA	preferential trade agreement
SMEs	small and medium enterprises
STEM	science, technology, engineering, and math
TFA	Trade Facilitation Agreement
TPR	Trade Policy Review
VAT	value added tax
WTO	World Trade Organization

OVERVIEW

The goal of this report is to improve the understanding of the impacts of trade and trade policy on gender equality, and to provide policy makers with evidence on the benefits of trade for women and with potential policy solutions. The report uses a conceptual framework that illustrates the diverse transmission channels through which trade and trade policy can affect women, according to three key economic roles they play: workers, consumers, and decision makers. The report also gathers and analyzes new data[1] to show how trade and trade policy can affect women and men differently—in wages, consumption, and welfare, and in the quality and quantity of jobs available to them. New empirical analysis based on these data suggests that expanding trade can act as an impetus for countries to improve women's rights and boost female participation in the economy.

The report comes amid the COVID-19 pandemic that has laid bare the economic opportunities and challenges women face, some of which are driven by trade. For example, trade in goods and services, especially online, has helped women to mitigate the negative impact of the crisis. At the same time, women's specialization in the manufacture of apparel and the provision of touristic services has left them more vulnerable to the trade shock of this crisis (box O.1). Overall, because some trade links have already broken and near-term trade growth remains weak, women are in danger of losing a sizable share of the economic gains they have reaped as a result of trade.

Box O.1 Early evidence on the impact of COVID-19 on trade and women

The COVID-19 pandemic poses serious health and economic challenges for all countries. Early evidence suggests that the pandemic is likely to hit women more than previous economic downturns have, especially in low-income countries (WTO 2020). Trade is one channel through which women experience this effect because of the sectors in which they work.

For example, women account for 60 to 80 percent of the workforce in the global value chain (GVC) for apparel, which has been severely affected by the pandemic. The large volume of order cancellations and the temporary closure of retail shops have buffeted the global garment industry, resulting in factory shutdowns in Bangladesh, Cambodia, Vietnam, and other countries (Devnath 2020). The entire global supply chain is experiencing job losses, from those picking fibers used to make textiles to those selling the finished fashion product in a physical shop or online (BoF and McKinsey & Company 2020). Given that seasonal factors drive a large amount of clothing spending, a significant share of the revenues will be permanently lost as a result of the lockdown (Dennis 2020).

Sectors such as tourism and hospitality—in which women are particularly active as employers or employees—have been hit hard by international travel and trade restrictions imposed by countries to contain the pandemic. These sectors are also expected to experience a relatively slow recovery because of lower consumer confidence and the likelihood of longer restrictions on international movement of people (UNWTO 2020). Other sectors, including food services and handicrafts, that depend on tourism and employ a large share of women have also been hurt.

The lockdown and social distancing measures have led some companies to adopt or increase teleworking in order to ensure continuity of their activities. A large number of women, however, simply cannot telework, especially women working in sectors like light manufacturing or retail that require face-to-face interactions (Adams-Prassl et al. 2020). Much lower information technology literacy rates and a much higher burden of childcare, because of school closure, also prevent women from telecommuting. In addition, lower financial resources put the survival of women-owned businesses at greater risk.

As this report demonstrates, women are often more economically vulnerable than men and thus are less likely to be resilient in the face of the crisis. As economies emerge out of the crisis, it is important that governments generate long-term gender-inclusive growth by addressing the constraints that women face. Although most of this report was prepared prior to the onset of the COVID-19 pandemic, policy makers can draw on the report's lessons to find ways that trade can continue to benefit women.

Trade improves the lives of *women*

In an integrated world, the competitive pressure generated by trade raises the cost of discrimination against women. Countries that do not allow women to fully participate in the economy are less competitive internationally—particularly those countries with export industries that globally have high female employment rates (World Bank 2011).

The novel analysis produced for this report confirms that trade can substantially improve economic outcomes for women, by increasing employment and wages, creating better jobs, and lowering costs. But the positive effects of trade will materialize only if the barriers that hold women back are lifted and appropriate policies to deal with adjustment costs are put in place. Highlights from the analysis include the following:

- Firms that engage in international trade employ more women. In developing countries women make up 33.2 percent of the workforce of firms that trade internationally, compared with just 24.3 percent of nonexporting firms and 28.1 percent for nonimporting firms (figure O.1). Women are also better represented in firms that are part of global value chains (GVCs), and that are foreign owned. Women constitute 36.7 percent of the workforce of GVC firms and 37.8 percent of the workforce of foreign-owned firms—10.9 and 12.2 percentage points more, respectively, than the proportion for non-GVC and domestically owned firms. In countries such as Morocco, Romania, and Vietnam, women represent 50 percent or more of the workforce of exporting firms—which have created jobs for more than 5 million women, roughly 15 percent of the female population working in these countries.

Credit: © Frame China/ Shutterstock.com. Used with permission; further permission required for reuse.

Figure O.1 Average female labor share is higher for manufacturing firms integrated into global trade

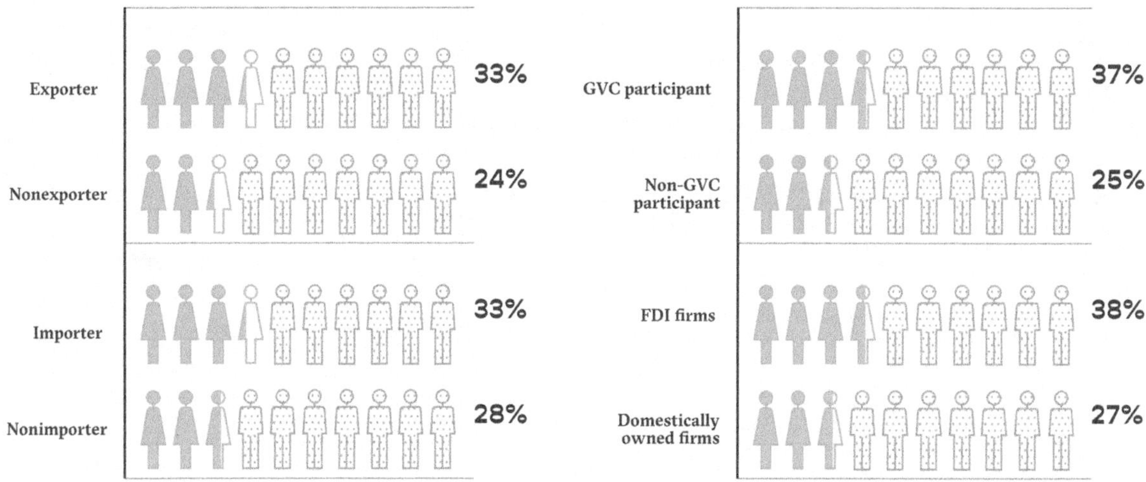

Source: Rocha and Winkler 2019, based on World Bank Enterprise Surveys.
Note: The graph shows weighted averages by firm type, using the number of permanent workers as weights. Exporters are firms with an export share (direct or indirect) of at least 10 percent of total sales. Importers are firms with an imported input share of at least 10 percent of total inputs. GVC (global value chain) participants are firms that are classified as both exporters and importers. FDI (foreign direct investment) refers to firms with a foreign ownership share of at least 10 percent.

- Trade increases women's wages and increases economic equality. Globally, women take home a smaller share of wages. When developing countries double their manufacturing exports—typical for developing countries that open themselves to trade—women's share of total manufacturing wages rises by 5.8 percentage points on average, through a combination of increased employment and higher salaries. In Africa, freer trade could help close the wage gap, especially for skilled women workers. Analysis on the implementation of the African Continental Free Trade Area (AfCFTA) suggests that, by 2035, wages for skilled and unskilled female labor would be 4.0 percent and 3.7 percent higher (relative to baseline), respectively, compared with a 3.2 percent increase for all males (World Bank, forthcoming). That increase translates roughly to an extra two weeks' pay each year—enough for a woman earning US$5 a day to pay for one family member's personal supplies, school supplies, and uniform for an entire school year.

- Trade creates better jobs for women. In both developing and emerging economies, workers in sectors with high levels of exports are more likely to be employed formally—giving them opportunities for benefits, training, and job security. For women, the probability of being informal goes from 20 percent in sectors with low levels of exports to 13 percent in sectors with high levels of exports (figure O.2). Women's rates of informality also decline more sharply relative to men's (with an overall 7-percentage-point reduction for women compared to 4 percentage points for men).

Figure O.2 Women are less likely to be in informal jobs if they work in trade-integrated sectors

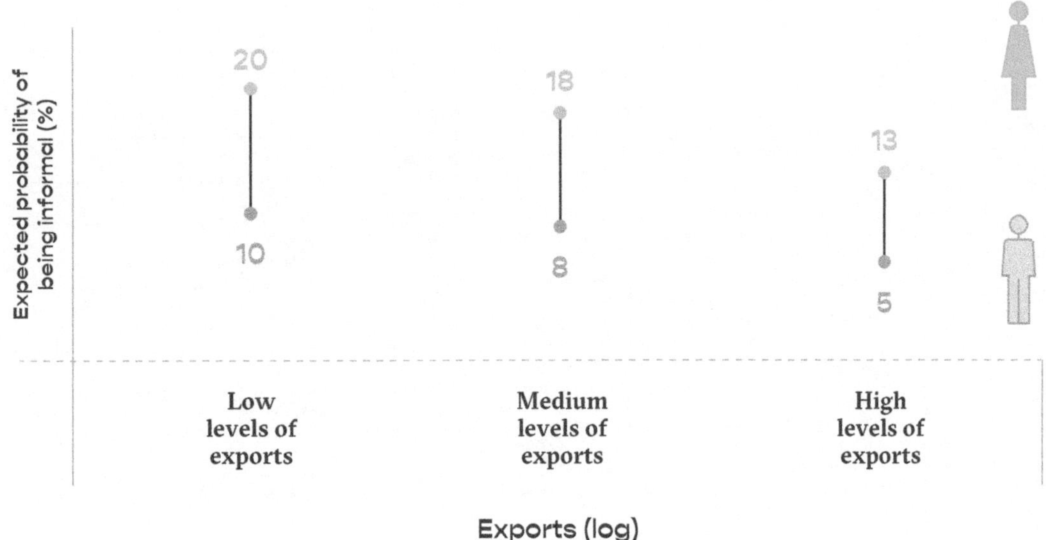

Source: World Bank Household surveys for the most recent available years, https://www.enterprisesurveys.org/en/data; World Bank Gender Disaggregated Labor Database (GDLD), http://datatopics.worldbank.org/gdld/.
Note: The graph shows the expected probability that a woman will have an informal job, defining informality as being a nonpaid worker. Low, medium, and high refer to the observations falling under the 25th percentile, between the 25th and 75th percentiles, and above the 75th percentile, respectively. See annex 1A (chapter 1 of this report).

· Trade openness can increase women's welfare. Evidence from the United States suggests that products specifically consumed by women face a higher tariff burden (Gailes et al. 2018). This higher burden is the result of higher applied tariffs and greater spending on imported goods by women consumers. In the textile sector, for instance, the tariff burden on women's apparel was US$2.77 billion higher than on men's clothing, and this gender gap grew about 11 percent in real terms between 2006 and 2016. As a result, tariff liberalization would lower the costs for women consumers and raise their welfare. A recent study for a sample of 54 developing countries suggests that eliminating import tariffs could result in a rise in real income for female-headed households relative to male-headed households in more than three-quarters of the countries considered. Compared with male-headed households, female-headed households tend to spend a larger share on agricultural goods (food), which are usually subject to higher tariffs, and to have a lower share of their income coming from wages. Other sources of income in female-headed households include income from the production of household services for own consumption (including meals, clean clothes, and childcare), social transfers in kind, and current transfers received (other than social transfers in kind). They could therefore gain up to 2.5 percent more real income than male-headed households through the removal of import tariffs (figure O.3). In countries such as Burkina Faso or Cameroon, eliminating trade policy bias would mean a gain for women equivalent to annual expenditure on education or health.

Figure O.3 The current tariff structure benefits male-headed households in 78 percent of countries assessed

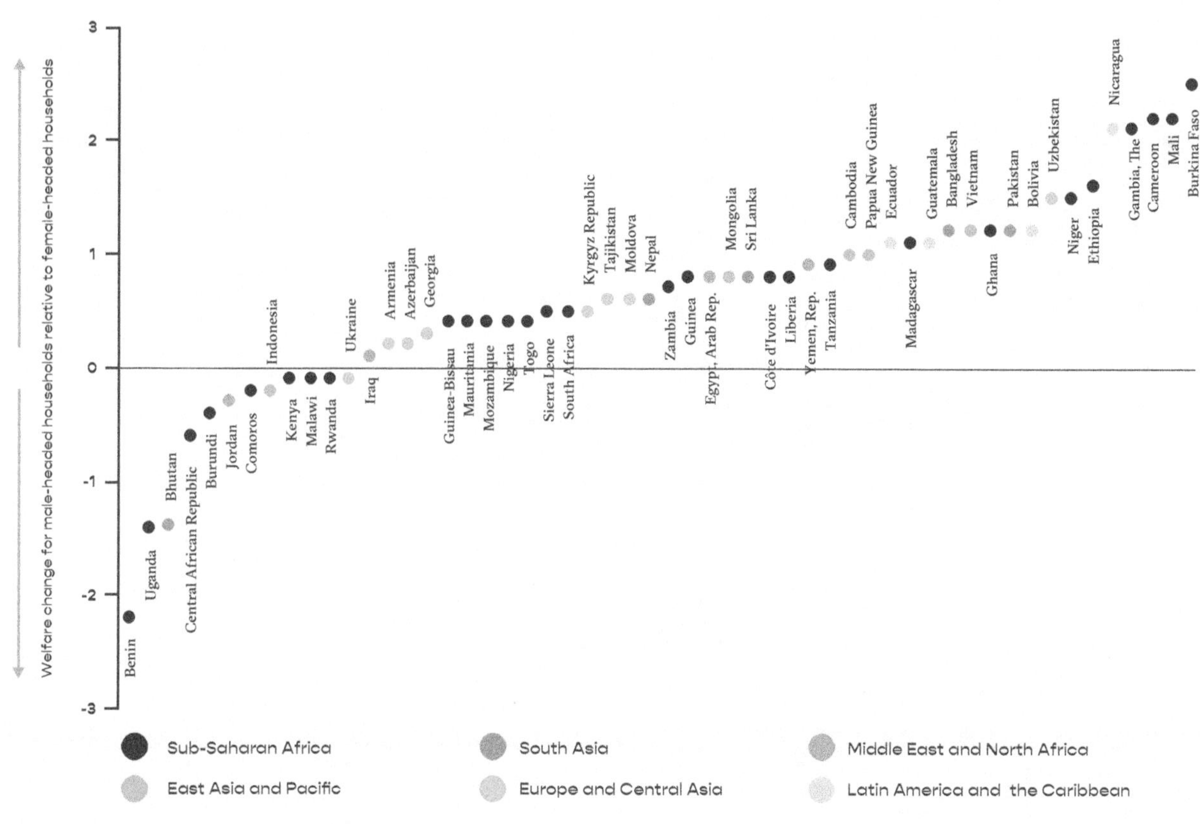

Source: Based on estimates by Depetris-Chauvin and Porto, forthcoming.
Note: The male-to-female gender bias is computed as the difference in the welfare gain, in terms of real income, from trade liberalization for female-headed households versus male-headed households. For each country, the index combines the structure of protection with the patterns of expenditure shares and income shares. World Bank country naming conventions used.

The changing nature of trade creates new opportunities for *women*

Empirically, countries that are more open to trade, as measured by the ratio of trade to gross domestic product, have higher levels of gender equality (figure O.4). Trade liberalization is linked to greater accumulation of education and skills (that is, human capital), and increased gender equality (Schultz 2007). Trade can also create incentives for countries to expand women's legal rights and their access to crucial resources such as education and technology. Improved women's rights have also promoted more trade. This has led to a virtuous circle between increased trade and gender equality. In contrast, high levels of gender inequality are linked to lower product and export diversification. This is especially true in lower-income countries, where gender gaps in education and the labor market decrease potential innovation (Kazandjian et al. 2019).

Figure O.4 Countries that are more open to trade have higher levels of gender equality

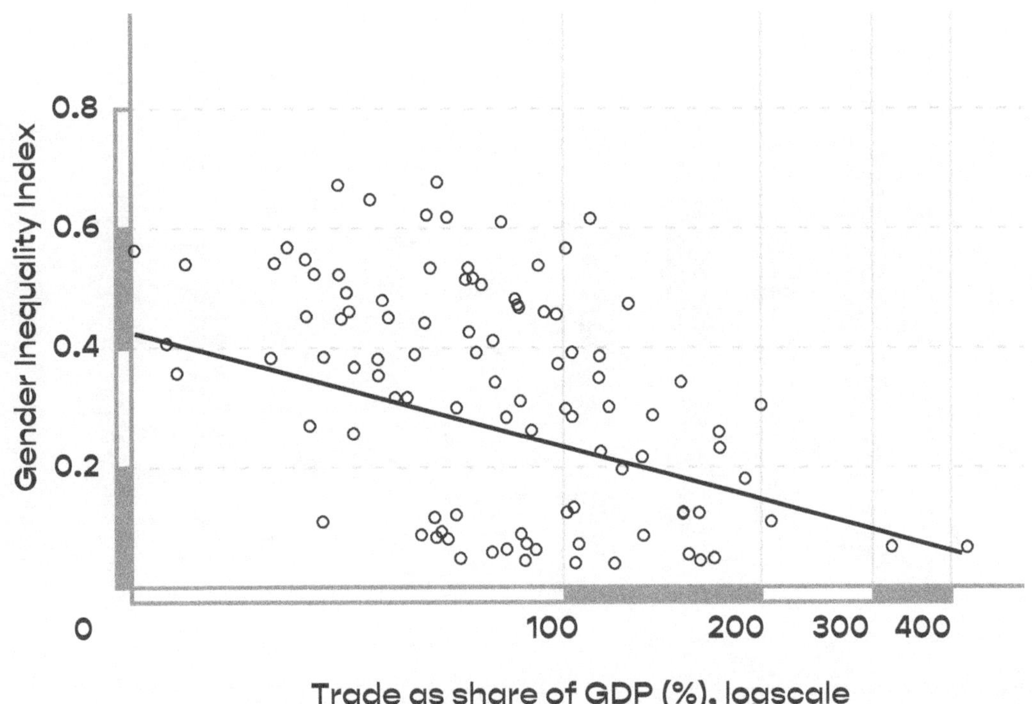

Source: Figure created using data from the United Nations Development Programme's Gender Inequality Index dataset, http://hdr.undp.org/en/data, and World Bank World Development Indicators, https://datacatalog.worldbank.org/dataset/world-development-indicators.
Note: The Gender Inequality Index measures gender inequalities in three important aspects of human development—reproductive health, measured by maternal mortality ratio and adolescent birth rates; empowerment, measured by proportion of parliamentary seats occupied by females and proportion of adult females and males aged 25 years and older with at least some secondary education; and economic status, expressed as labor market participation and measured by labor force participation rate of female and male populations aged 15 years and older.

The growing role of services in the global economy and trade, the rise of GVCs, and the adoption of new digital technologies create new and powerful opportunities for women to better reap the benefits of trade. Improving women's productivity in these sectors is essential to close the gender gap, especially for the most vulnerable women.

The servicification of the economy

Services play an increasingly important role in job creation, economic output, and trade in countries at all development levels. Services now create most jobs globally, and they do so earlier in the development process. This trend can be referred to as servicification. Since 2005, the average global growth of services trade was about 17 percent higher than the average growth of trade in goods (WTO 2019).

The service economy, including services trade and investment, provides an important source of inclusive growth (Ngai and Petrongolo 2017). Between 1991 and 2017, employment shares in the services sector expanded by 13 and 15 percentage points for female and male workers, respectively. More than two-thirds of women in upper-middle- and high-income countries were employed in the services sector in 2017, up from 45 percent in 1991. In low- and lower-middle-income countries, the proportion of women in the services sector jumped to 38 percent from 25 percent over the same period. Male workers followed a similar but less drastic trend (figure O.5).

Figure O.5 Female employment has shifted into services, 1991 versus 2017

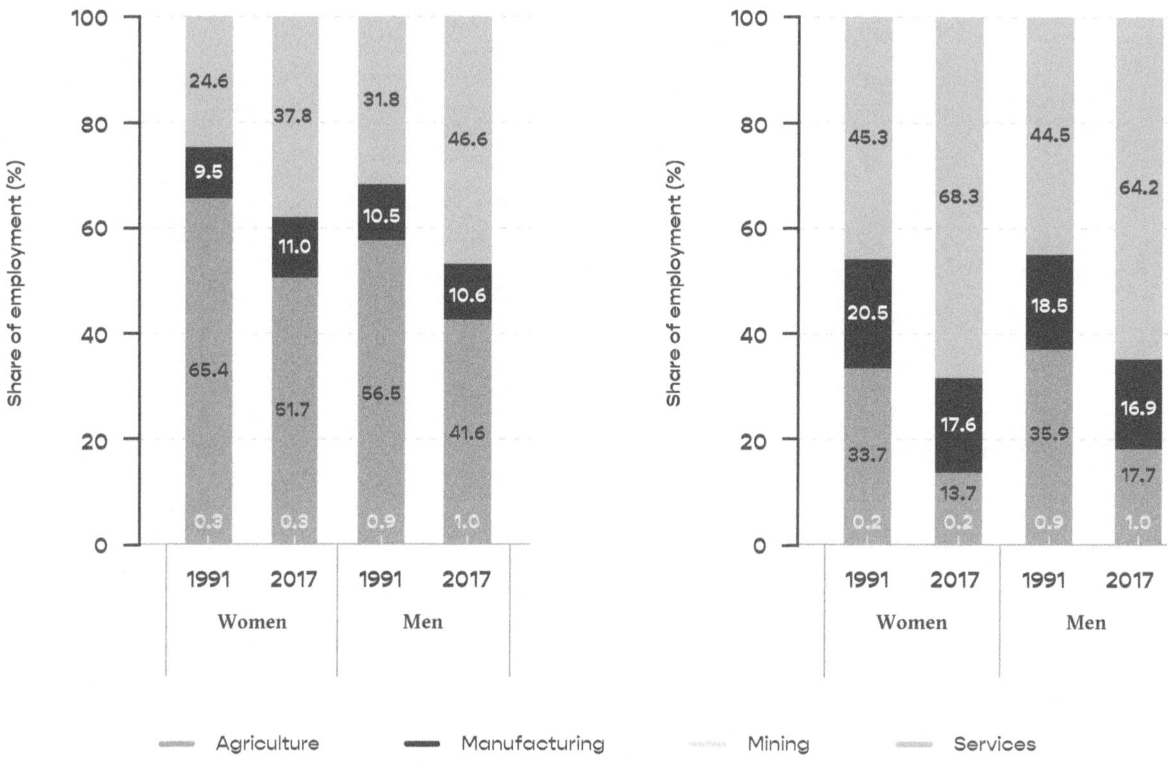

Source: International Labour Organization Department of Statistics, https://www.ilo.org/shinyapps/bulkexplorer46/?lang=en&segment=indicator&id=EMP_2EMP_SEX_ECO_NB.
Note: Employment by sector based on modeled estimates from the International Labour Organization, May 2018. Construction and utilities are included as Services.

As the development level of a country increases, so do the skills demanded within services, which has led to women's occupying an increasing proportion of high-skill services jobs such as corporate managers and health and teaching professionals. Today women represent almost 40 percent of high-skilled service workers in high-income countries, a 33 percent increase since 1991. In low-income countries women have seen an 11 percent increase in high-skill services work since 1991. Although this share represents just 3 percent of highly skilled workers in low-income countries, the employment growth potential continues to increase.

The rise of GVCs

International trade is increasingly dominated by GVCs, which spread different stages of production across countries. GVCs can provide an opportunity for export growth, employment, higher incomes, and knowledge and technology transfers. Women working in GVCs have a 10-percentage-point higher probability of holding a formal job relative to women working in sectors that are not highly integrated into GVCs.

Across the world, firms that both export and import tend to employ more women than firms that do not participate in GVCs (figure O.6). Foreign-owned firms as well as firms that export or import also have higher female labor shares on average than firms that do not. The relationship is strongest for GVC participants. GVC jobs can also have positive, indirect effects on other aspects of women's livelihoods, such as education. In Bangladesh, for example, young women in villages exposed to the garment sector—an export-intensive

Figure O.6 GVC firms employ more women than non-GVC firms

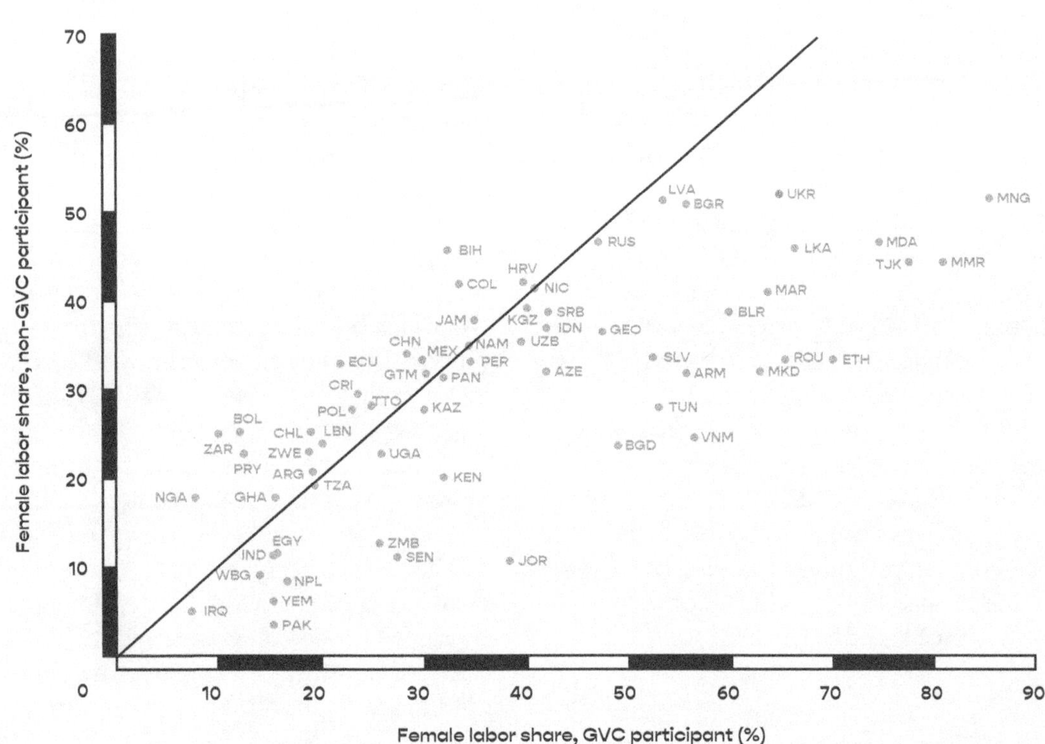

Source: Rocha and Winkler 2019, using data from World Bank Enterprise Surveys for the most recent available years, https://www.enterprisesurveys.org/en/data.
Note: Each dot represents a country-year observation. The x axis plots the employment-weighted share of female workers in total workers within firms that both export and import (GVC participant) within each country-year. The y axis plots the employment-weighted share of female workers in total workers within firms that do not export and import (nonparticipant). For a list of country codes go to https://www.iso.org/obp/ui/#search/code/. GVC = global value chain; WBG = World Bank Group.

sector—delay marriage and childbirth, and young girls gain an additional 1.5 years of schooling (Heath and Mobarak 2015).

The challenge in GVCs is to ensure that women have better access to higher-skill tasks and occupations. Female workers still tend to be concentrated in low-skill roles and nonmanagerial jobs. The spread of more inclusive management practices presents an opportunity for GVCs to open more roles for women, especially as countries upgrade their economies into high-tech and capital-intensive industry segments for the export market.

The rise of digital technologies and trade

The growing capability and accessibility of digital technologies could help women gain even more from trade. Women tend to face disproportionately higher barriers to trade compared to men. In addition to discrimination, women face greater barriers to finance, higher costs of doing business, and more limited access to information and markets. New online platforms give women the opportunity to bypass these barriers and expand their entrepreneurial skills, as well as providing women with the flexibility that can help them manage work and other responsibilities.

Digital platforms in both developed and developing economies have witnessed a sharp rise in women-owned companies, in particular micro and small enterprises, over the years. Increasingly, education and health services are traded online, which not only increases women's access to these services but also provides women better employment opportunities in sectors where they face less discrimination.

Better policies can help *women* overcome the challenges of trade and maximize its benefits

The preponderance of evidence demonstrates the positive impact of trade on gender equality. For women to benefit, however, policy makers need to actively address the challenges that trade itself can create while introducing complementary policies that enable women to fully participate in the economy.

There are three main challenges in ensuring that increased trade positively impacts women. First, although the overall correlation between national income, trade, and gender equality is high, some countries have shown that growth does not necessarily depend on gender equality. Several resource-rich countries have become high-income without integrating women into the workforce. Gender equality may increase the gains from trade, but it is possible for countries to benefit from trade even while keeping discriminatory policies in place. Greater gender equality can promote trade and economic growth even further—including in those countries. The positive impact of trade on gender equality therefore hinges on governments' political will and commitment to sustain gender diversity and equality in the economy.

Second, although aggregate benefits from trade are positive, localized costs can, in the absence of relevant adjustment policies, negatively affect certain women depending on their roles in the economy, their skills, the sectors they work in, and their geographical region. Because women hold a disproportionate share of lower-skill jobs, they can be particularly vulnerable to trade-related shocks that directly expose female-dominated industries to foreign competition or layoffs resulting from the introduction of new technologies. Women agricultural workers are especially vulnerable to imports because women are more likely to be engaged in less-productive, subsistence farming.

Third, women still face a wide range of barriers that prevent them from gaining from greater trade opportunities. These challenges range from policy and legal obstacles and gender-biased sociocultural norms to higher tariff and nontariff barriers and lack of access to technology, finance, and education.

These challenges are magnified by a lack of sex-disaggregated data. Given the complexity and specificity of the relationship between trade and gender, sex-disaggregated data are necessary to assess how different policies and obstacles affect women and men differently. Although more work and resources are needed to improve data availability for analysis, improved data collection around trade and gender can help policy makers to develop and implement transparent and effective targeted responses and policies.

Maximize women's gains from trade through policies that increase women's market access

Trade policy itself is a critical determinant in lowering the trade costs faced by women and improving women's access to international markets. Discriminatory trade policies that make women-dominated industries less competitive and productive than their male counterparts are widespread. Women's market access can be increased by addressing tariff and nontariff measures that hurt women traders and consumers, improving trade facilitation that enables women to trade as safely and easily as men, and expanding access to trade finance that empowers women to connect with international markets.

Lower tariff and nontariff barriers

Although most applied tariffs are relatively low, particularly in high-income countries, tariffs remain high on some products that governments consider to be sensitive. Female workers, particularly in developing economies, are affected by stubbornly high tariffs on agricultural goods. Similarly, tariffs on textiles, which are subject to higher tariffs than similar manufactured goods, strike a double blow against women as both the biggest consumers and the most frequent workers in the sector (Taylor and Dar 2015). A study on India shows that products produced largely by women face on average 6-percentage-point higher tariffs than products produced largely by men in export markets (Mendoza, Nayyar, and Piermartini 2018).

Similarly, discriminatory and nontransparent nontariff measures hurt women traders. Nontariff measures raise the compliance costs associated with procedures, regulations, and standards, which can be particularly burdensome for small enterprises with little experience in trade—as is the case for many women-owned firms. Eliminating the gender-related tariff differentials (for the same products) or reducing or removing altogether the relevant applied tariffs would help women business owners to access more and bigger markets.

Reduce barriers to services trade

Trade costs in services are almost double those in goods, and a large share of these costs results from policy barriers (WTO 2019). Having more open services for trade therefore offers a potentially large scope of gains for an economy in general and women in particular. A lack of competition in services decreases the productivity of services firms and increases operating costs of all firms in the economy.

Services play a key role as production inputs for farmers, manufacturing firms, and other services firms. When services such as transport, finance, and energy are protected from competition, the productivity growth (and thus income) of an entire economy can be negatively affected. This negative effect has serious consequences for women, because services employ more women than manufacturing and because efficient services help address some of the constraints that women face. More efficient and less costly transport services and financial services, for example, help increase women's mobility while decreasing financial constraints.

Enhance cross-border trade through trade facilitation and trade finance

Women engaged in moving goods across borders face a number of challenges, including time and skill constraints, burdensome customs requirements, limited access to trade finance, and higher exposure to extortion and physical harassment. These challenges are particularly pronounced for small-scale women traders in developing and least-developed economies.

The design and implementation of effective trade facilitation measures hinges on identifying the specific challenges and barriers faced by cross-border traders, including women. The adoption and implementation of domestic policies in compliance with commitments established under the World Trade Organization (WTO) Trade Facilitation Agreement (TFA) can be a catalyst for women traders by creating predictable and efficient customs processes, reducing clearance times and trade costs, reducing the opportunity for fraudulent practices at the border, and increasing the involvement of women in trade facilitation decision mechanisms.[2]

Limited access to trade finance, in particular short-term credit, is a global problem that affects women disproportionately and can limit opportunities for women traders. Improving women's access to trade finance can contribute to empowering women-owned and managed firms.

Increase women's capacity to engage in international trade

The extent to which women can take advantage of trade opportunities depends on more than trade policies. Investments in education, health systems, and infrastructure can provide women with the human capital they require to benefit from trade, particularly as workers. Improving access to education, financial resources, digital technologies, and information can further reduce some of the constraints that disproportionately affect women. On a macro level, functioning capital and labor markets, macroeconomic stability, and effective governance—including the reduction of gender imbalances—are key to maximize the gains from trade.

For women to fully benefit from trade, changes in sociocultural attitudes are necessary. Trade policies cannot overcome discriminatory legal and sociocultural barriers that prevent women from opening a bank account, running their own businesses, working in certain sectors, or crossing borders. Such discriminatory legal and sociocultural barriers often raise the costs of formalization for women traders and female entrepreneurs, forcing them to earn a living through the informal sector. Informality reduces job security and access to resources, including training and financial support.

Ensure that vulnerable women are not left behind

As governments elaborate trade policy, it is important to ensure that certain vulnerable segments of women are not left behind. Benefitting from economic progress involves adjusting to economic change and so does gaining from trade. Greater trade and technological innovation can cause disruption in some sectors as economic activity shifts to more productive areas where a country has a comparative advantage. Women can be particularly vulnerable to this type of disruption because

Credit: © Syda Productions/ Shutterstock .com. Used with permission; further permission required for reuse.

four out of five women globally work in low- to medium-skill jobs that could be more exposed to the risk of automation.

Well-targeted and adequately financed trade adjustment assistance through a mix of labor, competitiveness, and compensation policies can help workers manage the cost of adjusting to trade, while making sure that the economy captures as much as possible the benefits from these changes (Bacchetta, Milet, and Monteiro 2019; WTO 2017). Beyond improving economic efficiency, adjustment policy offers a way to compensate those who lose out from the dislocation or to maintain political support for innovation and trade openness.

Collective efforts to promote trade and gender equality

Over time, governments, international organizations, and some private sector companies have increasingly incorporated a gender-trade perspective into their activities. This practice has been spurred in part by pressure from civil society—particularly from women's organizations, which have been active in raising their concerns related to gender and trade at the national, regional, and international levels.

Several governments have adopted more gender-responsive policies. In preparation for trade negotiations, some national, regional, and local governments use a gender impact assessment system to determine whether any new law, policy, or program is likely to have an impact on the state of equality between women and men. Some countries have used trade-related international cooperation to address gender discrimination. Several countries have adopted nonreciprocal preferential trading schemes that impose lower tariffs on imports from certain developing and least-developed economies of a broad range of products, including goods produced, exported, and consumed predominantly by women, such as clothing. Some of these schemes provide for the withdrawal of tariff reduction in case of violations of international conventions, some of which address women's conditions.

In parallel, a limited but increasing number of preferential trade agreements (PTAs)—namely 80 agreements, of which 69 are notified to the WTO and in force—refer explicitly to women and gender-related issues (Monteiro 2018). Like most other types of provisions in PTAs, gender-related provisions vary greatly in terms of structure, location, language, and scope. The most common type of gender-related provisions found in PTAs promote cooperation on specific gender-related issues, such as labor discrimination. Despite increased explicit references to gender in PTAs, more effort is needed to gauge the effectiveness of these provisions in advancing women's economic empowerment.

Women's economic empowerment cannot be fully materialized, however, without the engagement of the private sector. Some companies, in particular some retailers, brands, and suppliers, have adopted voluntary gender-related initiatives that promote women's access to training for skills development, health services, maternity benefits, education, leadership, and financial management. Some companies have also established lists of potential certified women-owned business suppliers with a view to diversifying their suppliers base (Scott 2017). Some of these private-led initiatives are part of government partnerships or international initiatives.

Both the World Bank and WTO, through their different functions and activities, play a role in promoting trade as a tool for greater gender equality. Going forward, governments, business, and international organizations can collectively advance a gender-inclusive trade agenda. In particular, international institutions can support trade and gender equality through the maintenance and strengthening of open, rules-based, and transparent trade. Ongoing WTO negotiations and joint initiatives related to services, agriculture, electronic commerce, and micro, small, and medium enterprises could further empower women in the world economy. In addition, impact evaluations of international assistance, including Aid for Trade with a gender component, can provide feedback on the kinds of interventions that are most effective in promoting gender equality in trade. Further analysis and technical assistance should continue to take advantage of increasing access to sex-disaggregated data to identify priority sectors, skills, and markets in which women have a comparative advantage.

Notes

1 As part of this project, the World Bank has created a Gender Disaggregated Labor Database (GDLD) that has been used to produce some of the evidence presented in this report. The dataset is available at http://datatopics.worldbank.org/gdld/.

2 The TFA, which entered into effect in 2017, aims to promote trade facilitation through improved transparency, simplified and automated procedures, coordinated border management, and consultative mechanisms (WTO 2015).

References

Adams-Prassl, Abi, Teodora Boneva, Marta Golin, and Christopher Rauh. 2020. "Inequality in the Impact of the Coronavirus Shock: Evidence from Real Time Surveys." CESifo Working Paper 8265, Munich Society for the Promotion of Economic Research - CESifo GmbH, Munich.

Bacchetta, M., E. Milet, and J.-A. Monteiro, eds. 2019. *Making Globalization More Inclusive: Lessons from Experience with Adjustment Policies.* Geneva: World Trade Organization.

BoF (The Business of Fashion) and McKinsey & Company. 2020. "The State of Fashion 2020 Coronavirus Update." McKinsey. https://www.mckinsey.com/~/media/McKinsey/Industries/Retail/Our%20Insights/Its%20time%20to%20rewire%20the%20fashion%20system%20State%20of%20Fashion%20coronavirus%20update/The-State-of-Fashion-2020-Coronavirus-Update-final.ashx.

Dennis, Steve. 2020. "Coronavirus Shutdowns Came at the Worst Possible Time for Fashion and Luxury Retail." *Forbes*, April 21, 2020. https://www.forbes.com/sites/stevendennis/2020/04/21/covid-19-and-fashion-and-luxury-retails-lost-season.

Depetris-Chauvin, N. D., and G. Porto. Forthcoming. "The Gender Bias of Trade Policy in Developing Countries." Working Paper, World Bank, Washington, DC.

Devnath, Arun. 2020. "European Retailers Scrap $1.5 Billion of Bangladesh Orders." *Bloomberg,* March 22, 2020 (updated March 23, 2020). https://www.bloomberg.com/news/articles/2020-03-23/europe-retailers-cancel-1-billion-of-bangladesh-garment-orders.

Gailes, A., T. Gurevich, S. Shikher, and M. Tsigas. 2018. "Gender and Income Inequality in United States Tariff Burden." Economics Working Paper No. 2018-08-B, U.S. International Trade Commission, Washington, DC.

Heath, R., and A. M. Mobarak. 2015. "Manufacturing Growth and the Lives of Bangladeshi Women." *Journal of Development Economics* 115 (C): 1–15.

Kazandjian, R., L. Kolovich, K. Kochhar, and M. Newiak. 2019. "Gender Equality and Economic Diversification." *Social Sciences* 8 (4): 118.

Mendoza, A., G. Nayyar, and R. Piermartini. 2018. "Are the 'Poor' Getting Globalised?" Policy Research Working Paper 8609, World Bank, Washington, DC.

Monteiro, J.-A. 2018. "Gender-Related Provisions in Regional Trade Agreements." WTO Staff Working Paper No. ERSD-2018-15, World Trade Organization, Geneva.

Ngai, L. R., and B. Petrongolo. 2017. "Gender Gaps and the Rise of the Service Economy." *American Economic Journal: Macroeconomics* 9 (4): 1–44.

Rocha, N., and D. Winkler. 2019. "Trade and Female Labor Participation: Stylized Facts Using a Global Dataset." Policy Research Working Paper 9098, World Bank, Washington, DC.

Schultz, T. P. 2007. "Does the Liberalization of Trade Advance Gender Equality, in Schooling and Health?" In *The Future of Globalization: Explorations in Light of Recent Turbulence,* edited by E. Zedillo, 178–208. London: Routledge.

Scott, L. 2017. "Private Sector Engagement with Women's Economic Empowerment: Lessons Learned from Years of Practice." Saïd Business School, University of Oxford.

Taylor, L. L., and J. Dar. 2015. "Fairer Trade, Removing Gender Bias in US Import Taxes." *The Takeaway* 6 (3): 1–4.

UNWTO (United Nations World Tourism Organization). 2020. "International Tourist Arrivals Could Fall by 20–30% in 2020." UNWTO, Madrid. https://www.unwto.org/news/international-tourism-arrivals-could-fall-in-2020.

World Bank. 2011. *World Development Report 2012: Gender Equality and Development.* Washington, DC: World Bank.

———. Forthcoming. "Africa Continental Free Trade Area: Economic and Distributional Effects." World Bank, Washington, DC.

WTO (World Trade Organization). 2015. *World Trade Report 2015: Speeding Up Trade: Benefits and Challenges of Implementing the WTO Trade Facilitation Agreement.* Geneva: WTO.

———. *2017. World Trade Report 2017: Trade, Technology and Jobs.* Geneva: WTO.

———. *2019. World Trade Report 2019: The Future of Services Trade.* Geneva: WTO.

———. 2020. "The Economic Impact of COVID-19 on Women in Vulnerable Sectors and Economies." WTO Information Note, WTO. https://www.wto.org/english/tratop_e/covid19_e/covid19_e.htm.

Chapter 1

THE IMPACT OF TRADE ON *WOMEN* IN THEIR DIFFERENT ROLES

Key messages

- The increase in trade since the 1990s has reshaped the global economy—leading to higher living standards and lower poverty, particularly in developing countries—but has come with costs, such as job displacement. It has expanded opportunities for women and led to changes in their role in society, but the channels through which trade affects gender inequality are not well understood.

- A lack of sex-disaggregated data has hampered research into trade and gender links. Given the complexity and specificity of the relationship between trade and gender, sex-disaggregated data can demonstrate trade policy's potential impact on women and help policy makers to develop appropriate, evidence-based responses and policies.

- New empirical analysis for this report confirms that trade benefits women in several ways:

  » Firms that engage in international trade employ more women. In developing and emerging countries, women make up 33 percent on average of the workforce of firms that trade, but just 24 percent for nonexporting firms and 28 percent for nonimporting firms. Foreign-owned firms and those that are part of global value chains also employ more women. In countries such as Morocco, Romania, and Vietnam, women represent 50 percent or more of the workforce of exporting firms—which have created jobs for more than 5 million women, roughly 15 percent of the female population working in these countries.

  » Trade increases women's wages and increases economic equality. Globally, women take home a smaller share of total wages. When developing countries double their manufacturing exports—typical for developing countries that open themselves to trade—women's share of total manufacturing wages rises by 5.8 percentage points on average, through a combination of increased employment and higher salaries. Analysis on implementation of the African Continental Free Trade Area suggests that opening to trade can increase women's salaries relative to men's, helping to close the gender wage gap and decrease gender inequality. By 2035, wages for skilled and unskilled female labor would be 4.0 percent and 3.7 percent higher (relative to baseline), respectively, compared with a 3.2 percent increase for all males. That increase translates roughly to an extra two weeks' pay each year—enough for a woman earning US$5 a day to pay for one family member's personal supplies, school supplies, and uniform for an entire school year.

» Trade creates better jobs for women. In both developing and emerging economies, workers in sectors with high levels of exports are more likely to be employed formally—with opportunities for benefits, training, and job security. Women's probability of being informal goes from 20 percent in sectors with low levels of exports to 13 percent in sectors with high levels. Women's rates of informality also decline more sharply than men's (an overall reduction of 7 percentage points for women compared to 4 percentage points for men).

» Trade openness can increase women's welfare. Analysis for a sample of 54 developing and emerging countries suggests that eliminating import tariffs could raise real income for female-headed households compared to male-headed households in more than three-quarters of the countries considered. Female-headed households tend to spend a larger share of income on agricultural goods (food), which are usually subject to higher tariffs, and to have a lower share of income coming from wages. They could therefore gain up to 2.5 percent more real income than male-headed households through the removal of import tariffs. In countries such as Burkina Faso or Cameroon, eliminating trade policy bias would mean a gain for women equivalent to annual expenditure on education or health.

Introduction

Over the past three decades, the world has become increasingly integrated. Trade in goods as a share of gross domestic product (GDP) increased from about 43 percent in 1995 to almost 60 percent in 2017. Tariffs have also progressively fallen since the establishment of the General Agreement on Tariffs and Trade (GATT) in 1948. Unilateral liberalization and eight rounds of multilateral negotiations have significantly reduced tariffs applied by World Trade Organization (WTO) members. Applied most favored nation (MFN) rates have fallen from levels over 10 percent in 1995 to slightly over 7 percent in 2017 (figure 1.1). Countries that are open to international trade tend to grow faster, innovate, improve productivity, and provide higher income and more opportunities to their people.

Open trade also benefits lower-income households by offering consumers more affordable goods and services. Integrating with the world economy through trade and global value chains (GVCs) helps drive economic growth and reduce poverty—locally and globally.

Figure 1.1 Trade openness and liberalization increased in the 1990s and 2000s

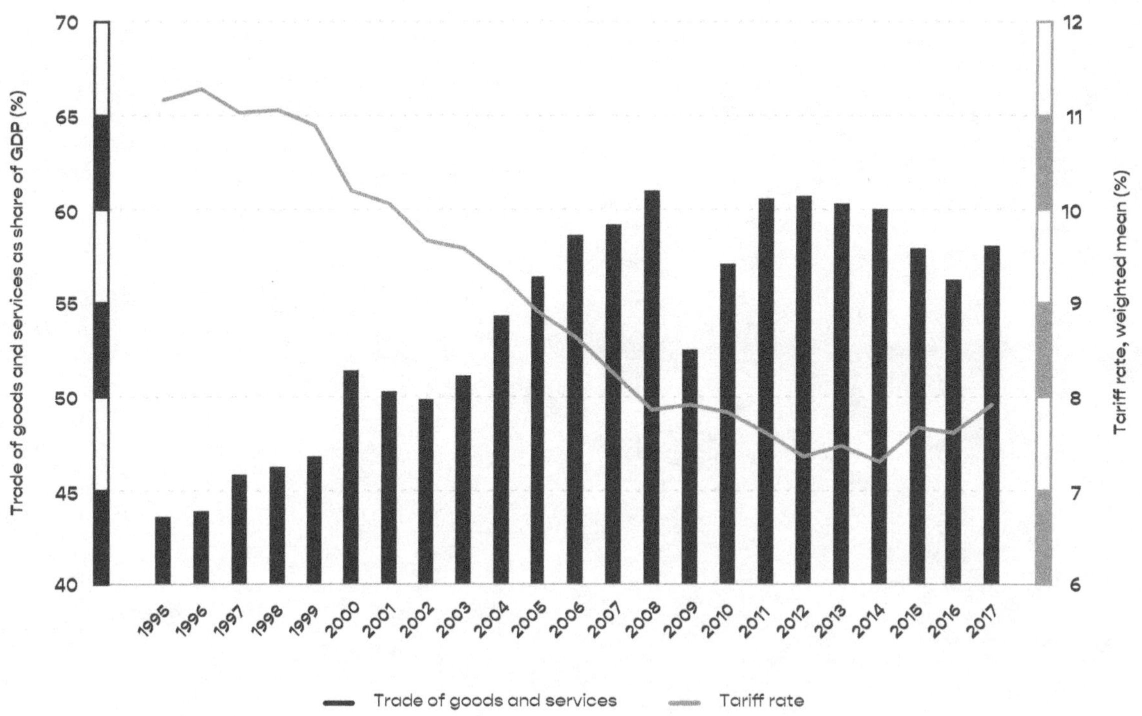

Source: World Bank World Development Indicators, https://datacatalog.worldbank.org/dataset/world-development-indicators.
Note: Trade is the sum of exports and imports of goods and services measured as a share of gross domestic product (GDP). To avoid sample selection bias, tariffs have been calculated for a balanced subsample of countries and missing data have been interpolated. The subsample includes 82 countries with applied most favored nation rates in at least 15 years between 1995 and 2017.

International trade has played an important role in the global improvement of gender equality over time (see box 1.1 for discussion of gender equality and other key terms used throughout this report). Trade liberalization has been linked to increased trade, greater accumulation of education or skills (that is, human capital), and increased gender equality (Schultz 2007). Openness to trade in countries, as measured by their trade-to-GDP ratio, is positively correlated with gender equality (figure 1.2, panel a) and women's legal rights (figure 1.2, panel b).

Figure 1.2 Countries that are more open to trade have higher levels of gender equality, 2017

Source: Figures created using data from the United Nations Development Programme's Gender Inequality Index dataset, http://hdr.undp.org/en/data; World Bank Women, Business and the Law Index dataset, https://wbl.worldbank.org/en/resources/data; and World Bank World Development Indicators, https://datacatalog.worldbank.org/dataset/world-development-indicators.
Note: The Gender Inequality Index measures gender inequalities in three important aspects of human development—reproductive health, measured by maternal mortality ratio and adolescent birth rates; empowerment, measured by proportion of parliamentary seats occupied by females and proportion of adult females and males aged 25 years and older with at least some secondary education; and economic status, expressed as labor market participation and measured by labor force participation rate of female and male populations aged 15 years and older. The Women, Business and the Law Index measures global progress toward gender equality in the law.

The more a country is integrated globally, the more trade can act as an impetus for that country to improve women's rights and boost female participation in the economy. The competitive pressure that comes with trade makes gender inequality more costly in an integrated world. Countries that discriminate against female workers are less competitive internationally—particularly those countries with export industries that have high female employment rates (World Bank 2011). Gender inequality is also linked to lower levels of diversification and innovation of produced and exported goods. This situation is especially true in lower-income countries where women are generally less educated and have fewer employment opportunities than men, reducing women's potential to generate ideas that translate into greater productivity and job creation (Kazandjian et al. 2019).

The ready-made garment sector in Bangladesh showcases how trade has transformed the lives of women over the past 30 years. The sector has expanded on average by 17 percent per year since 1980 and represents over three-quarters of Bangladesh's export earnings. The reason the garment sector has been so transformational is that it offered formal job opportunities to women outside their homes for the first time, directly increasing women's incomes and labor force participation. The sector now employs 3.6 million workers, an estimated 53 percent of them women (Moazzem and Radia 2018). The garment trade has also indirectly increased gender equality. Bangladeshi parents with access to garment factory jobs are more likely to keep younger daughters at school because basic education enhances young women's chances to work in factories in the future (Heath and Mobarak 2015).

Box 1.1 Key terms used in this report

What do we mean by gender equality?

Gender refers to the social, behavioral, and cultural attributes, expectations, and norms associated with being a man or a woman. Gender equality refers to how these aspects determine how women and men interact with each other and the resulting differences in power between them (World Bank 2011). This report focuses on three key aspects of the relationship between gender equality and trade: the economic opportunities that women have through participation in the economy (employment, entrepreneurship), the generation and accumulation of income (capital, assets, wages), and consumption and related decisions affecting individual and household well-being.

Why is gender equality important?

Women and girls account for half the world's population and therefore represent half of its potential. Gender equality is central to all areas of a healthy society, from reducing poverty to promoting health, education, welfare, and well-being of girls and boys. Reducing the gender gap promotes economic development. Societies are unable to unlock their potential and meet the challenges of rapid economic and technological change without harnessing the skills and ideas of their entire population. Achieving gender equality and empowering all women and girls is the fifth Sustainable Development Goal of the United Nations 2030 Agenda for Sustainable Development.

How is gender equality measured?

There are many ways to measure gender inequality, including employment, wages, health, and education. Some measures seek to combine different aspects of gender inequality into an overall assessment of how women fare compared to men. Such tools include the United Nations Development Programme's Gender Inequality Index and the World Bank's Women, Business and the Law Index.[a] Although this report refers to both indexes, its analysis focuses on specific aspects of inequality that are directly affected by trade, such as the wage gap, the employment gap, and the productivity gap. It also addresses aspects of gender inequality, such as education and societal discrimination against women, that occur outside of the workplace and that can affect the extent to which women can benefit from trade.

What are the economic roles of women?

Women perform a wide range of economic roles, many of which are affected by and affect trade directly and indirectly. As workers and business owners, women are important participants in the productive sector of economies that are affected by international trade. As consumers, they are affected by changes in employment, wages, and prices associated with trade openness. As decision makers, women's use of income and the important life choices they make for themselves or their family, such as enrolling in higher education or having children, can be affected by trade.

a. For more information on the Gender Inequality Index, see http://hdr.undp.org/en/content/gender-inequality-index-gii; for more information on the Women, Business and the Law Index, see https://wbl.worldbank.org/.

Recent evidence from Indonesia also suggests that women benefit from trade. Reducing tariffs on imports corresponded with increased female participation in the labor force and more equitable distribution of household duties. Lower tariffs were also correlated with delayed marriage and reduced fertility of less skilled female workers. Trade liberalization also led to an expansion of sectors that employ relatively more women in the affected region (Kis-Katos, Pieters, and Sparrow 2018).

Trade and its impact on women are changing. Trade is no longer limited to importing and exporting final goods. The rise of GVCs requires the importing of goods that are used for the production of intermediate and final exports of goods and services. This expansion has dramatically increased specialization, ranging from production of commodities (for example, agriculture and mining) to limited manufacturing (for example, assembly of ready-made parts), advanced manufacturing and services (for example, circuitry and robotics), and innovative activities (for example, research and development). The type of trade specialization has consequences for gender inequality because women and men frequently have different levels of skills, which affects their competitiveness in the labor market. Specialization into more sophisticated trade is associated with reduced gender inequality with regard to reproductive health, empowerment, and economic status (figure 1.3).

Figure 1.3 Gender inequality falls as countries specialize into more sophisticated GVCs

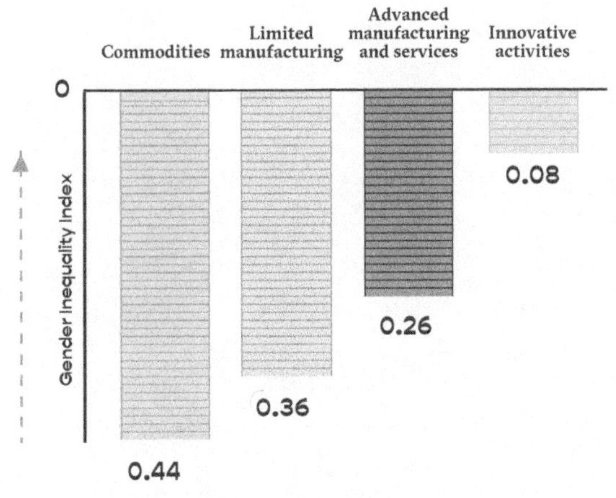

Source: Figure created using data from the United Nations Development Programme's Gender Inequality Index dataset, http://hdr.undp.org/en/data, and from World Bank 2019.
Note: The graph shows the average Gender Inequality Index for 145 countries in 2017 by level of specialization into global value chain (GVC) taxonomy group (see box 1.3 in World Bank 2019).

Despite the preponderance of evidence that demonstrates the positive impact of trade on gender equality, there are two important caveats. First, development itself is not a proxy for global integration and rising gender equality. Although the overall correlation between income and gender equality is high, some countries have shown that prosperity does not depend on gender equality. Several resource-rich countries as well as some economies in East Asia have become high-income without integrating women into the workforce.

Second, trade liberalization is not universally beneficial to women. Aggregate benefits from trade are positive, but localized costs can negatively affect women's livelihoods. Because women hold a disproportionate share of lower-skill jobs, they can be particularly vulnerable to trade-related shocks—such as trade liberalization that directly exposes female-dominated industries to foreign competition or layoffs due to the introduction of new technologies. Women agricultural workers are especially vulnerable to imports because they are more likely to be engaged in less productive, subsistence farming. The negative impacts of trade on certain groups of women demonstrate the ways that ostensibly gender-neutral trade policy, such as lowering a tariff, can affect men and women differently, depending on their roles in the economy, their skills, the sector they work in, and their geographical region.

As workers, producers, and consumers, women perform a wide range of economic roles that determine how they are affected by international trade. As employees and business owners, women are participants in the productive sector of economies that are affected by trade. Trade directly affects their employment, wages, and productivity through the job opportunities available to them, the level of competition in different sectors of the economy, and the introduction of new labor-saving technologies. As consumers, women are affected directly as trade lowers prices for purchases of goods and increases competition in traded sectors and indirectly because those lower prices and increased competition affect women's job opportunities and incomes. Trade influences women's life choices around education, marriage, and fertility by shifting incentives to acquire skills and changing the economic dynamics within families and communities.

A clearer and more systematic understanding of the different channels through which trade and trade policy affect women can help policy makers design policies that reduce negative impacts on women and improve gender equality. This report uses a conceptual framework based on the different roles women play in the economy to clarify the effects of trade policy on women.[1] The main objective of this framework is to improve understanding of the diverse dimensions and transmission channels through which trade can affect women. It illustrates the different factors that trade policy has on women's empowerment, business ownership, participation in labor markets, and consumption.[2] It provides new evidence on the relationship between trade and women in their different life roles to inform more gender-equal trade policy making. Given the simultaneous roles women play, the framework helps isolate the role of trade in gender equality.

The next section of this chapter describes the impact of trade on women's participation in the labor market. The chapter then focuses on women as producers and business owners to explore the productivity dimension of the gender gap. The final section describes the effects that trade can have on women consumers and decision makers by looking at how women's income and spending patterns are influenced by trade.

How trade affects *women* workers

International trade has a positive effect on gender equality by helping women move into the formal economy and get jobs with better conditions and benefits. Firms that are more integrated into the world economy have higher shares of female employment. Industries that are more integrated into the global economy have a lower gender wage gap.

Despite these positive effects, the impact of more open trade on individual female workers can differ widely depending on where they work, where they live, and their specific characteristics. Female workers may lose their jobs if they work in industries that face foreign competition. Better technology driven by trade competition can open job opportunities for women in previously closed industries. But that same technology may also reduce the demand for low-skilled—often female—labor.

One way to gauge how trade affects women is to compare women's and men's participation rates in the workforce (that is, their labor share). The share of women in the labor force increases with countries' specialization in more sophisticated trade. The female labor force represents only 39 percent of the total labor force on average in 2015 for countries specializing in commodities, but the percentage increases slightly with specialization into more sophisticated trade. The female labor share reaches over 45 percent on average for countries specializing in innovative activities, such as many Western European countries, Israel, Singapore, and the United States, among others (figure 1.4); however, even Finland, the country with the highest female labor share among this group (48 percent), has still not reached parity between women and men.

Figure 1.4 The female labor share increases as countries specialize into more sophisticated trade and GVCs

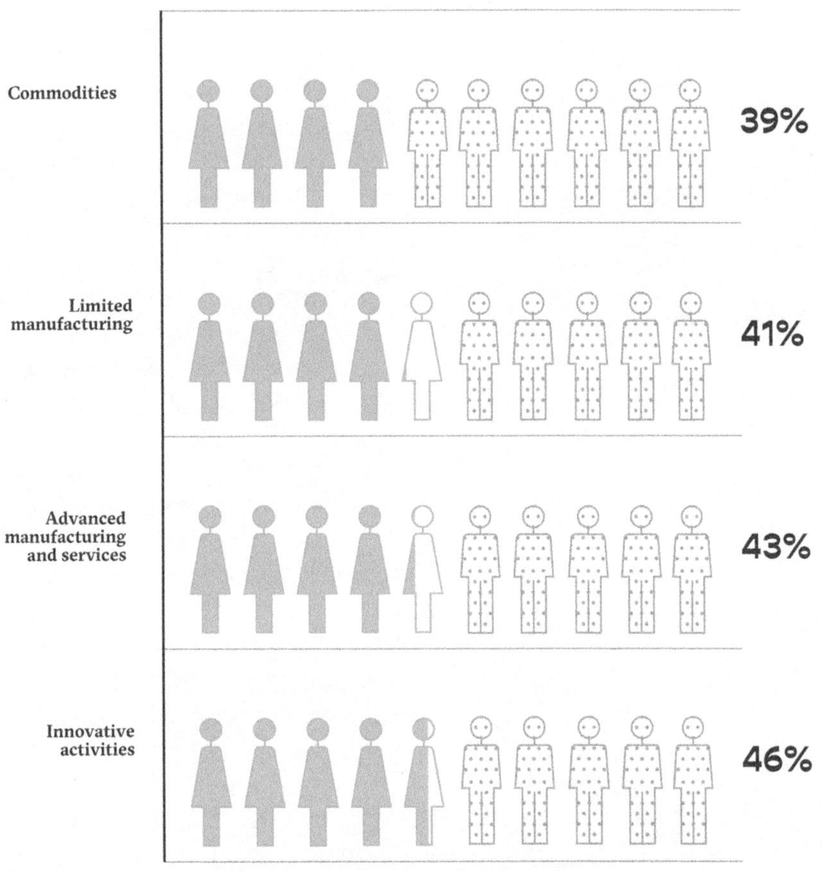

Source: World Bank World Development Indicators, https://datacatalog.worldbank.org/dataset/world-development-indicators); World Bank 2019.
Note: The graph shows the average (mean) female share in the total labor force in 2015 for 145 countries by level of specialization in global value chain (GVC) taxonomy group (see box 1.3 in World Bank 2019).

Specialization in more sophisticated trade is also correlated with more equal pay between men and women. The gender wage gap falls sharply for countries specializing in limited manufacturing or advanced manufacturing and services compared to the gap for those specializing in commodities; that gap declines further for countries in the innovative activities group (figure 1.5). The sharp decline in the gender wage gap between the commodities and limited manufacturing groups could also be related to the level of women's employment in informal activities, which is higher in countries with less sophisticated trade. This difference implies that countries' specialization into limited manufacturing creates more formal jobs with higher pay for women relative to men.

Female employment has evolved

Industrialization and the rise of international trade have corresponded with the entry of women in the workforce. Women's roles as workers in the period of early industrialization consisted mainly of providing services that created human capital, in sectors such as education

Figure 1.5 As trade participation involves more sophisticated trade and GVCs, the male-to-female wage ratio declines

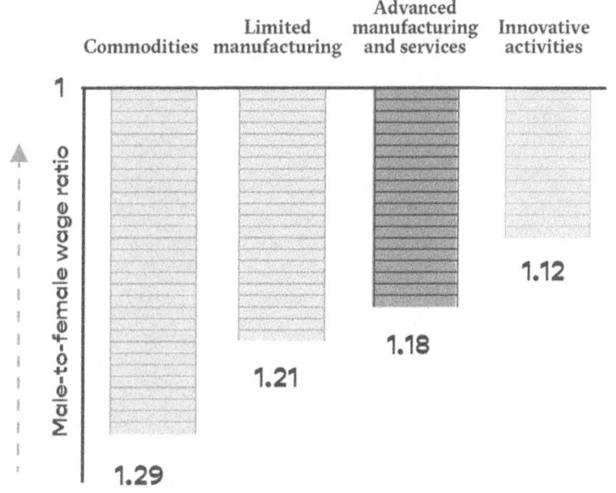

Source: World Bank Gender Disaggregated Labor Database (GDLD), http://datatopics.worldbank.org/gdld/; World Bank 2019.
Note: The graph shows the average (mean) male-to-female wage ratio across 69 countries by global value chain (GVC) taxonomy group (see box 1.3 in World Bank 2019).

and health. As specialization increased, women found roles that were traditionally dominated by men as well as entirely new professions based on new technologies.

The past three decades of rapid global integration have accelerated the trend of women taking on ever more complex roles in the economy. Many more women are in the labor market today, and they are more likely to be found in better jobs in manufacturing and services. Meanwhile, women have moved out of low-paying, less productive jobs in the agriculture sector. Although they increasingly occupy high-skill jobs, about 80 percent of women still occupy low- to medium-skill roles. Women also remain overrepresented in informal work, especially in developing countries and in the agriculture sector. It is also well documented that women—even those with equivalent education and experience—earn on average less than men in all advanced societies.

Female employment has increased

More female workers participate in the labor market today, particularly in high- and middle-income countries. Female employment-to-population ratios in 2017 were higher for most countries than in 1991, as suggested by the location above the 45-degree line in figure 1.6. High- and upper-middle-income countries experienced the largest growth in female employment-to-population ratios between 1991 and 2017. Morocco and North Macedonia showed remarkable increases

Figure 1.6 The female employment-to-population ratio increased in most economies between 1991 and 2017

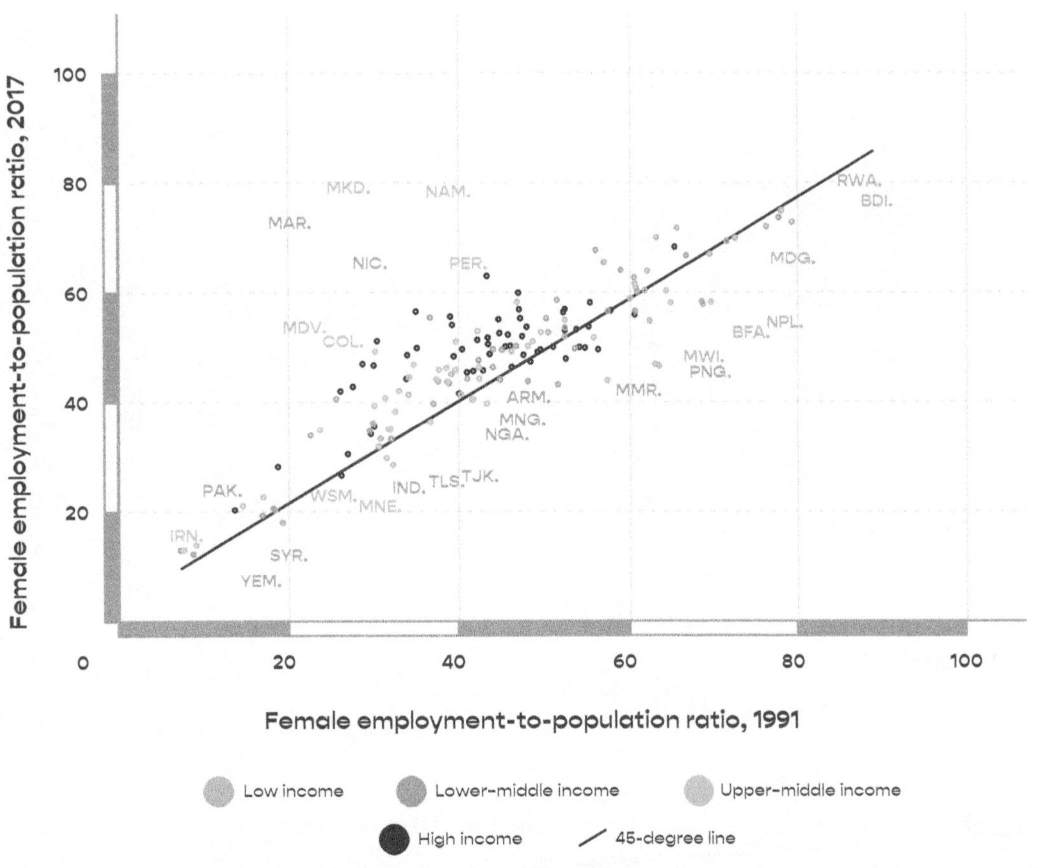

Source: International Labour Organization Department of Statistics, https://www.ilo.org/shinyapps/bulkexplorer46/?lang=en&segment=indicator&id=EAP_2WAP_SEX_AGE_RT_A.
Note: The employment-to-population ratio expresses the number of employed persons as a percent of the total working-age population. Country income groups determined using World Bank 2018 income classification. For a list of country codes go to https://www.iso.org/obp/ui/#search/code/.

in women's employment, increasing by over 50 percentage points each.

Despite the global increase in women's participation in the labor market over the past 25 years, fewer than one in two women works. The average global female employment-to-population ratio increased from 45.0 to 47.9 percent between 1991 and 2017. This increase contrasts with the male employment-to-population ratio, which declined from 71.0 to 67.8 percent over the same period. The percentage of female employment is surprisingly low, particularly because it includes subsistence farmers and informal jobs.[3] The eight economies with the lowest rates of women's labor force participation are exclusively in the Middle East and North Africa. The female employment-to-population ratio was only 10 percent or lower in Jordan, the Syrian Arab Republic, West Bank and Gaza, and the Republic of Yemen.

The landscape of women's jobs is shifting from agriculture to services

In many countries, women continue to be employed overwhelmingly in agricultural work. Female agricultural workers are among the poorest groups of workers in the world. They are

Figure 1.7 Women's employment is shifting into services and away from agriculture, 1991 versus 2017

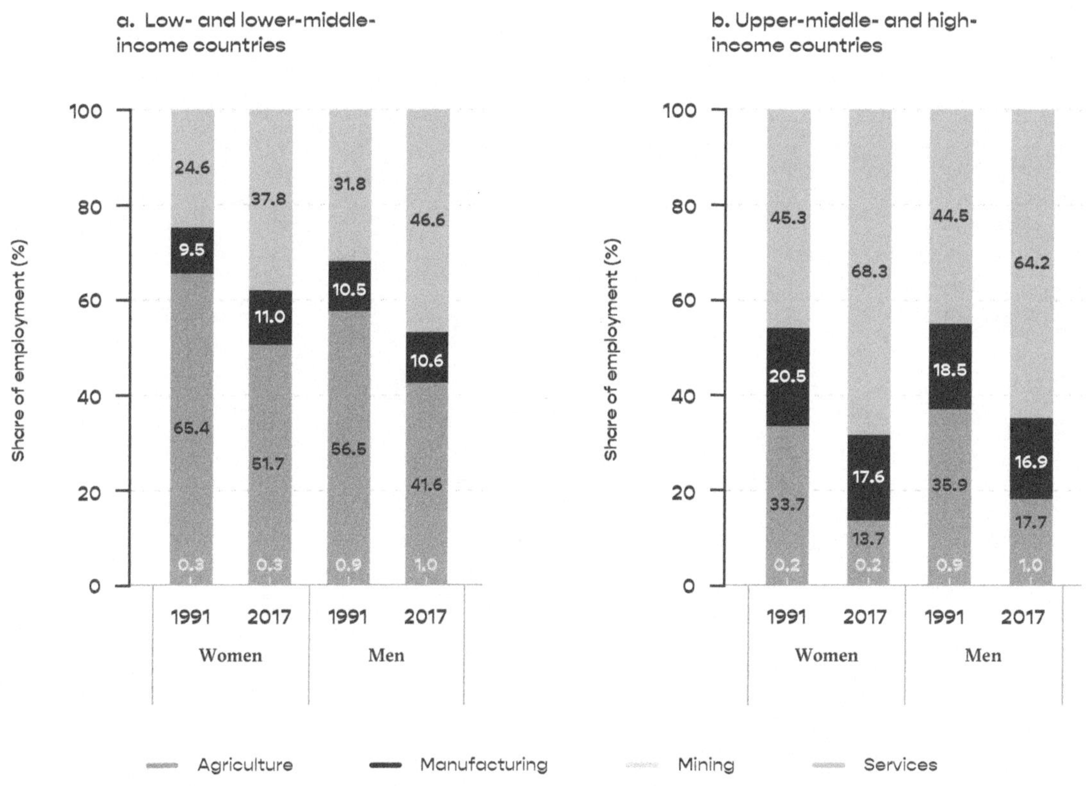

Source: International Labour Organization Department of Statistics, https://www.ilo.org/shinyapps/bulkexplorer46/?lang=en&segment=indicator&id=EMP_2EMP_SEX_ECO_NB.

Note: Employment by sector based on modeled estimates from the International Labour Organization, November 2018. Construction and utilities are included as Services.

most likely involved in subsistence agriculture to meet their own or their family's needs. This work is especially concentrated in the world's least developed countries (figure 1.7, panel a). In Sub-Saharan Africa, over half of the female workforce in 2017 was employed in agriculture (figure 1.8), and almost one-third of the female workforce in East Asia and Pacific was in agriculture. More than three-quarters of the female population in Burundi, Cambodia, the Lao People's Democratic Republic, Madagascar, Nepal, Rwanda, and Tanzania worked in agriculture in 2017.

Women's jobs are moving from agriculture, however, to both manufacturing and services. Work opportunities for women in manufacturing and especially in services have increased. The share of female manufacturing employment in low- and lower-middle-income countries was 11 percent in 2017, a 1.4-percentage-point increase since 1991 (figure 1.7, panel a). In Sub-Saharan Africa, East Asia and Pacific, the Middle East and North Africa, and South Asia, women's employment in agriculture has declined by more than 15 percentage points since 1991 (figure 1.8). The services sector has created even more new employment opportunities for female and male workers alike. Between 1991 and 2017, employment shares in the services sector of low- and lower-middle-income countries expanded by 13 and 15 percentage points for female and male workers, respectively (figure 1.7). Although Asia follows the global trend of structural transformation into services, its progress still trails the Middle East and North Africa, Latin America and the Caribbean, Europe and Central Asia,

Figure 1.8 Agriculture still accounts for much of female employment in certain regions, 1991 versus 2017

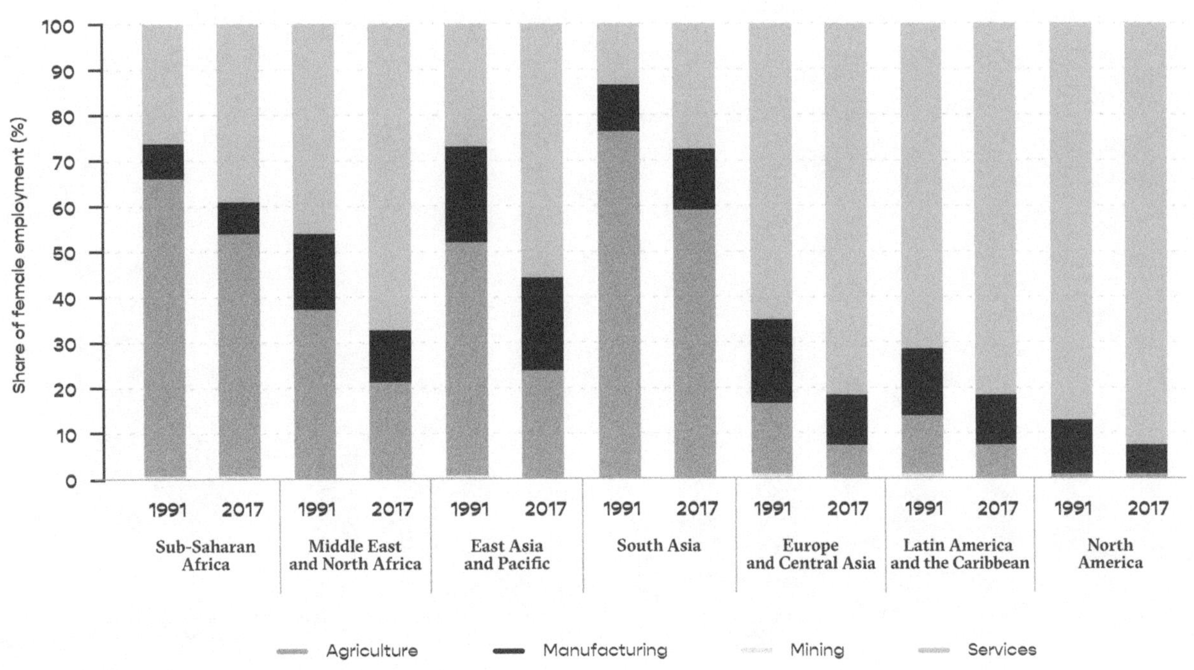

Source: International Labour Organization Department of Statistics, https://www.ilo.org/shinyapps/bulkexplorer46/?lang=en&segment=indicator&id=EMP_2EMP_SEX_ECO_NB.
Note: Employment by sector based on modeled estimates from the International Labour Organization, November 2018.

and especially North America—where women's employment is roughly between 80 and 90 percent in services (figure 1.8).

In upper-middle- and high-income countries, the share of female employment has declined in both agriculture and the manufacturing sector over the past 30 years, but it has increased in the services sector. The share of female workers in agriculture fell from 34 to 14 percent over the period 1991–2017. Similarly, the share of female workers in manufacturing declined by 3 percentage points to less than 18 percent. By contrast, female employment in the services sector expanded from 45 to 68 percent. Male workers in developed countries followed a similar, but less drastic, trend. Their decline in manufacturing employment share was only 1.6 percentage points, whereas their increase in services employment was 20 percentage points (figure 1.7, panel b).

In both low- and high-income countries, the increase in service jobs was stronger in more tradable services such as wholesale and retail, financial and business, and administrative services—such as rental and leasing, travel agency, and tour operator activities (figure 1.9).

Figure 1.9 More tradable services have provided the strongest job growth for both genders, 1991 versus 2017

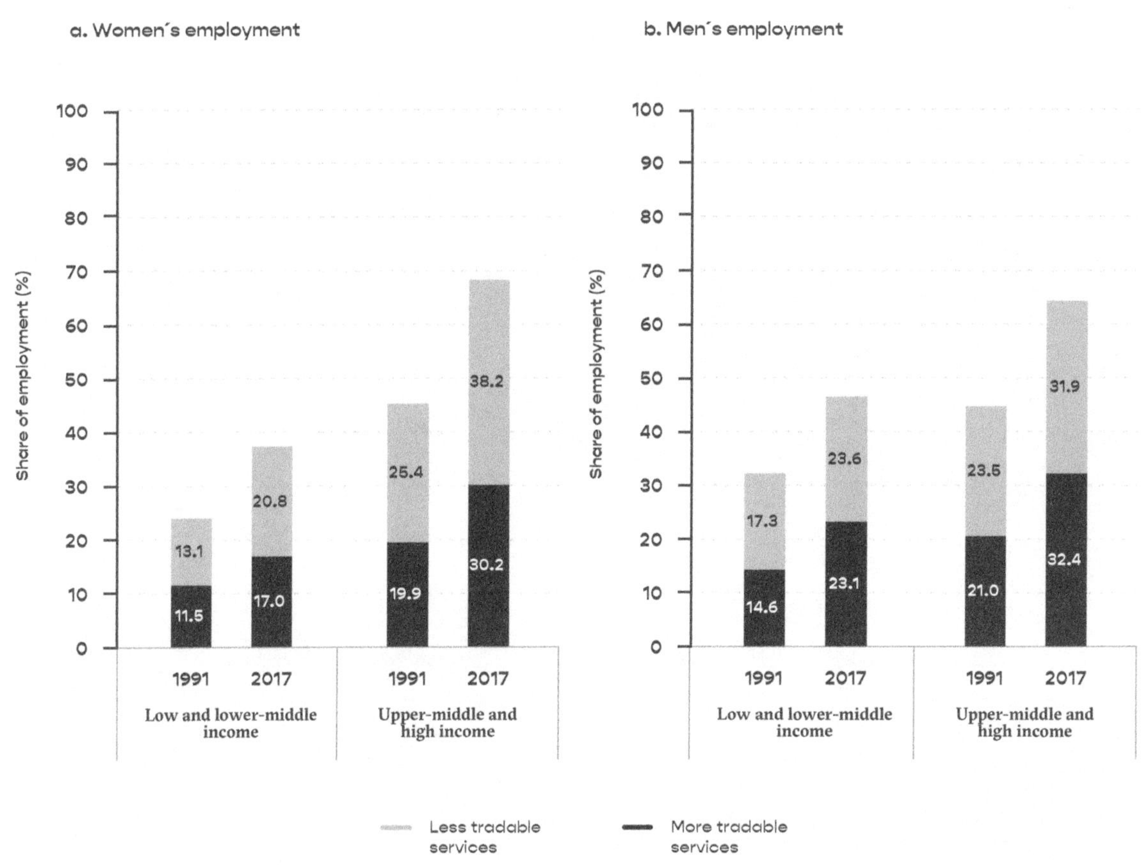

Source: International Labour Organization Department of Statistics, https://www.ilo.org/shinyapps/bulkexplorer46/?lang=en&segment=indicator&id=EMP_2EMP_SEX_ECO_NB.

Note: Employment by sector based on modeled estimates from the International Labour Organization, November 2018. More tradable services include wholesale and retail trade, transportation and storage, information and communication, financial and insurance activities, and business and administrative services. Income levels defined using the World Bank income classification for 2018.

Where do women work?

Women work mainly in low- to medium-skill occupations

Women are increasingly moving from medium-skill to high-skill jobs (figure 1.10). Despite this increase, 80 percent of women globally still occupy medium- and low-skill jobs. The share of skilled female employees increases with income and reaches almost 40 percent in high-income countries, but only 3 percent in low-income countries, in 2017 (figure 1.11). In all country groups—but especially in low-income countries—most of the female workforce is employed in medium-skill jobs. The services sector, independent of gender, tends to employ more educated workers, but their employment share is lower in developing countries. Over 14 percent of male and 16 percent of female employees working in the services sector have postsecondary education, compared to only 2.7 and 2.1 percent, respectively, in the manufacturing sector (figure 1.12).

In low- and lower-middle-income countries, women occupy fewer high-skill jobs compared to their counterparts in upper-

Credit: ©ProStockStudio/ Shutterstock.com. Used with permission; further permission required for reuse.

middle- and high-income countries. More-educated female workers tend to work as service and market sales workers, clerks, technicians, and professionals.[4] Service and market sales workers require only 7 years of education on average in lower-income countries compared to over 10 years in higher-income countries. Skilled agricultural and elementary occupations (for example, occupations that involve simple and routine tasks) employ the largest shares of women in developing countries, requiring only 4 to 5 years of education on average (figure 1.13).[5]

Trade is linked to more formal jobs for women

Evidence shows that trade can help women move into the formal economy, offering them better working conditions, more frequent access to health or retirement benefits, and better occupational safety and health standards. Women who are employed formally are also more shielded from extortion, bribery, and

Figure 1.10 Women's presence in high-skill roles has expanded, 1991 vs. 2017

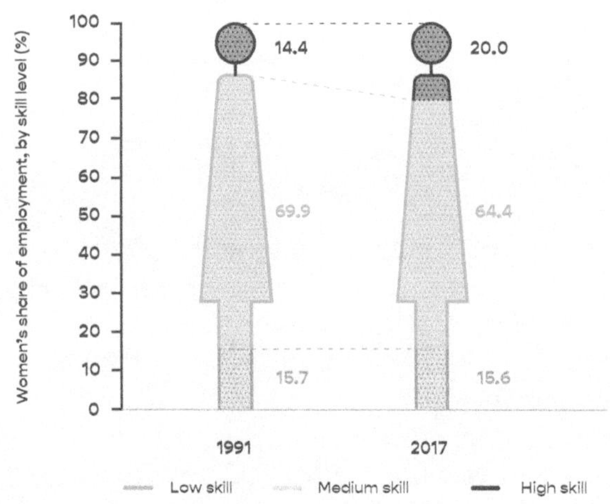

Source: International Labour Organization Department of Statistics, https://www.ilo.org/shinyapps/bulkexplorer11/?lang=en&segment=indicator&id=EMP_2EMP_SEX_OCU_NB_A.

Note: Employment by sex and occupation based on modeled estimates from the International Labour Organization, May 2018. Data presented by occupation are based on the International Standard Classification of Occupation (ISCO) and classified into three broad skill levels: Low skill refers to elementary occupations. Medium skill refers to occupations such as clerical support workers; service and sales workers; skilled agricultural, forestry, and fishery workers; craft and related trades workers; and plant and machine operators and assemblers. High skill refers to managers, professionals, and technicians and associate professionals.

Figure 1.11 Low-income countries have very few women in high-skill jobs

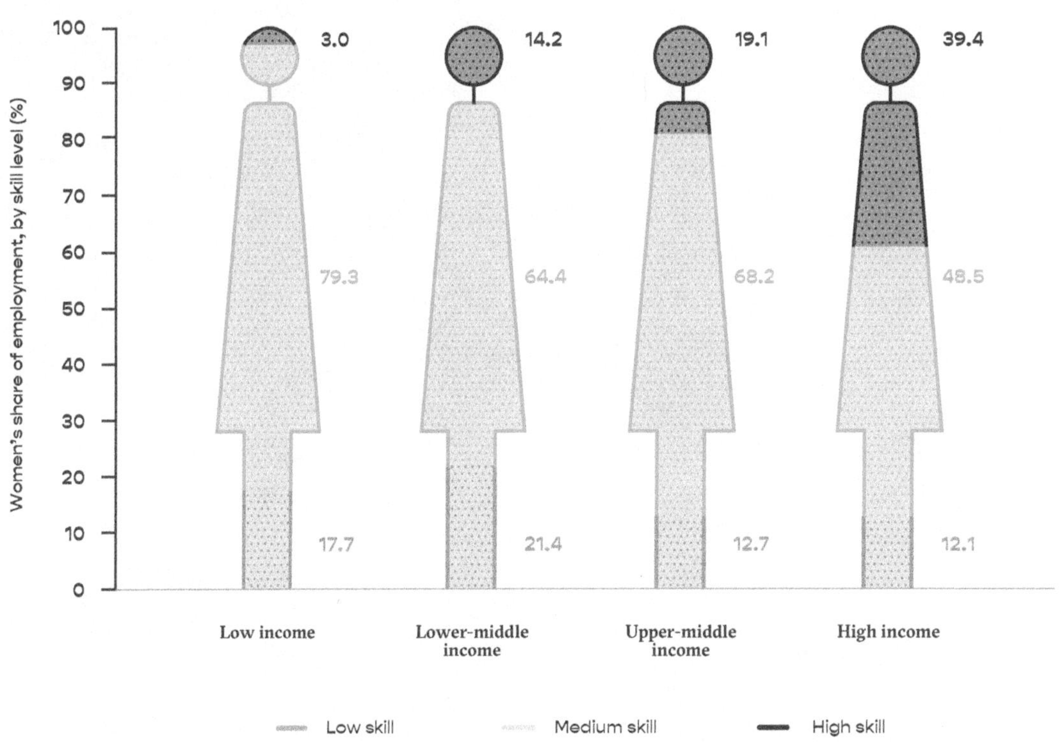

Source: International Labour Organization Department of Statistics, https://www.ilo.org/shinyapps/bulkexplorer11/?lang=en&segment=indicator&id=EMP_2EMP_SEX_OCU_NB_A.

Note: Employment by sex and occupation based on modeled estimates by the International Labour Organization, May 2018. Data presented by occupation are based on the International Standard Classification of Occupation (ISCO) and classified into three broad skill levels: Low skill refers to elementary occupations. Medium skill refers to occupations such as clerical support workers; service and sales workers; skilled agricultural, forestry, and fishery workers; craft and related trades workers; and plant and machine operators and assemblers. High skill refers to managers, professionals, and technicians and associate professionals.

harassment. The ability of formal workers to organize into trade unions further strengthens their positions in many countries. In addition, formal enterprises offer higher productivity and quality jobs largely because of workers' access to technology, education, market information, and training (ILO 2006).

Female workers are less likely to be informal if they work in sectors that trade more or are more integrated into GVCs. A household-level analysis across a sample of 31 developed and emerging countries finds that higher export values and GVC integration (both backward and forward) are linked to a lower probability of working informally, and this effect is higher for women compared to men. (figure 1.14).[6] The findings hold for two types of informality—(i) being unpaid and (ii) working without a contract—controlling for other worker-level determinants of informality including age, education level, marital status, and occupation (see methodology described in annex 1A).[7] Women's probability of being informal goes from 20 percent in sectors with low levels of exports or with low GVC integration to 13 percent in sectors with high levels of exports or high GVC integration. Women's rates of informality also decline more sharply than men's (an

Figure 1.12 Service sector jobs require higher education levels for women and men

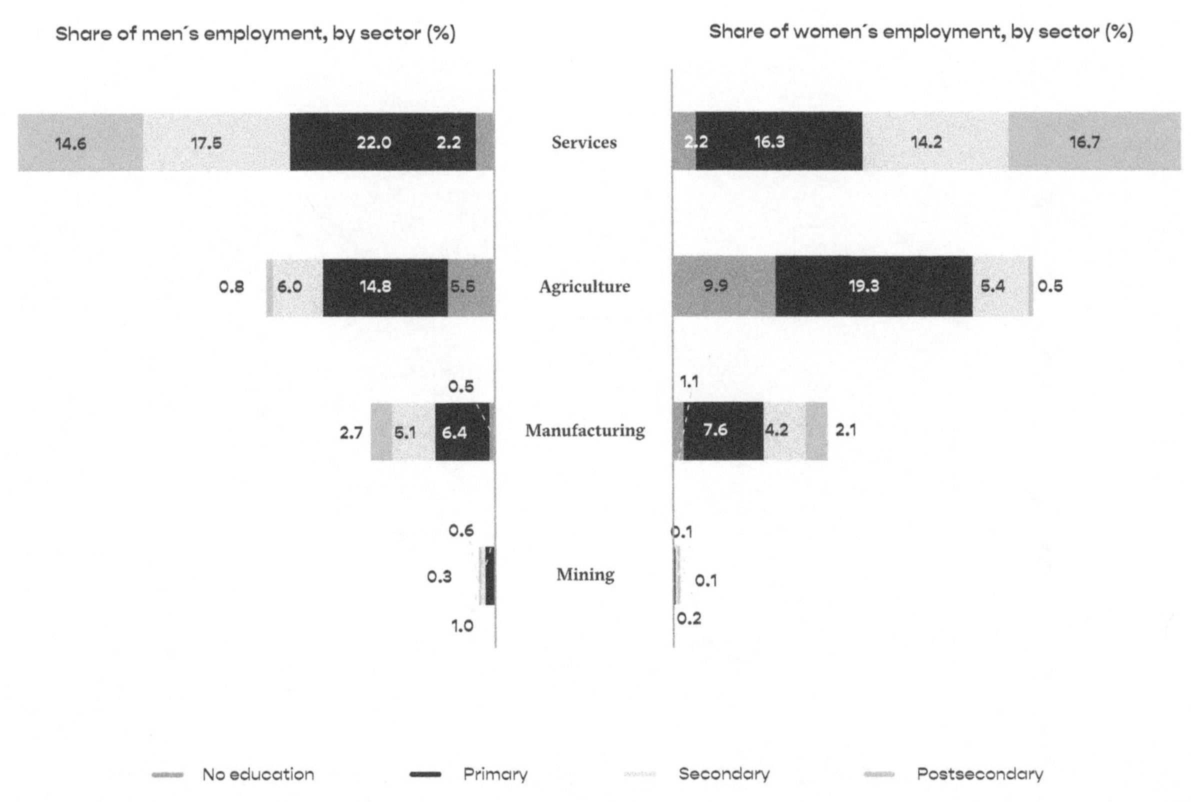

Source: World Bank Household Surveys for the most recent available years.

overall reduction of up to 7 percentage points for women compared to up to 4 percentage points for men) (figure 1.14).[8]

Regions that are less integrated into GVCs—particularly Sub-Saharan Africa and South Asia—have higher rates of informal employment for women. The share of informal employment in Sub-Saharan Africa is 86.4 percent for men and 92.1 percent for women. Similarly, the shares of informal employment in South Asia are 86.8 and 90.7 for men and women, respectively. In Latin America and the Caribbean, the share of informal workers is also slightly lower for men (52.3 percent) compared to women (54.3 percent) (figure 1.15). Women are more exposed to informal employment in more than 90 percent of Sub-Saharan African countries, 89 percent of South Asian countries, and almost 75 percent of countries in Latin America and the Caribbean (ILO 2018). These regions also tend to be specialized in commodities trade, as opposed to more sophisticated trade participation in other regions (see the first part of this section, "How trade affects women as workers").

Analysis for Mexico between 1993 and 2011 suggests that the tariff cuts that took effect beginning in 1993 under the North American Free Trade Agreement (NAFTA) increased the probability of working formally in the manufacturing sector, for both female and male workers. But these effects were not uniform. Formality increased for workers

Figure 1.13 Skilled agricultural and elementary occupations have the largest shares of women in low- and lower-middle-income countries

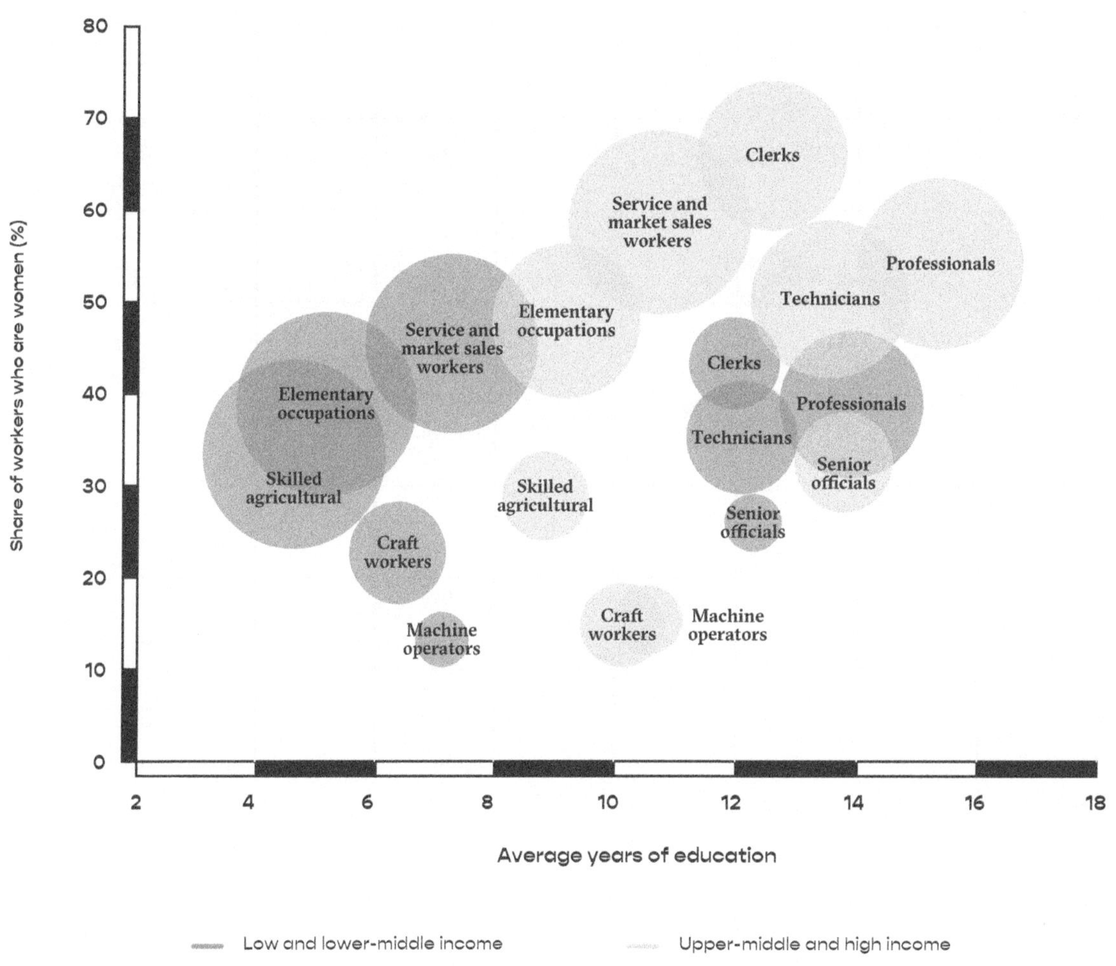

Source: International Labour Organization Department of Statistics, https://www.ilo.org/shinyapps/bulkexplorer11/?lang=en&segment=indicator&id=EMP_2EMP_SEX_OCU_NB_A.

Note: Circle size indicates the share of female employment. Classification of occupations comes from the International Standard Classification of Occupations (ISCO). Elementary occupations involve the performance of simple and routine tasks that may require the use of handheld tools and considerable physical effort. Most occupations in this major group require low skills (skills at the first ISCO skill level). Professionals increase the existing stock of knowledge, apply scientific or artistic concepts and theories, teach about the foregoing in a systematic manner, or engage in any combination of these activities. Competent performance in most occupations in this major group requires high skills (fourth position in the ISCO skill scale: ISCO-08). Income level defined using the World Bank income classification for 2018.

employed by large firms and decreased in small firms. In the services sector, the impact of trade liberalization on female formal employment was negative (Ben Yahmed and Bombarda 2018). In Brazil, tariff reductions during the period 1987–94 reduced the gender gaps in employment and labor force participation. Trade liberalization in the tradable male-intensive sector led to a contraction and decline in overall employment, but more so for male workers. It also fostered the relocation of male workers into the less tradable informal sector (Gaddis and Pieters 2017).

Figure 1.14 Women are less likely to be in informal jobs if they work in trade-integrated sectors

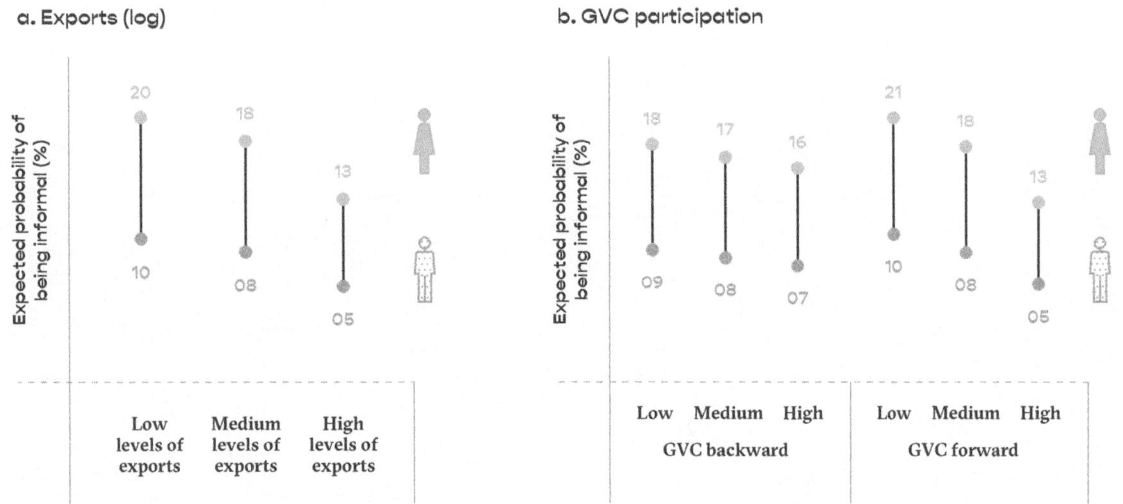

Source: World Bank Household Surveys for the most recent available years; World Bank Gender Disaggregated Labor Database (GDLD), http://datatopics.worldbank.org/gdld/.
Note: The graph shows the expected probability of a woman having an informal job, defining informality as being a nonpaid worker. Low, medium, and high refer to the observations falling under the 25th percentile, between the 25th and 75th percentiles, and above the 75th percentile, respectively. All regressions control for the common determinants of informality such as age, education level, marital status, and occupation. The model also includes country and sector fixed effects to control for unobservable shocks as specified in equation (1A.1) of annex 1A. All results shown are significant at the 10 percent level. Exporters are firms with an export share (direct or indirect) of at least 10 percent of total sales. GVC = global value chain.

Trade and technology affect the employment gap

In developing countries, international trade increases labor force participation and wages for women who get jobs in export industries, thereby reducing the employment and wage gap with men. The overall impact of trade on women workers, however, depends on the sector in which women are employed and on how these industries are affected by trade.

Gains from trade arise through the reallocation of resources in an economy, including the movement of workers from one sector to another.[9] This sectoral reallocation positively affects female workers who find jobs in tradable sectors that pay better wages (Bussolo and De Hoyos 2009). Export industries such as garments, where developing countries have comparative advantage, are a prime example of how women's concentration in low-value-added, low-wage, and labor-intensive work can bring into the workforce women who were previously employed informally or not employed at all (Otobe 2015).

Sectoral reallocation does not come without costs. Empirical studies show, however, that men and women face different costs of switching jobs across sectors—because of different social, geographical, and skills mobility. In the United States, for instance, it is relatively more costly for men to switch into the services industry, whereas women face relatively higher costs in moving into agriculture and mining and manufacturing sectors (Brussevich 2018). Trade liberalization can increase the probability of women leaving the labor market rather than moving to another sector. Analysis of the effect of import competition on family decisions in countries such as China suggests that, even though men and women can be equally affected by the negative trade shock in terms of earnings or job losses, women are more likely to

Figure 1.15 Informal employment remains at high levels in several regions

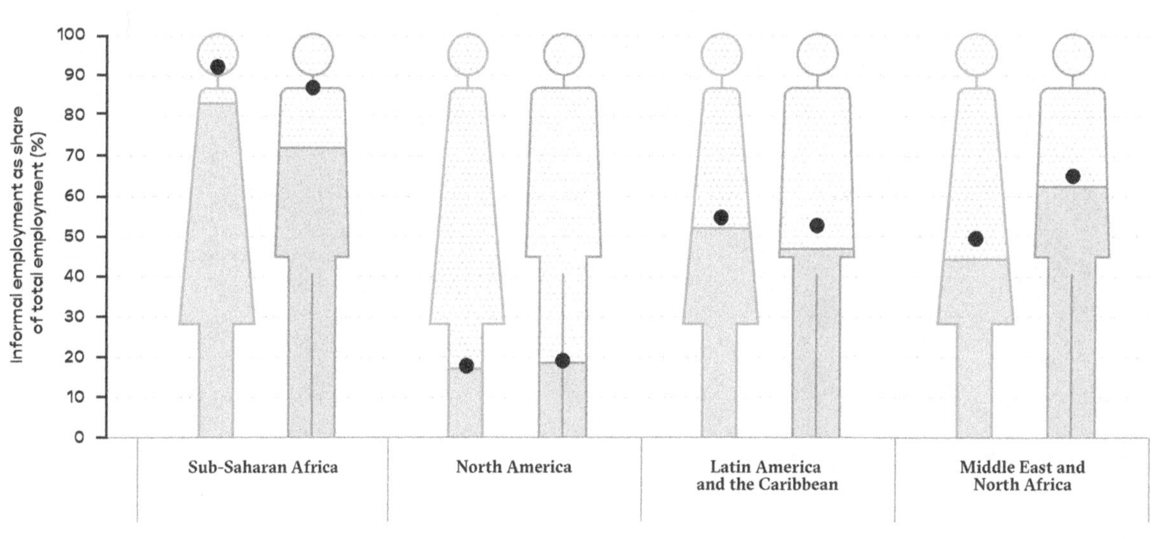

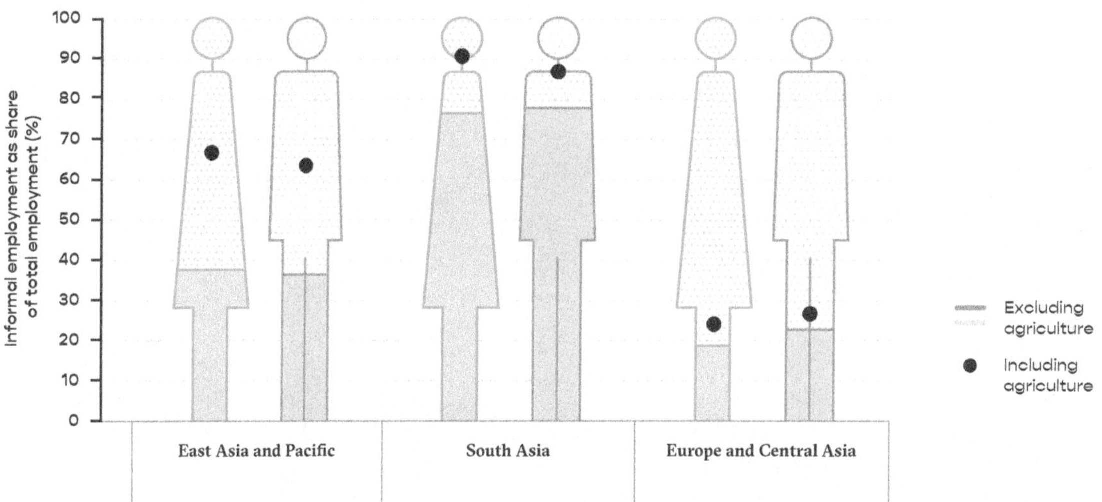

Source: ILO 2018.

leave the labor market and focus on family activities. That likelihood is reflected in a decrease in female labor force participation and a rise in birth rates and parental leave for married women (Keller and Utar 2018).

Technological change is another transmission channel through which trade affects women in the labor market. Trade liberalization may trigger the introduction of new technologies by firms in reaction to increased competition from foreign firms. Easier access to better-quality inputs can spur this technological upgrading, which, in turn, could affect men and women in the workplace differently. The effect depends on the tasks they perform (for example, blue-collar or white-collar tasks) and if these tasks have a complementary relationship with new technologies. Traditional technology generally requires more physically demanding blue-collar tasks, whereas modern technology is characterized by more computerized production processes and higher levels of productivity. The introduction of modern computerized production technologies that rely less on physical strength makes blue-collar women relatively more productive compared to more traditional technology.

The wider adoption of new, less physically demanding technologies in a country increases the share of women in blue-collar jobs and raises their relative wages. Evidence for a positive effect of trade-induced technological change on female blue-collar employment and wages has been found for Mexico following the entry into force of NAFTA (Juhn, Ujhelyi, and Villegas-Sanchez 2014). But the effect of trade-induced technology on women's wages and employment depends on the type of technology (whether it affects routine-type occupations or increases robotization or the purchase of computerized machinery and equipment). If technological upgrading increases a firm's capital intensity (that is, its use of capital per unit of labor), employed labor expenses represent a lower share of costs, disincentivizing firms to look for cheap low-skill labor. As a result, female employment and possibly wages fall, because women tend to be less skilled and less expensive than men. Analysis for 16 countries in South Asia and Latin America and the Caribbean between 1985 and 2007 finds that the productivity of the manufacturing sector (a proxy for the technological conditions of production) corresponded with a decrease in the female employment share in manufacturing (Tejani and Milberg 2016).

Figure 1.16 Trading manufacturing firms in developing and emerging countries show a significantly higher female wage share than nontrading firms

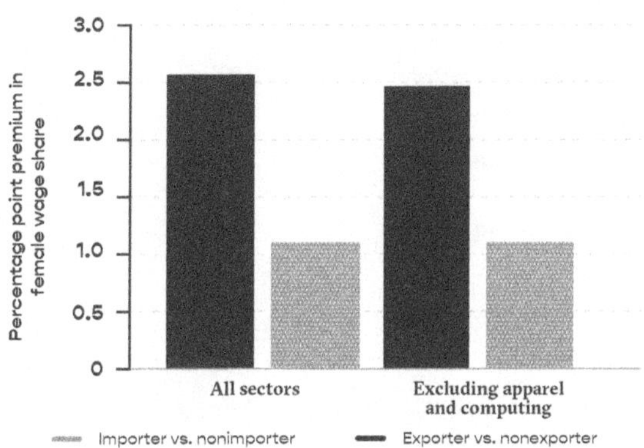

Source: Rocha and Winkler 2019, based on World Bank Enterprise Surveys for the most recent available years, https://www.enterprisesurveys.org/en/data, and World Bank Gender Disaggregated Labor Database (GDLD), http://datatopics.worldbank.org/gdld/.

Note: The graph shows mean differences between exporters and nonexporters and between importers and nonimporters, using firm's female share in total wages as dependent variable. Exporters are firms with an export share (direct or indirect) of at least 10 percent of total sales. Importers are firms with an imported input share of at least 10 percent of total inputs. All regressions control for firm output, capital intensity, total factor productivity, and relative wages at the sector level (all in natural logarithms) as well as country-sector, subnational region, and year fixed effects as specified in equation (1B.1) of annex 1B. All results shown are significant at the 10 percent level.

New evidence on the impact of trade on female employment

Manufacturing exports are linked to a higher female wage share in developing countries

Globally, women earn less than men and take home a smaller share of total wages. This inequality can discourage women from joining the workforce and limits women's power over their own life choices, such as pursuing education, buying a home, or starting a business. Trade can help decrease inequality between men and women by increasing women's share of wages. In developing countries, exporting firms show a significantly higher female share in total wages than nonexporting firms do.[10] Women account for 23 percent of all wages for manufacturing exporters compared to just 15.5 percent for nonexporters in 30 developing and emerging countries, according to firm-level analysis drawn from World Bank Enterprise Surveys.[11] Among all firms, women's share of wages is 2.5 percentage points higher in exporting firms compared to nonexporting firms (figure 1.16).[12] Women's share of total wages increases because exporting firms both pay better wages and increase the demand for labor. Doubling the value of exports in a country's manufacturing sector would increase the average female wage share by 5.8 percentage points on average. In other words, a 100 percent increase in export values in the manufacturing sample would equal an increase in the average female wage from a current level of 24 percent to roughly 30 percent.

Although increases in exports across all industries show an increase in the average female wage share, the apparel sector exhibits a particularly strong positive relationship because of women's opportunities in that sector.[13] A similar pattern arises in some services sectors. Doubling export values in non-male-intensive services sectors (such as construction and transportation) would increase the female wage share by over 2.7 percentage points, from the current share of 34.8 percent to 37.5 percent. Excluding more tradable sectors such as wholesale trade, transport, post and telecommunications, and financial intermediation and business activities from the services sample also suggests a positive relationship between exports and the female wage share (figure 1.17).

Trading is linked to a higher female labor share

Trade is positively and significantly correlated with an increase in the female share of the workforce. The female labor share for total workers is about 4 percentage points higher in exporting firms compared to nonexporting firms in developing and emerging countries (see annex 1B). By contrast, the average female labor share for total workers is only 2 percentage points higher for importing firms than for nonimporting firms, outlining the importance of the export channel even when

Figure 1.17 In developing countries, an increase in manufacturing exports is significantly linked to increases in the female wage share

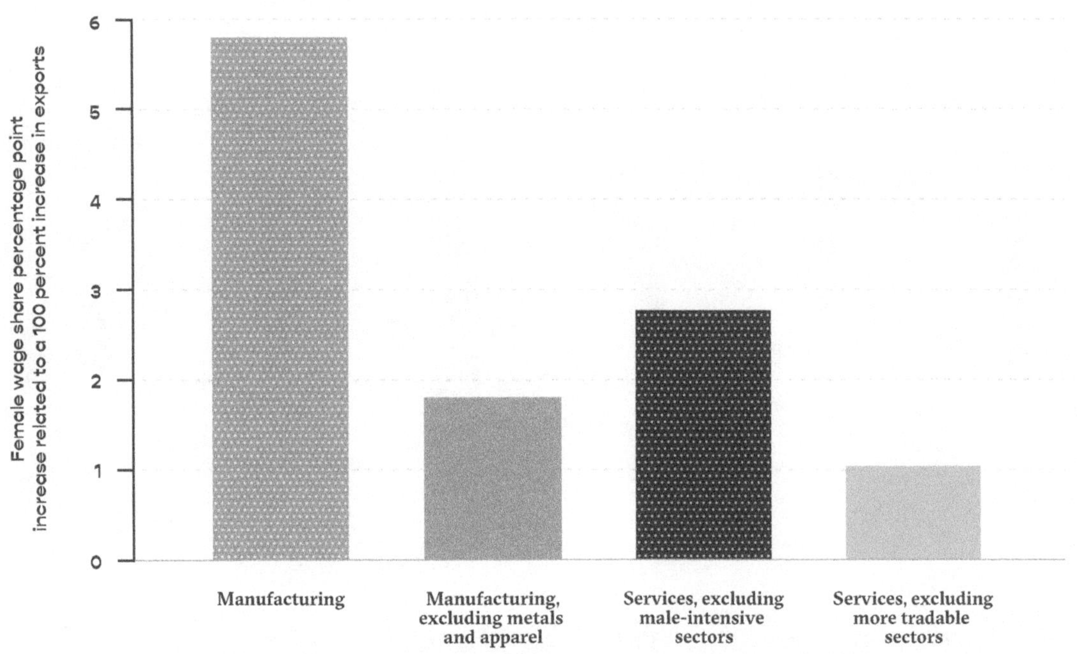

Source: Calculations based on Borin and Mancini 2015, using Eora Global Supply Chain Database, https://worldmrio.com/, and World Bank Gender Disaggregated Labor Database (GDLD), http://datatopics.worldbank.org/gdld/.
Note: Cross-sectional regression analysis including 50 low- and middle-income countries using the female wage share as dependent variable and export values (in natural logarithms) as independent variable, controlling for output, the relative wage ratio of male to female workers, and fixed-year and fixed-sector effects. Manufacturing sectors cover 9 Eora sectors; services sectors cover 12 services sectors. Analysis includes only sectors with an export value of at least US$1 million. Regression coefficient for total services sectors is insignificant. Male-intensive services sectors include recycling, construction, maintenance and repair, and transportation. More tradable services sectors include wholesale trade, transport, post and telecommunications, and financial intermediation and business activities.

accounting for non-female-intensive sectors such as apparel and computing (figure 1.18).[14]

Firms that are more integrated into the world economy have higher shares of female employment. Women make up 33 percent of the workforce of exporting firms compared to just 24 percent for nonexporting firms and 28 percent for nonimporting firms, according to an analysis of 29,000 manufacturing firms across 64 developing and emerging countries using World Bank Enterprise Surveys. This finding holds across most countries (figure 1.19), and shares are highest in Eastern European and Central Asian countries and countries that trade more and are more integrated into GVCs. For example, in countries such as Morocco, Romania, and Vietnam, exporting firms employ 50 percent or more women. These firms have created jobs for more than 5 million women, roughly 15 percent of the female population working in these countries. Women constitute 36.7 percent of the workforce of GVC firms and 37.8 percent of the workforce of foreign-owned firms—10.9 and 12.2 percentage points more, respectively, than the proportion for non-GVC and domestically owned firms (figure 1.20).[15]

The level of female employment differs by skills

Globally, the female labor share of exporters relative to nonexporters is relatively high in manufacturing industries that use less technology. This phenomenon is referred to as the female labor share premium. Low-

Figure 1.18 In developing and emerging countries, trading firms in manufacturing show a significantly higher female labor share than nontrading firms

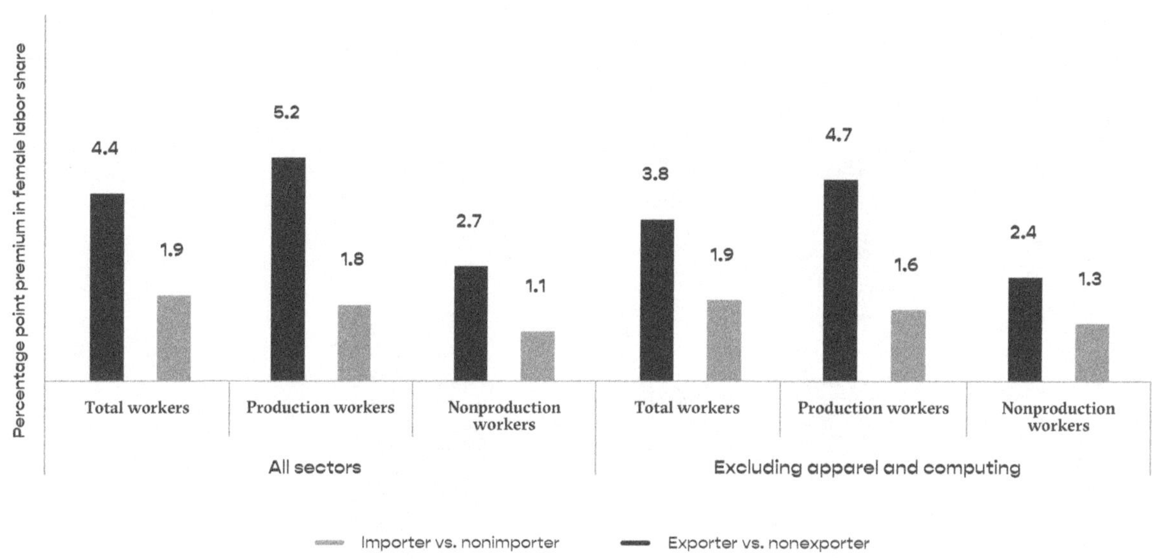

Source: Rocha and Winkler 2019, based on World Bank Enterprise Surveys for the most recent available years, https://www.enterprisesurveys.org/en/data, and World Bank Gender Disaggregated Labor Database (GDLD), http://datatopics.worldbank.org/gdld/.
Note: The graph shows mean differences in female labor share between exporters and nonexporters and between importers and nonimporters for total, production, and nonproduction workers. Exporters are firms with an export share (direct or indirect) of at least 10 percent of total sales. Importers are firms with an imported input share of at least 10 percent of total inputs. All regressions control for output, capital intensity, and total factor productivity (all in natural logarithms) as well as country-sector, subnational region, and year fixed effects as specified in equation (1B.2) of annex 1B. All results shown are significant at the 10 percent level.

tech industries like food and beverages, or textiles and clothing, show the largest positive correlation between exporting and the female share of employment. Exporters operating in low-tech industries have a female labor share that is on average 5.7 percentage points larger than the share for nonexporters in the same industries, controlling for other factors that could explain this difference. The female labor share premium for exporters relative to nonexporters in medium-tech industries drops to 2.6 percentage points, whereas that in medium- to high-tech industries is even lower (figure 1.21). These findings suggest that the positive relationship between exporting and the female labor share is stronger for tasks that appear to have a higher demand for more low-skilled workers.[16]

Female ownership and management have a positive effect on female employment

Female-owned and female-managed exporters employ a higher percentage of women than do firms owned and managed by males and nonexporting firms owned and managed by both sexes. In exporting firms with a female top manager, the share of women workers is 8 percentage points higher relative to nonexporting firms, and the premium for exporting firms with a male top manager is only 4 percentage points (figure 1.22). The correlation between importing and the female labor share is eight times higher for importing firms with a female top manager compared to those with a male top manager. The results underline the importance of female corporate leadership for female employment (World Economic Forum 2017).

Figure 1.19 Average female labor share across developing and emerging countries is higher for manufacturing firms that export

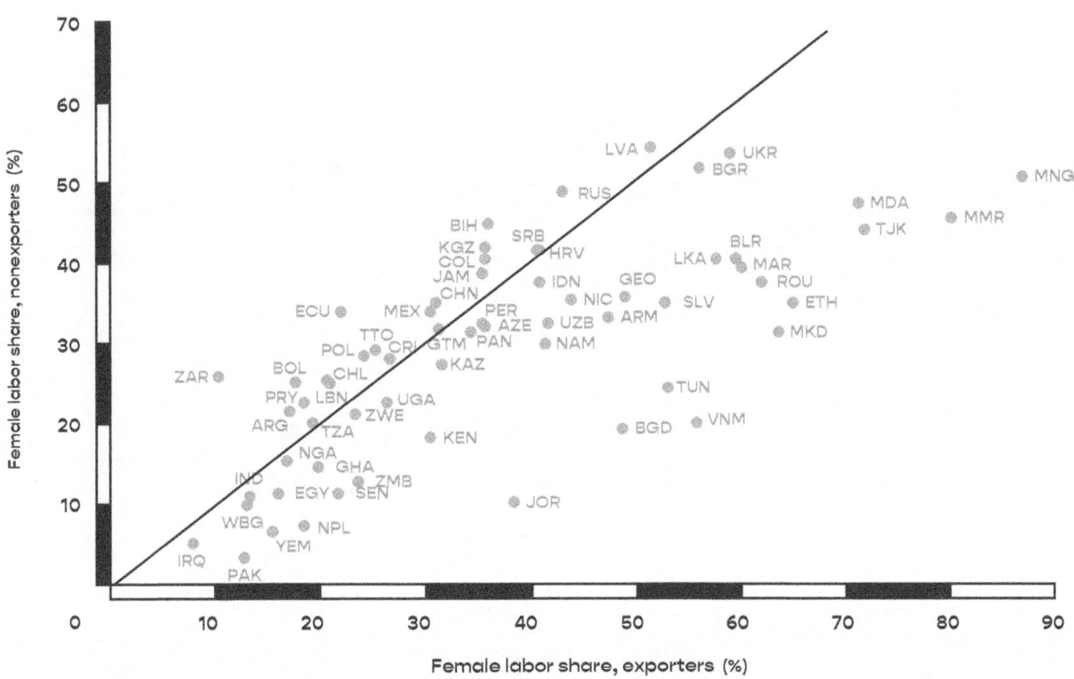

Source: Rocha and Winkler 2019, based on World Bank Enterprise Surveys for the most recent available years, https://www.enterprisesurveys.org/en/data.
Note: The graph shows weighted averages by country, using the number of permanent workers as weights. Exporters are firms with an export share (direct or indirect) of at least 10 percent of total sales. For a list of country codes go to https://www.iso.org/obp/ui/#search/code/.

New simulation model shows trade liberalization can boost female employment in some developing countries

Trade liberalization reforms not only increase exports, imports, and GDP but also—in developing countries with a comparative advantage in female-intensive sectors, such as textiles and apparel—significantly expand female employment.[17]

The implementation of the African Continental Free Trade Area (AfCFTA) agreement—the largest free trade area in the world, connecting 54 countries and 1.3 billion people—would create better-paying jobs for female workers, particularly for the skilled. As a result of output expansion in key female-labor-intensive sectors across the continent, notably in services (increase of US$149 billion in output), wages for female workers would grow faster as compared to those of male workers. By 2035, wages for skilled and unskilled female labor would be 4.0 and 3.7 percent higher (relative to baseline), respectively, compared with a 3.2 percent increase for all males. For a woman earning US$5 a day, this increase is enough to pay for one extra family member's personal supplies, school supplies, and uniform for an entire school year. The results vary by country, however, reflecting the heterogeneity of economic conditions in Africa. A few selected cases could even lead to worsening of the gender or skill wage gap. Overall, these results on wages are upper-bound estimates that serve to highlight the importance of implementing complementary policy reforms that support labor mobility and equality of opportunities (World Bank, forthcoming).

1.20 Average female labor share in developing and emerging countries is higher for manufacturing firms integrated into global trade

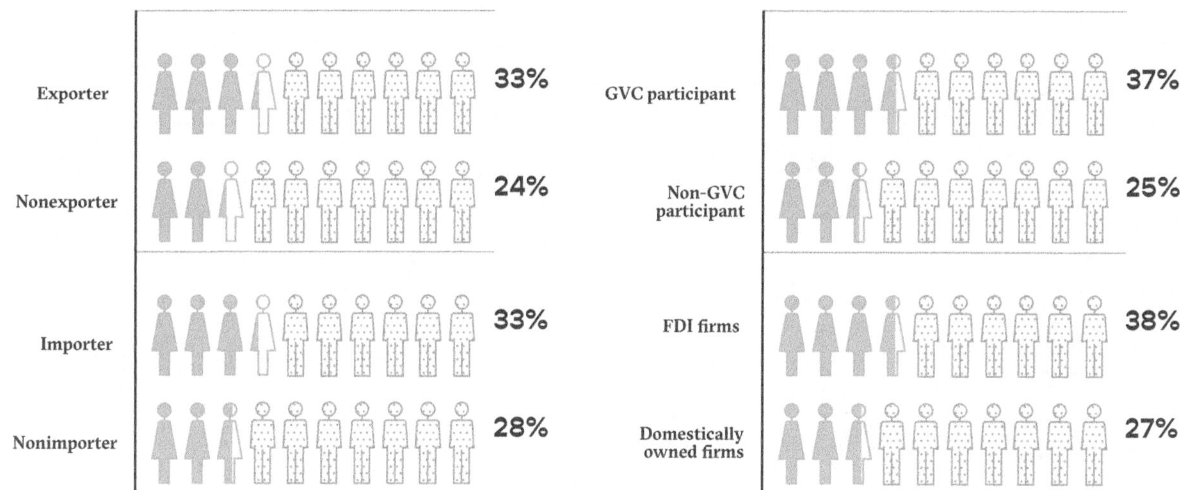

Source: Rocha and Winkler 2019, based on World Bank Enterprise Surveys for the most recent available years, https://www.enterprisesurveys.org/en/data.
Note: The graph shows weighted averages by firm type, using the number of permanent workers as weights. Exporters are firms with an export share (direct or indirect) of at least 10 percent of total sales. Importers are firms with an imported input share of at least 10 percent of total inputs. GVC (global value chain) participants are firms that are classified as both exporters and importers. FDI (foreign direct investment) refers to firms with a foreign ownership share of at least 10 percent.

Figure 1.21 The female labor share premium in exporting firms is higher in low-technology manufacturing sectors

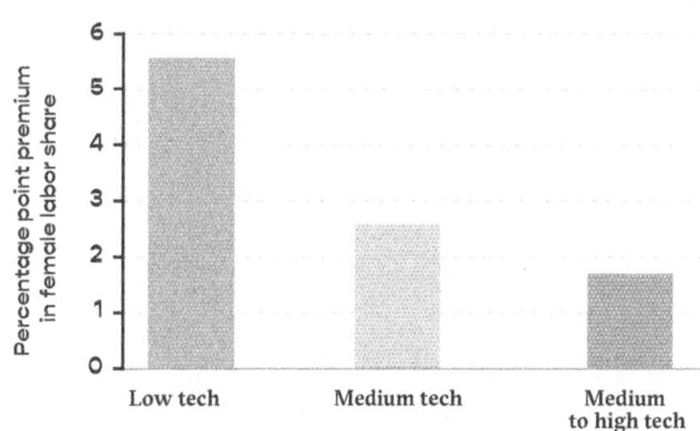

Source: Rocha and Winkler 2019, based on World Bank Enterprise Surveys for the most recent available years, https://www.enterprisesurveys.org/en/data, and World Bank Gender Disaggregated Labor Database (GDLD), http://datatopics.worldbank.org/gdld/.
Note: The graph shows the percentage point premium (mean difference) between exporters and nonexporters by sectoral technology intensity, using a firm's female labor share as dependent variable. All regressions control for output, capital intensity, and total factor productivity (in natural logarithms) as well as country-sector, subnational region, and year fixed effects. All results shown are significant at the 10 percent level.

Figure 1.22 In the manufacturing sector, trading firms managed by women have a higher female share of the workforce than nontrading firms

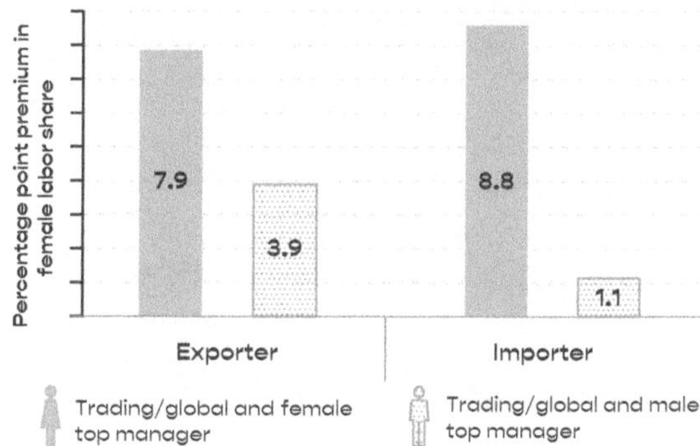

Source: Rocha and Winkler 2019.
Note: The graph shows the percentage point premium (mean difference) in the female labor share between exporters and nonexporters and between importers and nonimporters, for firms with a male and female top manager. All regressions control for output, capital intensity, and total factor productivity as well as country sector, subnational region, and fixed-year effects. All results shown are significant at the 10 percent level.

Credit: ©Monkey Business Images/ Shutterstock.com. Used with permission; further permission required for reuse.

Figure 1.23 The wage gap between female and male workers still exists

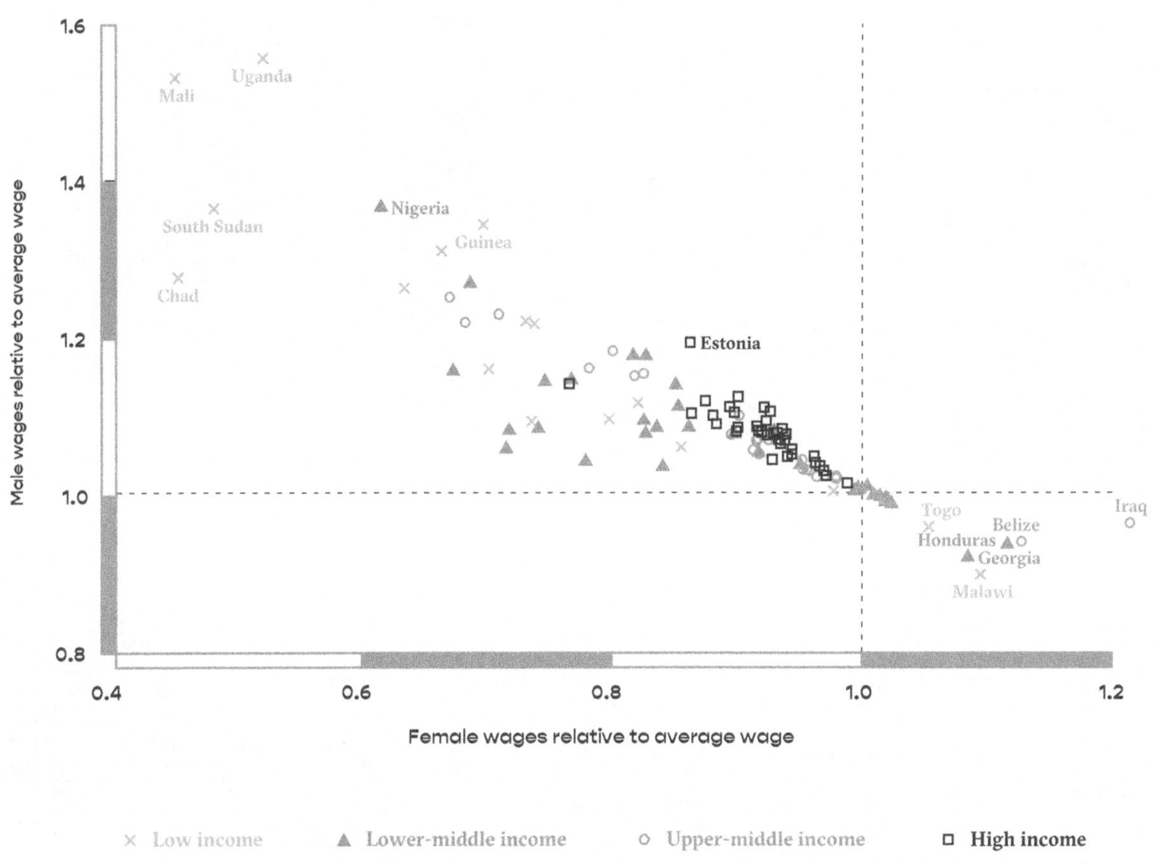

Source: International Labour Organization Department of Statistics, https://www.ilo.org/shinyapps/bulkexplorer3/?lang=en&segment=indicator&id=EAR_4HRL_SEX_OCU_CUR_NB_A; World Bank Household Surveys for the most recent available years.
Note: Information on male and female wages is provided on a weekly basis. Wages are aggregated across individuals using simple averages. Figure shows most recent data available by country (mainly between 2014 and 2016); some exceptions have information between 2001 and 2013.

Patterns of the declining—but continuing—gender wage gap

Since the 1960s the pay gap between women and men has narrowed substantially, particularly in developed countries, but has not disappeared (Cozzi et al. 2018). The lower gender wage gap over time has been linked to increases in demand for female labor as a result of countries' integration into female-intensive GVCs such as apparel, increases in capital stock and its complementary relationship with female labor, and increased decision-making power for women's consumption.

Almost all countries have a wage gap, with male average wages higher than total average wages (figure 1.23). The gender wage gap is particularly high in Mali and Uganda, where men earn 50 to 60 percent more than the average worker, and in Guinea, Nigeria, and South Sudan, where male wages are between 30 and 40 percent higher. A few countries—mainly in Latin America and the Caribbean and Sub-Saharan Africa—pay higher average wages for female workers. Georgia, Iraq, and Malawi, for example, have more highly educated women than men; and, in Honduras and Togo, less educated women earn more than similarly educated men.

The values provided in figure 1.23 are based on weekly average wages (hourly earnings

Figure 1.24 Men tend to work longer hours than women, especially in low-income countries

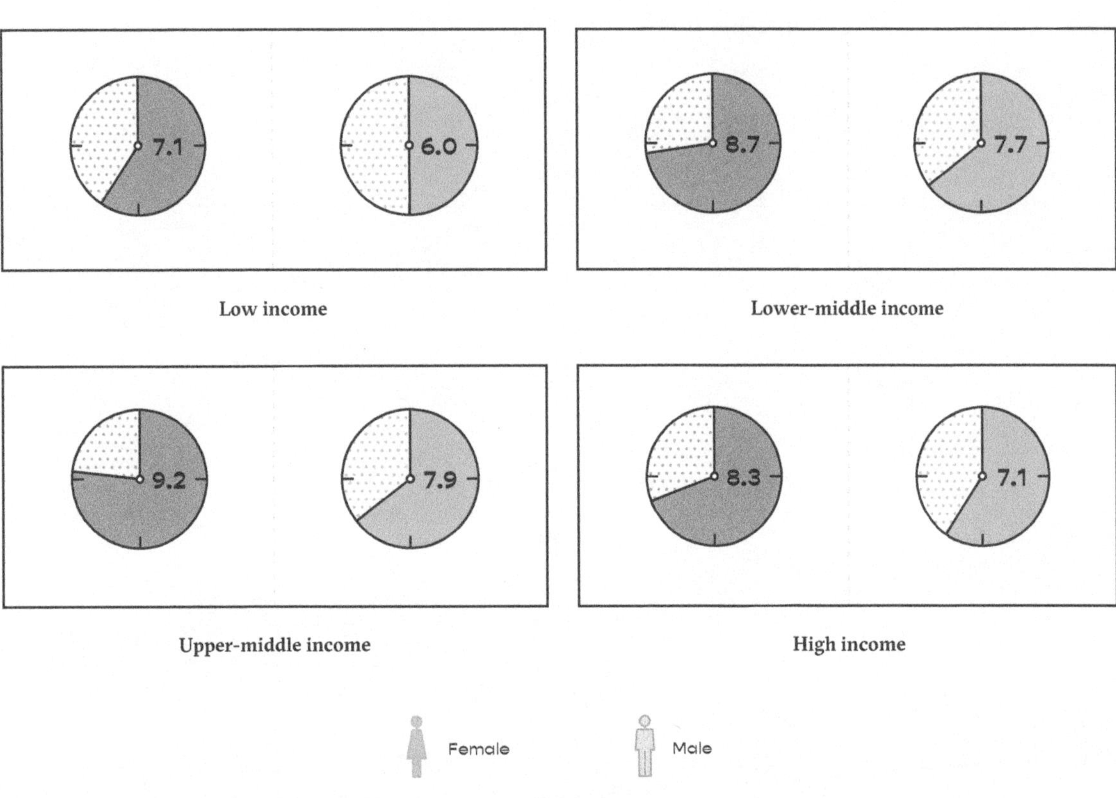

Source: World Bank Household Surveys for the most recent available years.
Note: Average number of hours worked during the last week for a sample of 65 countries.

data are unavailable). A major explanation for the calculated gender wage gap across countries could be the lower number of hours worked by women relative to men, especially in low-income countries (figure 1.24). Male workers spend on average between 16 percent and 21 percent more time at work, according to a sample of 65 countries from the World Bank Household Surveys. A higher gender wage gap can also reflect a country's comparative advantage in labor-intensive production. Countries with larger gender wage gaps have been shown to have higher comparative advantage in labor-intensive production on the basis of a sample of 40 countries over the period 1975–2000 (Busse and Spielmann 2006). This finding is in line with substantially lower wage gaps for middle-income countries relative to low-income countries (figure 1.25).

The gender wage gap tends to be lower in countries with higher levels of education, although some evidence suggests that it may increase for the most educated people. The gender wage gap is highest for workers with no education. It is smaller for workers with primary and secondary education and smallest for workers with postsecondary education (figure 1.26). Similarly, women's time spent at work relative to men increases with level of education (figure 1.27). Although men with no education spend 33 percent more time on work than do uneducated women, this difference falls to 17 percent

Figure 1.25 The wage gap is smaller for middle-income countries than for low-income countries

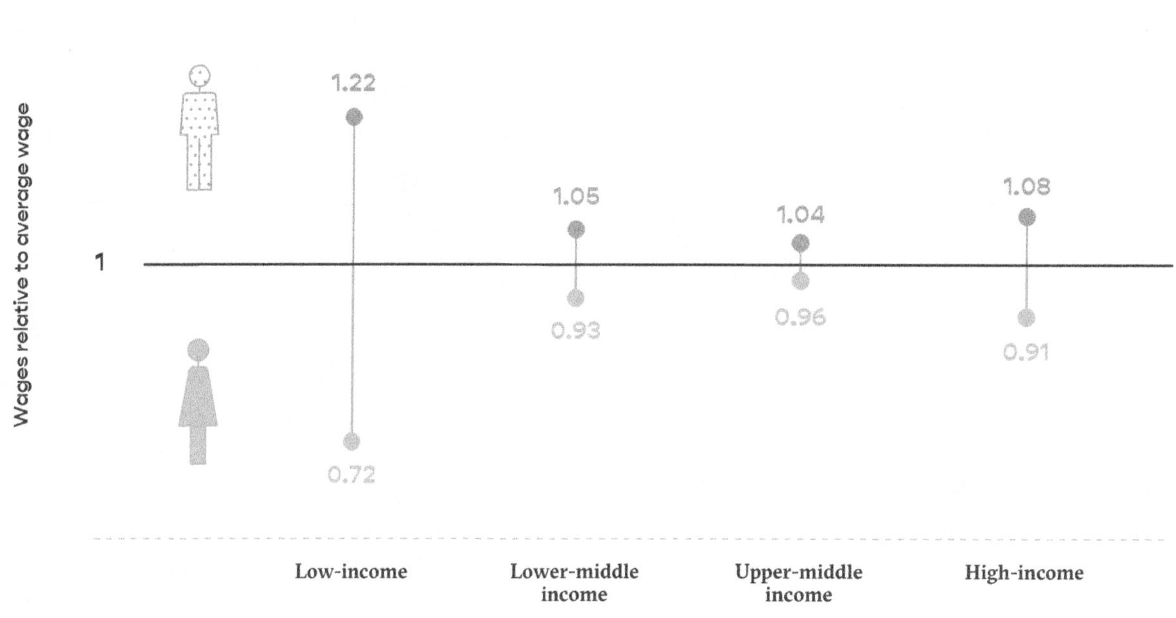

Source: International Labour Organization Department of Statistics, https://www.ilo.org/shinyapps/bulkexplorer3/?lang=en&segment=indicator&id=EAR_4HRL_SEX_OCU_CUR_NB_A, and World Bank Household Surveys for the most recent available years.
Note: Average weekly hours actually worked per employee. Figure shows most recent data available by country (mainly between 2014 and 2016); some exceptions have information between 2001 and 2013.

and 10 percent for workers with secondary and postsecondary education, respectively.

Female discrimination and trade

Discrimination against female workers is common but costly

Despite the increasingly important role women play in most economies, discrimination and bias continue to reduce women's ability to benefit from trade. According to the 2013 World Values Survey, 39 percent of surveyed individuals agreed that, "when jobs are scarce, men should have more right to a job than women" and 31 percent of them agreed that, "if a woman earns more money than her husband, it's almost certain to cause problems" (map 1.1).[18]

Gender bias, however, can be very costly. According to Becker's (1957) canonical model on discrimination, sectors facing higher levels of competition will have on average higher shares of women workers (because of less discrimination). The explanation for the model's finding is that, in more competitive markets, firms charging higher prices will tend to lose market share and will be forced to leave the market. Because these are precisely the firms with low shares of female employment, a necessary consequence is a rise in the share of female workers in the industry. In the context of international trade, a rise in international trade should lead to an increase in competition. A higher impact of international trade on the levels of competition is expected in more concentrated sectors (that is, sectors that are less competitive) than in less concentrated ones. Hence, more concentrated sectors experiencing a higher

Figure 1.26 Wage gaps between women and men decrease with higher levels of education

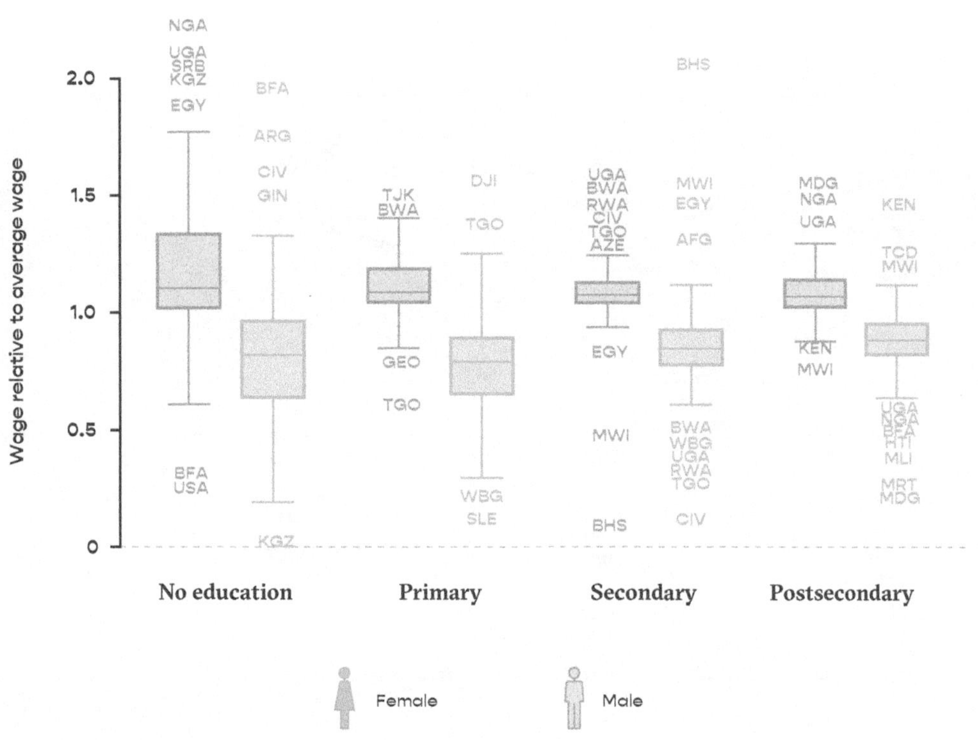

Source: World Bank Household Surveys for the most recent available years.
Note: Boxplot is a standardized way of displaying the distribution of data based on the five-number summary: minimum, first quartile, median, third quartile, and maximum. The central rectangle spans the first quartile to the third quartile; bold segment inside the rectangle shows the median; and "whiskers" above and below the box show the locations of the minimum and maximum. Outliers are plotted as individual points. For a list of country codes go to https://www.iso.org/obp/ui/#search/code/.

rise of international trade should see larger rises in female employment shares and larger reductions in the gender wage gap.

Becker's model has been confirmed in several empirical studies that illustrate the pro-competition and market size effects of trade liberalization. Empirical evidence suggests that, for a large cross-section of countries, gender wage discrimination falls with more economic development and trade (Oostendorp 2009). In the 1990s, Uruguay opened its economy to international trade with the creation of the Southern Common Market (Mercosur) with Argentina, Brazil, and Paraguay. The decline in import tariffs led to greater foreign competition and to reductions in the gender wage gap in trade-affected sectors. Better market access also reduced the gender wage gap in sectors that were already competitive or had a low level of concentration prior to trade liberalization. By contrast, access to foreign markets allowed firms in sectors dominated by a few (large) firms to increase the gender wage gap (Ben Yahmed 2017).

In Colombia, unilateral trade liberalization starting in 1984 and entry into WTO in 1995 led to a modification of hiring practices of firms in the manufacturing sector and to lower levels of discrimination against women. Firms affected by the greatest reduction in tariffs increased the female share of their workforce more than did firms in industries that faced little or no tariff reduction. Specifically, trade liberalization increased female employment by almost 7 percent in those sectors exposed to lower tariffs compared to sectors with no liberalization. In addition, the effect of tariff liberalization was larger

Figure 1.27 Women's time spent at work relative to men increases with a higher level of education

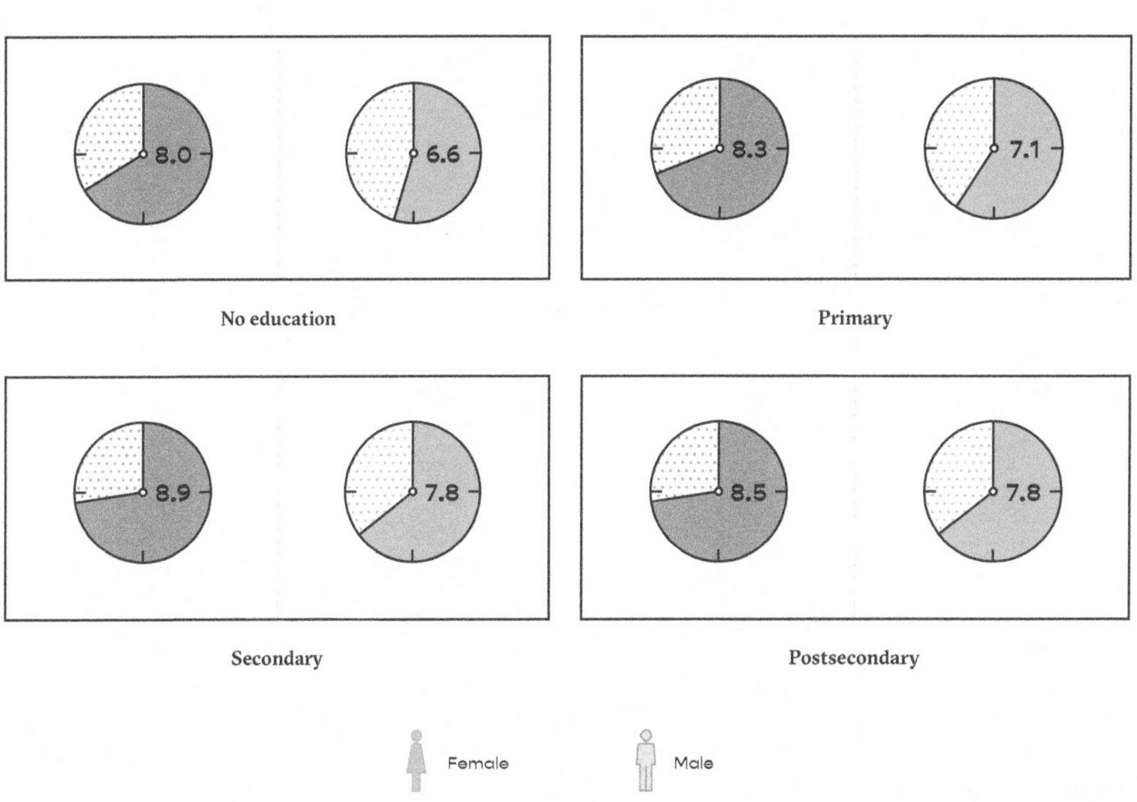

Source: World Bank Household Surveys for the most recent available years.
Note: Average number of hours worked during the last week for a sample of 65 countries.

for nonexporting firms—for example, firms that initially faced little competitive pressure (Ederington, Minier, and Troske 2009).

In the United States, increased trade openness between 1976 and 1993 lowered the gender wage gap because of the reduced ability of manufacturing firms to discriminate against women.[19] A similar pattern was found in German manufacturing, independent of women's skill level (Black and Brainerd 2004).

Trade can also potentially reduce discrimination against women by promoting the adoption of gender-related regulatory standards. Exporting economies that are more "women friendly" could benefit as a result of pressure from consumers and nongovernmental organizations that increases their products' international competitiveness (Greenhill, Mosley, and Prakash 2009). The underlying logic is similar to countries and sectors that have benefitted from adopting core labor standards or fair-trade practices. Countries competing for foreign direct investment (FDI) can improve their attractiveness as potential investment hosts by improving women's economic rights: such improvements are typically associated with greater labor supply and enhanced human capital quality and productivity.

Unilateral policies to decrease discrimination against females might put pressure on competing countries to make similar policy moves, thus leading to upward

Map 1.1 Discrimination against female workers persists in many countries

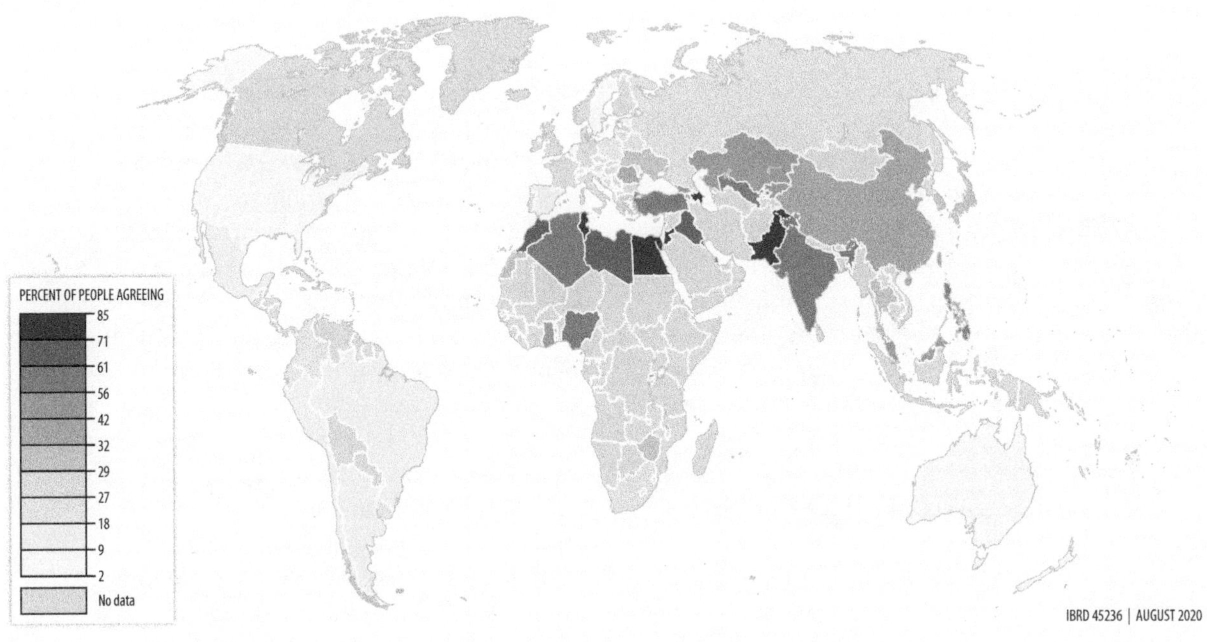

Source: World Values Survey 2013, http://www.worldvaluessurvey.org/WVSDocumentationWV6.jsp.
Note: Map shows responses to question V44 of the World Values Surveys, which asks respondents to agree or disagree with the statement: "When jobs are scarce, men should have more right to a job that women."

policy convergence on women's economic rights (Wang 2018). Some governments have established government procurement schemes that award contracts for services only to companies guaranteeing compliance with the principle of equal pay for men and women (box 1.2). Consumers and nongovernmental organizations in countries with better economic rights protection for women can also pressure their governments and the private sector to adopt stricter standards to ensure that imported goods or inputs follow the same ethical practices that are applied at home (Prakash and Potoski 2007). More stringent standards might create incentives for exporting countries to also improve protection of women's economic rights in order to ensure that the countries don't lose their market access (Neumayer and De Soysa 2011).

Empirical analysis performed for a sample of developing and developed countries between 1987 and 2007 suggests that stronger economic and social rights for women in one country spill over into a country with weaker rights when the two countries are connected via trade or FDI (Neumayer and De Soysa 2011). Additional analysis between 1999 and 2009 also confirms that governments tend to promote gender parity through protection of women's rights in response to similar policy choices by their economic competitors (Wang 2018).

Box 1.2 Procurement policy in support of women's equal pay

Government procurement represents 10 percent of Switzerland's gross domestic product and 25 percent of its expenditure. The Swiss government has set up a procurement policy giving preference in allocating its government contracts to companies that respect equal pay. For this purpose, Switzerland created a free tool to evaluate companies' equal pay policies. This tool, called Logib, requires companies to provide information (no older than 36 months) such as the salaries and gender of their employees. The requirements apply to bidders with 50 or more employees.

In addition, the Federal Office of Gender Equality (FOGE) conducts independent investigations to verify whether the companies are complying with equal pay requirements. If wage discrimination is identified in a company, the tender can be revoked or a penalty can be imposed. In 2018, the government conducted 104 controls, which revealed that less than one-half of the companies reviewed had no systematic discrimination and that 12.5 percent were violating wage equality conditions required for participation in federal public procurement. Switzerland allows those companies in violation of its procurement requirement to correct their policies. It is interesting to note that 50 percent of businesses found to be in violation of wage equality requirements checked their pay practices and raised women's wages. This tool won the United Nations prize for public service in 2012 (der Boghossian 2019).

Source: der Boghossian 2019.

Trade liberalization does not necessarily favor all women

The evidence above notwithstanding, there is also evidence that trade liberalization may reduce women's bargaining power to achieve wage gains. Trade liberalization influences the gender wage gap, but the direction depends on the sector of comparative advantage and the sectoral specialization and skill level of women relative to men.[20] Increased competition may reinforce discrimination by lowering women's bargaining power in the labor market (Darity and Williams 1985; Williams 1987).

In the Republic of Korea, competition from foreign trade in concentrated industries, such as food and chemical industries, is positively associated with wage discrimination against women (Berik, van der Meulen Rodgers, and Zveglich 2004). This result is in line with the theory that firms compete for export market share on the basis of absolute (rather than relative) costs of production. Trade liberalization stimulates the search for lower cost of labor, because firms compete to reduce absolute unit costs. Firms might then take advantage of gender inequalities and hire women (considered a cheap and flexible labor force) to reduce costs. Wages in this theory are determined by the relative bargaining power of groups of workers. As a result, even if female employment increases, women's pay might not necessarily improve.

Exporting firms often demand highly flexible employees (for working peculiar hours, taking late night phone calls, and engaging in international travel arranged at short notice). Women are at an increased risk of discrimination when they are perceived to be less flexible. This theory is confirmed in a study in Norway where the gender wage gap was found to be higher in exporting than in nonexporting firms. Interestingly, this effect is driven by college-educated workers, a result that suggests that women are particularly disadvantaged as they compete with men for jobs with higher levels of responsibilities (Bøler, Javorcik, and Ulltveit-Moe 2018). The study also shows that, when Norway introduced legislation allowing men to take longer paternity leave, in support of the argument that lack of flexibility is a major obstacle for women's career opportunities, the wage gap was reduced. Similarly, a recent analysis on the manufacturing sector in South Africa reports a higher gender wage gap for exporters attributed to this flexibility channel (Janse van Rensburg et al. 2019).

Evidence on trade, wages, and the gender wage gap

In aggregate, trade raises incomes and net welfare for both men and women; however, the evidence shows wide variations in these effects across industries and between groups of workers. The fact that women occupy lower-skill occupations on average could lead them to benefit less from trade than their male counterparts, who occupy higher-skill jobs. This disparity could lead to certain instances in which women increase their wages and incomes at the same time that the gap between men's and women's wages increases.[21]

As noted previously, firms that trade—by exporting, importing, or integrating into GVCs—have lower employment and wage gaps than nontrading firms (figure 1.28). Firm-level analysis for a sample of 64 developing and emerging countries from the World Bank Enterprise Surveys shows that the gender wage gap is smaller for firms that trade.[22] For firms involved in FDI, the relationship between female employment shares and average wages becomes positive. In other words, foreign firms that employ a higher share of women pay higher average wage rates, which could relate to cultural norms adopted in those firms. Increasing the female labor share by 10 percentage points is associated with 2.6 percent higher average wage rates of foreign firms. Interestingly, the correlation between the female labor share and average wages is even higher for FDI firms that offer training to their employees compared to FDI firms that do not train their workforce.[23]

Figure 1.28 The negative relationship between the female labor share and the average wage rate is smaller for trading firms

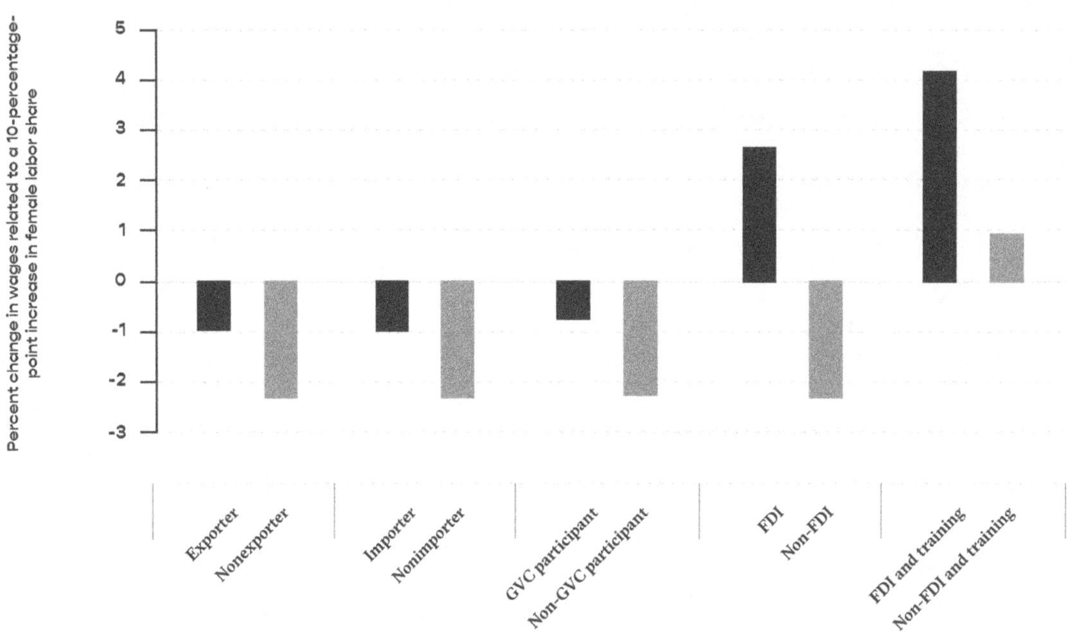

Source: World Bank Enterprise Surveys for the most recent available years, https://www.enterprisesurveys.org/en/data.
Note: The percent change in wages reflects the change related to a 10-percentage-point increase in the female labor share. The graph shows the results of regression analysis described in annex 1C using the firm's average wage rate (in natural logarithms) as dependent variable and the female labor share as independent variable. The model interacts exporter, importer, GVC (global value chain) participant, and FDI (foreign direct investment) dummies with the female labor share variable to assess the mediating role of trading/FDI status. Exporters are firms with an export share (direct or indirect) of at least 10 percent of total sales. Importers are firms with an imported input share of at least 10 percent of total inputs. GVC participants are firms that are classified as both exporters and importers. FDI refers to firms with a foreign ownership share of at least 10 percent. All regressions control for age, firm size, capital intensity, and skill intensity as well as country-sector, subnational region, and year fixed effects. All regressions are at least statistically significant at the 5 percent level.

Figure 1.29 The share of female-owned firms and exporters increases with the level of specialization of countries into more sophisticated trade

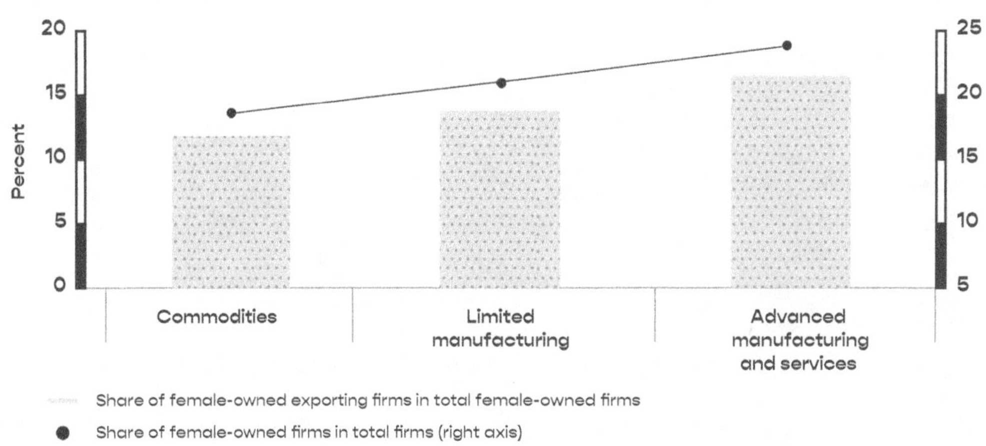

Source: World Bank Enterprise Surveys for the most recent available years, https://www.enterprisesurveys.org/en/data; World Bank 2019.
Note: The graph shows the average (mean) share of female-owned exporting firms in total female-owned firms (left axis) and the share of female-owned firms in total firms (right axis) for 1.5 million firms across 69 countries by GVC (global value chain) taxonomy group (see box 1.3 in World Bank 2019). Female-owned firms are defined as firms with a female ownership share of at least 50 percent.

How trade affects *women* producers and business owners

The rise of GVCs and the increase in digital technologies have opened opportunities for businesses to participate in and gain from trade. Advances in logistics have made it easier for small producers to get products, however small and specialized, to new markets; and the dispersion of advanced technologies across borders has made it possible for entrepreneurs to connect to business opportunities in foreign countries. Women producers and business owners, however, are frequently held back by a variety of constraints that reduce their productivity. Farmers and other agricultural workers—numerically the most important group of women producers—remain severely disadvantaged by domestic resource constraints, such as access to finance, and limited international market access due to high tariffs.

Like workers, women producers and business owners are affected by trade through sectoral reallocation and technological change. Female-owned businesses specializing in the production of goods or services in which a country has a comparative advantage tend to benefit from trade liberalization (see the earlier section, "Trade and technology affect the employment gap"). Similarly, if women's businesses invest in new technologies because of increased competition, they can increase their productivity. Both dynamics offer women business owners possible gains from trade, in addition to valuable export opportunities that arise from market opening abroad. The extent to which women benefit from trade depends on whether they are adversely affected by import competition and discrimination (either explicitly or through established social practices) and on the size of the company and women producers' access to information technology.

How countries integrate into 21st-century trade shapes the share of female business ownership and female traders. The share of majority-female-owned businesses increases from 18 percent for countries specializing in commodities to over 20 percent for countries in limited manufacturing, and to over 23 percent for countries in the advanced manufacturing and services group (figure 1.29, right axis). Among majority-female-owned firms, the share of exporters also grows with countries' upgrading along these groups. Although the share of exporters among female-owned firms is only 12 percent in countries specializing in commodities, it exceeds 16 percent in countries in the advanced manufacturing and services stage (figure 1.29, left axis). Despite improvements in female business ownership that come with more trade sophistication, these shares should not mask the fact that the share of female-owned exporters in all firms in advanced manufacturing and services countries is less than 4 percent, compared to 20 percent for nonexporters.

Female-owned global businesses are rare and less likely to trade than male-owned firms

The share of majority-female-owned exporters and importers is much smaller than that of male-owned traders.[24] An analysis of World Bank Enterprise Survey data covering over 35,000 manufacturing firms and over 31,000 services firms across 76 developing and emerging countries shows that, among exporting firms, males own 90 percent of manufacturers and 88 percent of services firms. Women-owned businesses also represent a lower share of GVC and FDI firms (figure 1.30). Female-owned firms are less likely than their male counterparts to export, to engage in GVCs, and to be foreign-owned. The difference tends to be larger for manufacturing firms.

Figure 1.30 A low percentage of firms is female-owned and global

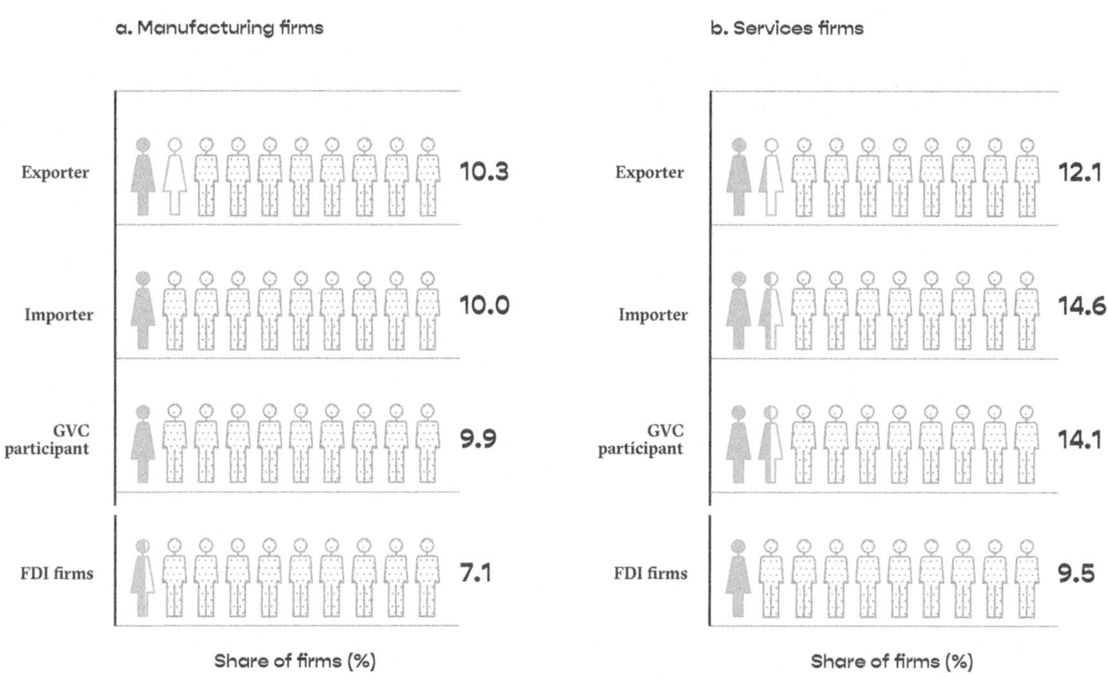

Source: World Bank Enterprise Surveys for the most recent available years, https://www.enterprisesurveys.org/en/data.
Note: Ownership by gender of at least 50 percent. Exporters are firms with an export share (direct or indirect) of at least 10 percent of total sales. Importers are firms with an imported input share of at least 10 percent of total inputs. GVC (global value chain) participants are firms that are classified as both exporter and importer. FDI (foreign direct investment) refers to firms with a foreign ownership share of at least 10 percent.

Firms with majority female ownership are less active in global markets than their male counterparts for three main reasons. First, female-owned manufacturing businesses tend to specialize in relatively more protected manufacturing sectors. Among majority-female-owned firms, 55 percent of manufacturing firms are concentrated in textiles and apparel and food products and beverages (figure 1.31, panel a). In services, majority-female-owned businesses are concentrated in retail and construction, which according to recent estimates are sectors with medium and high trade costs (figure 1.31, panel b) (WTO 2019).

Second, the size, productivity, skill intensity, and experience of female-owned businesses create additional barriers to export (see, for example, Aitken, Hanson, and Harrison 1997; Bernard and Jensen 1999; Clerides, Lach, and Tybout 1998; Greenaway and Kneller 2008; Roberts and Tybout 1997). Female-owned firms tend to pay lower wages (a proxy for average skill intensity), to have less experience, and to be significantly smaller, less productive, and younger (figure 1.32, panel a). They are also less likely to use the Internet and email or to have their own website (figure 1.32, panel b). The analysis also shows that these gender gaps are larger for manufacturing firms, except for labor productivity and age for which the gap is similarly high.[25] Chapter 2 further explores the constraints that prevent women-owned firms from participating in export markets.

Third, the underrepresentation of female trading firms could be a function of low female business ownership in general. The overall share of female-owned firms in the data sample is only 10.3 percent

Figure 1.31 More than 50 percent of female-owned businesses are concentrated in sectors with high barriers to cross-border trade, in both goods and services

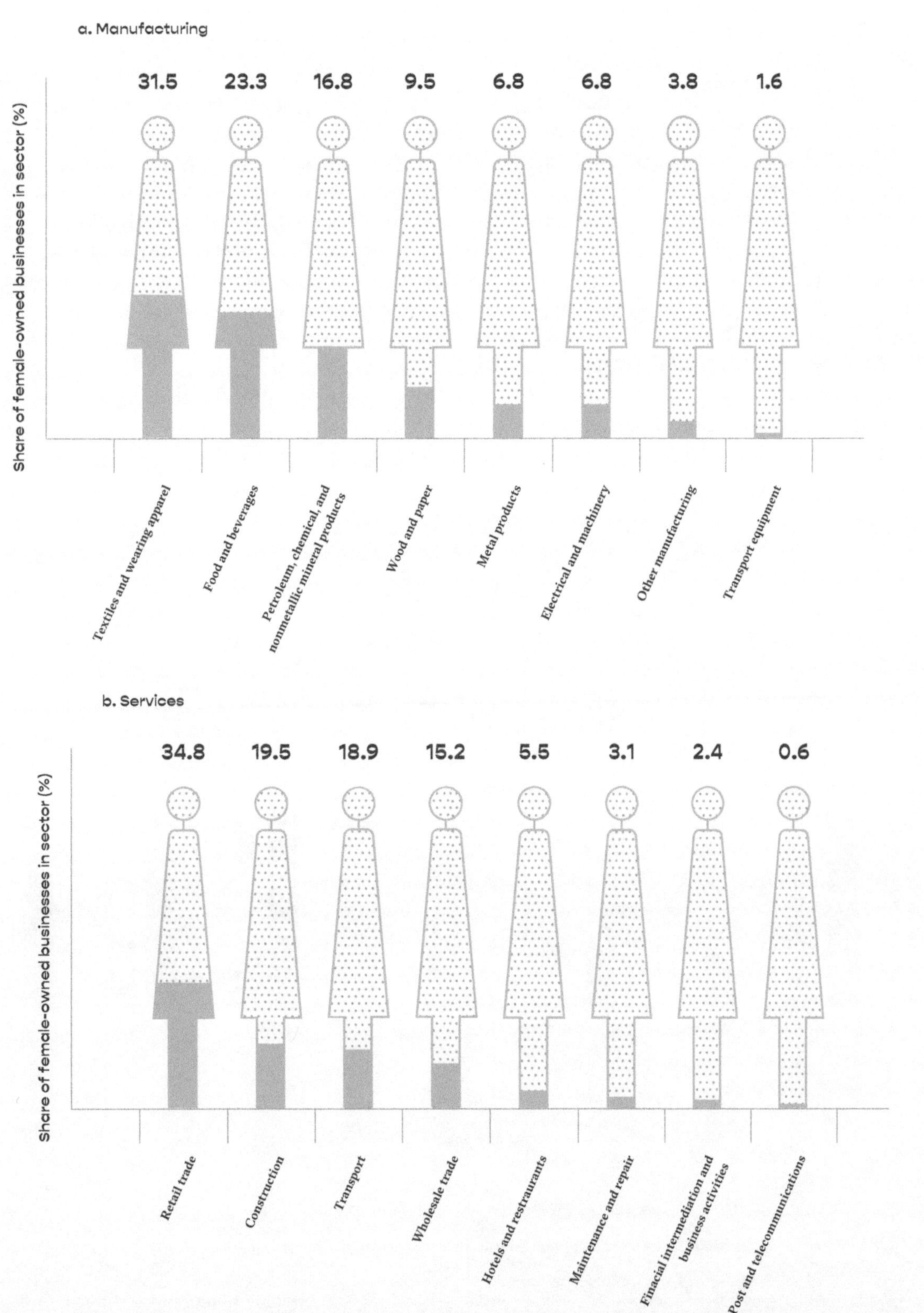

Source: World Bank Enterprise Surveys for the most recent available years, https://www.enterprisesurveys.org/en/data.
Note: Original International Standard Industrial Classification (ISIC) Rev. 3.1 sectors were aggregated to the sector classification of the Eora Global Supply Chain database.

for manufacturing firms. For services firms, this number is slightly higher (15.5 percent).[26] Among services firms, the highest shares of exports by small firms owned by women were in tourism and travel-related services, such as travel agencies, tour operators, hotels, and restaurants, as well as in transport. Tourism not only is an important source of female employment but also offers concrete opportunities for female business owners to trade internationally.

The role of trade in reducing the productivity gap of women farmers

Women make up 43 percent of the world's agricultural labor force. This share rises to over 50 percent in Sub-Saharan Africa and East Asia and Pacific; in countries such as Lesotho, Mozambique, and Sierra Leone, women constitute over 60 percent of the agricultural workforce (FAO 2011). Agriculture remains the most important source of employment and income for women in rural areas of developing countries. Despite women's strong representation in the agricultural labor force, a large body of analysis finds that female-managed plots or female-headed farming households achieve lower productivity than male farmers. Female farmers are less likely to produce cash crops—that is, crops that are sold for profit rather than consumed.

This gender gap in agricultural productivity in developing countries has been estimated to be about 20 to 30 percent—and even as high as

Figure 1.32 Majority-male-owned exporting firms perform better and are more digitally connected than female-owned exporting firms

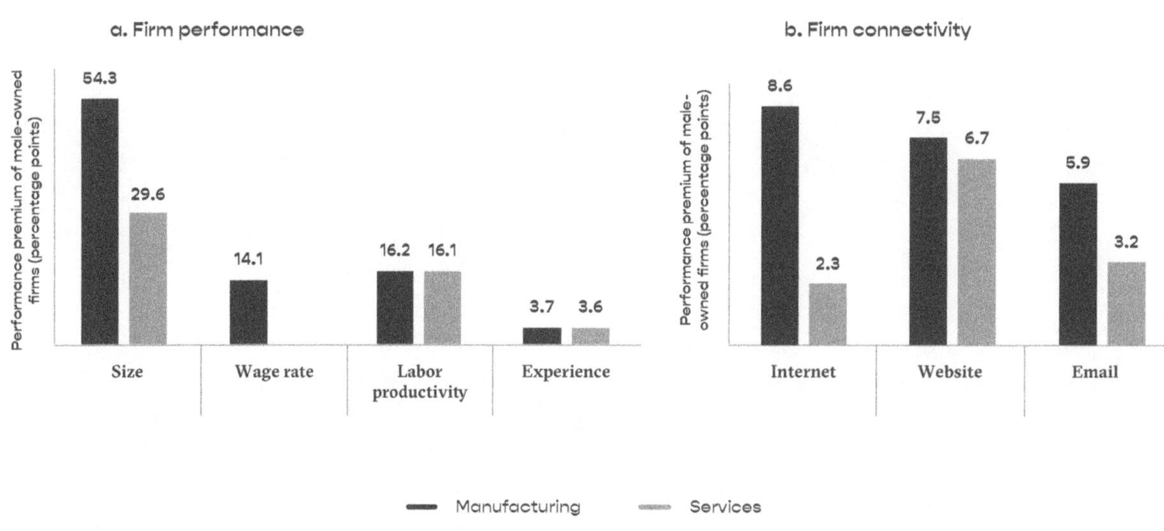

Source: World Bank Enterprise Surveys for the most recent available years, https://www.enterprisesurveys.org/en/data.
Note: Panel a shows the average premium in the performance indicators (shown on the vertical axis) for majority male-owned relative to female-owned firms. All regressions control for total factor productivity as well as country-sector, subnational region, and year fixed effects. The results shown are significant at the 1 percent level except for age (in manufacturing) which is significant at the 10 percent level. Wage rates are not available for services firms. Panel b shows the coefficients (mean differences) of separate regression models using the performance indicators shown on the vertical axis as dependent variables and male firm ownership as independent variable. The variables shown are in natural logarithms except for Internet, website, and email. Wage rates are not available for services firms. A positive value reflects lower performance for female-owned relative to male-owned firms. All regressions control for total factor productivity as well as country-sector, subnational region, and year fixed effects. All results shown are significant at the 1 percent level except for age (in manufacturing) and Internet (in services), which are significant at the 10 percent level.

40 percent (Kilic, Palacios-López, and Goldstein 2013). This result is consistent across crops and countries. Agricultural labor productivity in Malawi, for example, is found on average to be 44 percent lower on plots belonging to female-headed households than on male-owned plots (Palacios-López and López 2015). Reducing and eliminating this yield gap between women and men offers large potential increases in agricultural output and poverty reduction.

A range of studies shows that the gender of the farmer per se does not directly explain lower agricultural productivity. Rather it is gender differences in equality of opportunities—such as access to and use of agricultural inputs; the size of plots and ownership of land used for farming; access to markets and human and physical capital; and the role of institutions (formal and informal) in affecting farm management, crop choice, and marketing of agricultural produce—that explain the differences in productivity (see, for example, Horrell and Krishnan 2007; Kilic, Palacios-Lopez, and Goldstein 2013; Kinkingninhoun-Medagbe et al. 2010). Often these issues are interlinked with lack of access to finance, which affects the ability to purchase land and which, in turn, means that lack of property rights limits the incentive to invest in fertilizers and higher-yielding seeds. Most studies conclude that women farmers would be as productive as male farmers if they had the same access to land, inputs, and services and if they were treated by institutions in the same way. Estimates for Ethiopia show how reducing fertilizer logistics costs could increase fertilizer adoption and use intensity—thus benefitting agricultural productivity, especially for female-managed fields (box 1.3).

Box 1.3 Reducing fertilizer logistics costs and the gender gap in agricultural productivity in Ethiopia

Ethiopia has a 29.5 percent agricultural productivity gender gap (figure B1.3.1). On average, women managers use fewer inputs. Only 43 percent of female farm managers use chemical fertilizers compared to 53 percent of male farm managers. Additionally, the intensity of fertilizer use is lower on fields managed by women. Results suggest that increasing fertilizer use intensity can contribute to a reduction of the agricultural productivity gender gap because a given increase in the volume of fertilizer used will have a higher impact on productivity for female-managed fields.

Data from the Ethiopia Socioeconomic Survey (ESS) 2013–14 report that more than one-third of farmers living in the Ethiopian provinces/states of Benishangul-Gumuz, Dire Dawa, Gambella, Harari, and Somali did not use fertilizers because of nonavailability. The erratic and unpredictable availability of fertilizers is especially problematic in remote areas (Minten, Stifel, and Tamru 2014).

High fertilizer prices appear as a constraint to fertilizer adoption and use intensity. World Bank estimates suggest that the probability of fertilizer adoption increases by 0.77 percent for every Birr per kilogram decrease in the fertilizer price. Fertilizer use intensity increases by 2.8 kilograms per hectare for each decrease in fertilizer prices of one Birr per kilogram. Access to extension services and access to credit are also found to be key factors that increase the probability of adopting chemical fertilizer and its use intensity.

Figure B1.3.1 Farm managers' productivity distribution, by gender

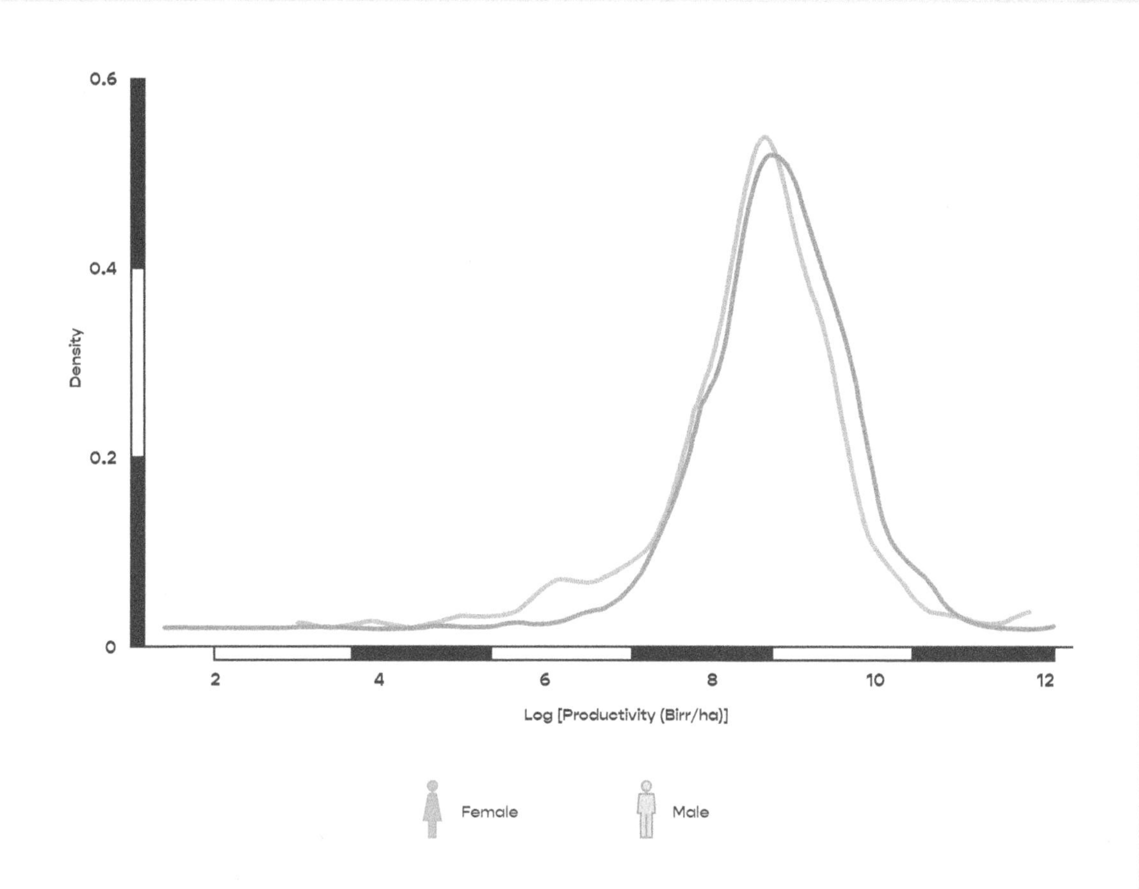

Source: World Bank Ethiopia Trade Logistics Project, https://www.worldbank.org/en/news/loans-credits/2017/03/31/ethiopia-trade-logistics-project.
Note: ha = hectare.

Transport costs account for 63 percent to 75 percent of the difference between fertilizer prices paid by Ethiopian farmers and the prices at the port of Djibouti (Rashid et al. 2013). Therefore, increasing competition in transport services and logistics is estimated to lower fertilizer prices and thus increase agricultural productivity, especially of female-managed fields. In particular, increasing competition in transport services through use of the recently constructed railway to Djibouti could reduce transport costs on the Djibouti–Addis Ababa corridor by 38 percent, which will potentially translate into a reduction of 3 percent in fertilizer prices at the cooperative level. This price reduction could lead to a 0.3 percent increase in fertilizer adoption and a 2 percent increase in fertilizer use intensity, which is expected to raise agricultural productivity by 0.35 percent for the average manager. The reduction of fertilizer prices will have a stronger effect on female managers' productivity (an increase of almost 1 percent). The government of Ethiopia has also decided to increase competition in the logistics sector by allowing foreign participation in the sector through joint ventures.

Source: World Bank Ethiopia Trade Logistics Project, https://www.worldbank.org/en/news/loans-credits/2017/03/31/ethiopia-trade-logistics-project.

How trade affects *women* consumers and decision makers

The influence of trade on consumption patterns and household decision making is well documented. By lowering prices, trade increases buying power of households. By increasing labor demand, trade can change the decisions within households to invest in education or to have additional children. But the way in which trade influences men and women differently is only beginning to be understood.

The analytical challenge here is to disentangle female consumption from household consumption and to take into account other variables that influence consumption decisions such as the bargaining power that women have in a household. This section attempts to illustrate the impact of trade on consumption patterns by using data on female-headed versus male-headed households. Although imperfect, this measure can provide some insights into how trade and trade policy can affect female consumption decisions and preferences as well as decisions such as pursuing education, getting married, or having children.

Trade liberalization and women as consumers

Consumption patterns differ between men and women

With the exception of staple foods, men and women consume different goods; and, on average, women and children consume a smaller share of household resources than men. Data on the consumption habits of individuals, such as the number of times that they consume meals together, are difficult to collect. Other consumption items, such as housing or consumer goods, are shared among household members and often cannot be allocated to specific individuals even in principle. Collecting data on individual-level consumption is costly and not always feasible in the context of large-scale household surveys. Even specialized datasets tend to individualize only some components of the overall consumption basket and thus provide a partial picture of sharing within households. Moreover, basing our understanding of gender inequalities on differences in the consumption of specific consumption items is problematic if preferences over those items differ between household members. For example, even if men disproportionately consume alcohol and tobacco, women might spend more on other items, so any subset of items cannot provide the full picture (Tian, Yu, and Klasen 2018).

Another methodology for identifying gendered consumption patterns is to compare female-headed with male-headed households. Even this methodology, however, comes with challenges regarding the composition of such households and the reflection of social norms in countries.[27] To overcome these challenges, new models that estimate intrahousehold differences in resource allocation are being proposed.[28]

Country-specific analysis suggests that, if women have money of their own and the freedom to spend it, they will provide better food for their households and support their children's education (UNICEF 2007). Evidence from India and Nepal shows that women's participation in household decisions decreases stunting among children and reduces child mortality.[29] A study of poor Brazilian households reveals that girls living with mothers who are educated and decision makers are more likely to be enrolled in school and kept out of the informal labor market. Evidence from rural Bangladesh indicates that the prevalence of undernutrition in children under five in female-headed households compared with male-headed households was significantly lower across income quintiles. In China, increases in female income translated into higher levels of spending on children's education (Qian 2008). In this context, trade, by influencing female bargaining power and consumption patterns, could significantly affect not only female welfare but also the welfare of the entire household.

Trade openness can increase women's incomes and consumption

Trade can affect women as consumers directly, through the alteration of relative prices of imported goods, and indirectly, through labor market outcomes (for example, changes in wages), which may influence their bargaining power within the household and therefore their empowerment. Trade openness has generally been found to have a positive impact on consumers, male and female, by providing access to cheaper goods and services and by increasing the variety of goods consumed. The impact of trade and trade policy on female or male consumers, however, depends on their different consumption and income patterns and on the underlying country context.

A recent study for a sample of 54 developing countries suggests that eliminating import tariffs resulted in a rise in real income for female-headed households compared to male-headed households in more than three-quarters of the countries considered. The largest difference, also referred to as gender bias of trade policy, is observed in Burkina Faso, Cameroon, The Gambia, Mali, and Nicaragua—where female-headed households could earn on average more than 2 percent more real income than male-headed households through the removal of import tariffs (figure 1.33). These results reflect the current structure of both the trade protection of the countries and the expenditure and incomes of their households.

Reducing tariffs can result in new taxes as governments compensate for revenue losses and in reduced real income depending on the new taxes imposed. This outcome is particularly relevant for low- and middle-income countries, which tend to rely heavily on tariffs (Lahey 2018). A strategy used by governments in low- and middle-income countries is to substitute tariffs with value added taxes (VATs). For example, in the case of Pakistan a general sales tax of 12 percent was introduced on imports and domestic products to compensate for the loss in tariff revenue due to trade liberalization policies at the end of the 1980s (Siddiqui 2009). From a gender perspective the important question is then related to the gender bias of different tax systems, but empirical evidence on the effect of trade on women as taxpayers is limited, mainly because of the absence of individual consumption-level data.[30]

Trade and women as decision makers

Trade, through changes in female earnings and job opportunities, affects decisions that women take in relation to their families. Households' decisions are in general the outcome of a process of deliberation between the father and the mother. But the bargaining power of each individual cannot be assumed to be equal. Research has shown that the income contributed by each of the parties affects intrahousehold dynamics, and that women's involvement in paid employment increases their control over how household budgets are spent. These bargaining models highlight that women can be empowered by improving their leverage, measured by the level of well-being they could assure themselves of independently of their spouses. Hence, if trade increases employment opportunities for women and reduces the gender wage gap, the result might be an increase in the share of expenditure of goods preferred by women.

An important challenge in this literature is the difficulty in observing the bargaining process. To date, investigating the impact of trade liberalization on women's bargaining power consists essentially of country case studies. Trade liberalization was found to have improved the relative income of women

Figure 1.33 The current tariff structure benefits male-headed households in 78 percent of countries assessed

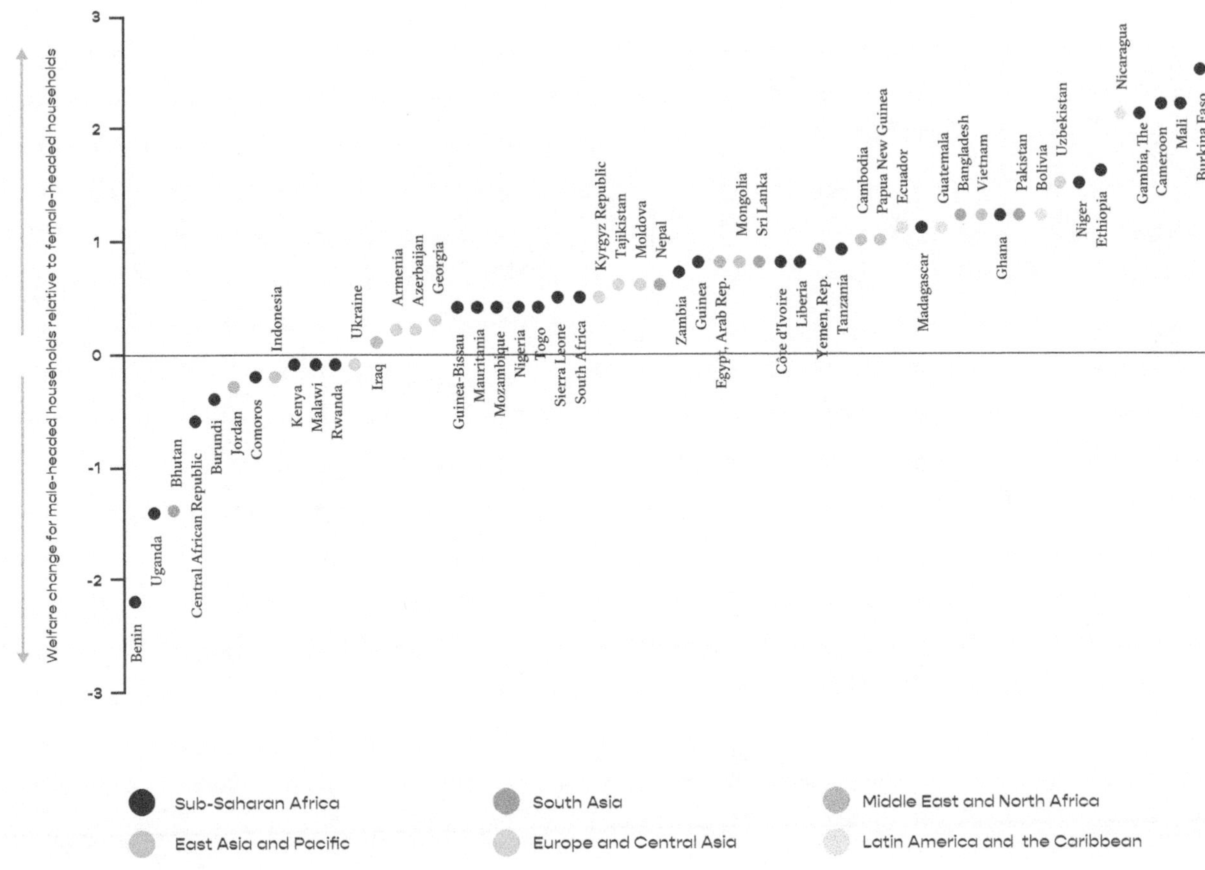

Source: Based on estimates by Depetris-Chauvin and Porto, forthcoming.
Note: The male-to-female gender bias is computed as the difference in the welfare gain, in terms of real income, from trade liberalization for female-headed households versus for male-headed households. For each country, the index combines the structure of protection with the patterns of expenditure shares and income shares. World Bank country naming conventions used.

in Mexico during the 1990s, which translated into expenditure shifts from goods associated with male preferences (men's clothing and tobacco and alcohol) to those associated with female preferences (women's clothing and children's education). Increased labor market opportunities in Mexico in the early 2000s were also found to have improved women's decision-making power, especially in choosing their work status or the money given to their parents independently of changes in the exposure of female and male labor to Chinese competition (Majlesi 2016).

When women can work independently, they increase their ability to make decisions within their families. This increased bargaining power may allow women to delay marriage or childbearing or increase investments in education, particularly for girls. The exact influence can vary between countries and regions.

Trade influences marriage and fertility decisions

Trade affects family decisions such as having children. With greater demand for women to join the workforce, fertility rates fall. Analysis across 146 countries over 50 years suggests that countries with a comparative advantage in female-intensive goods exhibit lower fertility

Figure 1.34 Women spend much more time on childcare than men do across all countries

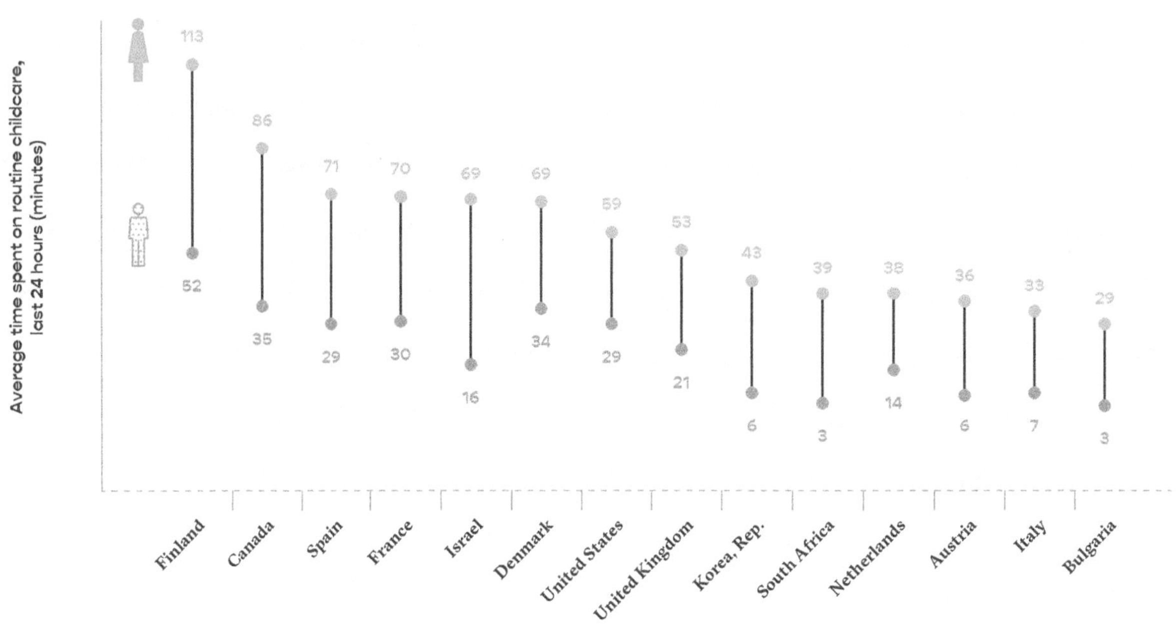

Source: Based on the Multinational Time Use Study (MTUS), https://www.timeuse.org/mtus.

rates. Trade liberalization induces an increase in female relative wages and, because it becomes more costly to raise a child, fertility rates decline (Do, Levchenko, and Raddatz 2016).

The decision to have children is influenced by women's opportunity cost of time, which encompasses, among others, the welfare that having a child provides and the time requirements of child rearing (Becker 1960). Although perceptions have changed, child rearing is still widely considered a woman's responsibility; therefore, a trade-off appears between having a child and working (see figure 1.34).

Analysis of the impact of the impressive growth in the export-oriented manufacturing industry on the lives of Bangladeshi women shows that girls exposed to the garment sector have delayed childbirth and marriage. These outcomes are explained by the fact that younger girls are more likely to be enrolled in school, in line with increased expected returns to human capital, and older girls are more likely to be employed outside the home in garment-proximate villages, consistent with the bargaining theory (Heath and Mobarak 2015). In India, the impact of trade liberalization starting in 1991 differs across socioeconomic strata. Birth rates increased among women with low socioeconomic status but decreased among women with high socioeconomic status. This outcome results because daughters of lower-status families are considered to yield "indirect utility" (for example, by providing old-age support), whereas daughters of high-status families are seen to provide "direct utility" (Anukriti and Kumler 2019).

The effects of trade shocks on bargaining power and household decisions are also confirmed for industrialized countries. In the United States, an adverse shock to male-intensive employment increased the fraction of young women who were never married and reduced the fraction currently married or formerly married; adverse shocks to female-intensive employment reduced the fraction of young women who have never married while raising the fraction who are divorced, widowed, or separated (Autor, Dorn, and Hanson 2018). A study in Denmark finds that import competition from China reduced labor market opportunities and thus led to more marriages, higher fertility, more parental leave-taking, and fewer divorces. This effect is mainly driven by women (Keller and Utar 2018).

Trade can also influence decisions to acquire education

Trade can influence the education decision-making process (and indirectly influence fertility) through three key mechanisms. First, trade can alter the opportunity cost of education. The opportunity cost of education refers to the earnings lost by choosing to invest in education. In particular, trade can raise the opportunity cost of education by raising wages in low-skill sectors, which hurts boys or girls more depending on which sector is affected and on the average level of education. In Mexico, for example, the growth of manufacturing exports between 1986 and 2000 has been found to have led to a reduction in educational attainment: for every 25 jobs created, one student—attracted by relatively high wage prospects—dropped out of secondary school and chose to enter the labor market. Although male and female schooling significantly declined with new export job arrival, female schooling declined less than male schooling (Atkin 2016). It is important that government policies address the potential risk of forgone schooling when they increase trade and employment opportunities.

Second, trade, often through its interaction with productivity and technology upgrading, increases the demand for higher skills in both developed and developing economies, resulting in higher wages for skilled workers and providing an incentive for further education to acquire higher skills. Depending on a country's comparative advantage sectors, higher returns to education can benefit women more. This outcome is especially true for trade in services where jobs generally require greater skills. The growth of the business process outsourcing industry in India, for instance, has generated new, high-paying job opportunities for young women who can speak English and use computers. The availability of new employment opportunities in this sector, where women represent almost 50 percent of the employment share, provided an incentive for families to invest in girls' human capital in anticipation of labor market returns in the future (Jensen 2012). Similarly, a recent analysis for India suggests that liberalization in services sectors is linked to increases in the average years of schooling as well as decreases in the gender education gap (that is, the gap in education between women and men) at the district level (Nano et al. 2019).[31] Analysis on the effect of the openings of ready-made garment factories in Bangladesh on women's educational attainment also suggests that young girls living close to villages where garment factories opened were more likely to be enrolled in school after the arrival of the garment sector (Heath and Mobarak 2015). Here, educational attainment increases as new vacancies are expected to continue and new jobs sufficiently reward school acquisition.[32]

Finally, trade raises income and can make the cost of schooling more affordable, which can benefit more girls. For instance, after the 1991 tariff reform, rural India experienced a significant increase in schooling and decline in child labor (Edmonds, Pavcnik, and Topalova 2010).[33]

Annex 1A

Econometric analysis on the determinants of informality, data, and methodology

Drawing on the World Bank Household Surveys, this analysis provides individual-level evidence based on a cross-section of 32 countries covering the period 2010–17. It quantifies the patterns of labor informality according to different measures of trade integration, controlling for the common determinants of informality such as age, education level, marital status, and occupation.

To provide more insights about the determinants or correlates of informality, this analysis assesses informality through regression analysis using a simple Probit regression model. The dependent variable of the regression model is a binary variable that takes a value of 1 if the worker is employed in the informal sector (that is, if the worker is a nonpaid employee or does not have a contract) and 0 otherwise. Separate regressions are provided for the full sample and for workers in sectors other than agriculture. The main independent variables used include (i) a rural dummy, (ii) demographic characteristics of the worker (a married dummy, and the worker's age), (iii) the highest educational level attained by the worker, (iv) occupation, (v) gender, and (vi) broad economic sector of employment.

The model is the following:

$$inf = \alpha + \beta_1\, rural + \beta_2\, age + \beta_3\, married + \beta_4\, edu + \beta_5\, occup + \beta_6\, broadSector + \beta_7 \ln Output + \beta_8\, trade + \beta_9\, gender + D_c + D_s + \varepsilon_{cs} \tag{1A.1}$$

The variable *gender* is a dummy variable taking the value of 1 for women, and 0 for men. *Rural* is a dummy variable taking the value of 1 if the worker lives in a rural area, and 0 if in an urban area, given that rural employment is associated with informal agricultural employment. *Married* is a dummy variable taking the value of 1 if the worker is married or living with a partner, and 0 otherwise. Country-sectoral output (in natural logarithm) controls for country-sector specific conditions. The *trade* variable refers to different measurements of a country-sector integration with the rest of the world: exports (in natural logarithm), exports over output, exports and imports over sectoral output, GVC backward integration (import content of exports over exports), and GVC forward integration (value of domestic production re-exported by the bilateral partners over exports). GVC integration measures follow the decomposition by Borin and Mancini (2015). The model also includes country and sector fixed effects to control for unobservable shocks.

Because of the cross-sectional nature of the data, results should not be interpreted causally.

Annex 1B

Econometric analysis on trade and labor demand, data, and methodology

Drawing on the World Bank Enterprise Surveys, this chapter provides firm-level evidence based on a cross-section of roughly 29,000 manufacturing firms across 64 developing and emerging countries covering the period 2010–17.[34] The Enterprise Surveys represent a comprehensive source of firm-level data in emerging markets and developing economies. One major advantage of the Enterprise Surveys is that the survey questions are the same across all countries. Moreover, the Enterprise Surveys represent a stratified random sample of firms using three levels of stratification: sector, firm size, and region. Sectors are determined on the basis of the International Standard Industrial Classification (ISIC) Rev. 3.1 classification of the main product or service.

A variable unit cost function *CV* is specified as follows:

$$CV = CV(Y, w^F, w^M, k, T),$$

where Y denotes the output and w^F and w^M are the exogenous wages for the variable input factors female labor L^F and male labor L^M. Capital is considered a quasi-fixed input factor in the form of capital intensity k. The technology shifter $T = T(tfp, trade)$ is defined as a function of total factor productivity (tfp) and trade.

Using the transcendental logarithmic (translog) form of a variable unit cost function as introduced by Brown and Christensen (1981) and applying Shephard's lemma, the following factor demand function can be derived:

$$S^F = \alpha + \beta_1 \ln Y + \beta_2 \ln(w^M/w^F) + \beta_3 \ln k + \gamma_1 \ln tfp + \gamma_2\, trade$$

where S^F is the cost share of L^F in variable costs CV, and in this case the female wage share. Because w^F and w^M are the only variable costs, CV is determined by the sum of the products of the variable factor costs with their respective factors, $CV = w^F L^F + w^M L^M = wL$, where w designates the average wage per labor input L, regardless of gender. A decrease of S^F can reflect a fall in L^F or a fall in w^F (or both), which implies a rise in S^M and thus an increase in L^M or in w^M or both. Hence, the composite term $S^F = w^F L^F / wL$ can be considered the relative demand for high-skilled labor.

Other control variables include output, Y. The coefficient sign of output Y, β_1, is not unambiguously predictable. An increase in Y normally leads to a higher overall wage bill and therefore to larger variable costs CV. If the cost increase is equally distributed between female and male labor, there should be no influence on S^F. If the wage bill of male labor increases more than proportionally—for example because of better bargaining power—the result is a higher L^M, w^M, or both; and S^F is expected to fall ($\beta_1 < 0$).

One expects a lower S^F and thus a lower cost share of L^F in variable costs CV when relative wages for male labor, w^M/w^F, as part of CV rise ($\beta_2 < 0$). An increase in the capital intensity, k, will increase S^F if capital is a substitute for male labor ($\beta_3 > 0$), but reduce S^F if capital is a substitute for female labor ($\beta_3 < 0$).

A higher tfp could increase labor demand in favor of female ($\gamma_1 > 0$) or male workers ($\gamma_1 < 0$). The influence of trade on S_{HS} is not easily predictable, because trade could increase the relative demand for female ($\gamma_2 > 0$) or male labor ($\gamma_2 < 0$).

In the absence of gender-specific wage data in the Enterprise Surveys, the model is modified in two ways. First, the analysis on trade and the relative demand for female workers (or female wage share) combines the Enterprise Survey dataset with sectoral wage data by gender, available from Household Surveys. This assumes equal relative wages across all firms in a sector. Such wage data are available for 30 countries in the Enterprise Surveys. The following female wage share equation is estimated:

$$S^F_{isrt} = \alpha + \beta_1 \ln Y_{isrt} + \beta_2 \ln(w^M/w^F)_{st} + \beta_3 \ln k_{isrt} + \gamma_1 \ln tfp_{isrt} + \gamma_2 trade_{isrt} + D_{cs} + D_r + D_t + \varepsilon_{isrt} \quad \text{(1B.1)}$$

Second, the analysis on trade and the female labor share assumes that $w^F = w^M = w$. Because $S^F = w^F L^F / wL$, the dependent variable becomes the female labor share in total employment, $femsh = L^F / L$. Similarly, the model no longer controls for relative wages, because we assume $\ln(w^M/w^F) = \ln 1 = 0$. Although assuming equal wage rates between female and male workers is a strong assumption, we argue that the fixed country-sector effects included in the model partially correct for it. This approach has the advantage of including all 64 countries in the analysis. The *female labor share* equation takes the following form:

$$fem\_sh_{isrt} = \alpha + \beta_1 \ln Y_{isrt} + \beta_2 \ln k_{isrt} + \gamma_1 \ln tfp_{isrt} + \gamma_2 trade_{isrt} + D_{cs} + D_r + D_t + \varepsilon_{isrt} \quad \text{(1B.2)}$$

Both models consider four types of trading firms. *Exporters* are firms with an export share (direct or indirect) of at least 10 percent of total sales. *Importers* are firms with an imported input share of at least 10 percent of total inputs. *GVC participants* are firms that are classified as both exporters and importers. *FDI* refers to firms with a foreign ownership share of at least 10 percent. The model also controls for country-sector, subnational region, and year fixed effects.

Annex 1C

Econometric analysis on the gender wage gap, data, and methodology

Drawing on the World Bank Enterprise Surveys, this chapter provides firm-level evidence based on a cross-section of roughly 29,000 manufacturing firms across 64 developing and emerging countries covering the period 2010–17 (see annex 1B). In the absence of matched employer–employee data that would allow for explicit testing for the existence and direction of a gender wage gap, this chapter follows the approach of Chen, Lai, and Wan (2013) who test implicitly how a firm's employment share correlates with its average wages. A negative (or positive) relationship between the female labor share and average wages suggests the existence of a gender wage gap. The role of trade is assessed using interaction terms between the female labor share and a firm's trade status.

Following the model by Chen, Lai, and Wan (2013), a firm's average wage rate, *wage*, is estimated as the following function:

$$\ln wage = \alpha + \beta_1 \ln age + \beta_2 \ln emp + \beta_3 \ln k + \beta_4\, skillsh + \beta_5\, femsh + \gamma femsh^{*} trade \qquad (1C.1)$$

The variable *age* designates the number of years a firm has operated (in natural logarithms) to measure experience. The next variable is employment, *emp* (in natural logarithms), to control for firm size. The variable *k* denotes capital intensity, measured as the replacement value of machinery in the firm divided by output (in natural logarithms); *skillsh* is the share of skilled production workers in total production workers; and *femsh* is the share of female workers in total employment (see annex 1B).

More experience ($\beta_1 > 0$), larger firm size ($\beta_2 > 0$), and a larger share of skilled production workers ($\beta_3 > 0$) are expected to be positively correlated with average wages. A larger capital intensity can be positively ($\beta_4 > 0$) or negatively ($\beta_4 < 0$) associated with the demand for labor and thus average wages, depending on whether capital and labor are complements or substitutes. Because of women's lower skill intensity, a higher female labor share is assumed to be negatively linked to average wages ($\beta_5 < 0$).

The most important element is the interaction term of the female labor share with the trade variable. Because of their higher productivity and possibly higher labor standards, trading firms are expected to show a lower wage gap compared to nontrading firms ($\gamma > 0$). The association between the female labor share and average wages for trading firms is given by the sum of $\beta_5 + \gamma$, whereas the correlation for nontrading firms is given only by β_5.

The model considers four types of trading firms: exporters, importers, GVC participants, and FDI firms (see annex 1B for definitions). The model also controls for country-sector, subnational region, and year fixed effects.

Notes

1 The analysis of the links between trade and gender is based on a selection of theoretical models and econometric studies. The case study literature on trade and gender, a third stream of literature, is rich and can provide insights into a narrow sector in a country. Because of that literature's narrow focus, however, it is difficult to draw general conclusions. For a thorough literature review (including case studies) on the impact of trade expansion on female employment, the gender wage gap, and female decision-making in developing countries, see, for example, Fontana (2009).

2 The overview of the possible channels linking trade reforms and gender presented in this framework is nonexhaustive and focuses on the main mechanisms that have been identified by both theoretical and empirical contributions in the economic literature.

3 The data from the International Labour Organization are based on labor force surveys that cover the entire noninstitutional population of a given country, all branches of economic activity, all sectors of the economy, and all categories of workers, including the self-employed, contributing family workers, casual workers, and multiple jobholders.

4 Professionals increase the existing stock of knowledge, apply scientific or artistic concepts and theories, teach about the foregoing in a systematic manner, or engage in any combination of these activities. Competent performance in most occupations in this major group requires skills at the fourth ISCO skill (ISCO-08).

5 Elementary occupations involve the performance of simple and routine tasks that may require the use of handheld tools and considerable physical effort. Most occupations in this major group require skills at the first ISCO skill level (ISCO-08).

6 Backward GVC participation refers to the import content embodied in a sector's exports, whereas forward GVC participation measures a sector's domestic value-added portion, which is used in bilateral partner countries for export production (that is, it excludes domestic value added that is consumed in the bilateral partner country). Both are measured as percent of the sector's gross exports.

7 Unpaid work refers to work performed by contributing family workers in small family enterprises, market activities carried out by women on their own account at or from home, casual or atypical work, and activities geared toward the production of goods for own final use by households (ILO 2013).

8 The average effects of trade liberalization on informality may be inconsistent, however, across all sectors within an economy if women, for example, lack skills to move across sectors and grab opportunities in expanding sectors. A study about the horticultural sector in Kenya, for example, suggests that trade liberalization there did not translate into higher levels of female formality in the horticultural sector. On the contrary, horticultural producers reduced the sourcing of goods from smallholders to large-scale farms and processing facilities and increased the use of casual labor (mainly female) to stay competitive after having been sheltered from international competition (Dolan 2005).

9 In the neoclassical theoretical framework, international trade is determined by comparative advantage originating from differences either in technology (Ricardo) or in factor endowments (Heckscher-Ohlin).

10 Analysis performed across a sample of 50 developing countries for which wage data by gender were available following the methodology described in annex 1B and using Eora data.

11 For the list of countries included in the analysis see figure 1.19. The regression model amends the models by Feenstra and Hanson (1995, 1997) that focus on offshoring and the relative demand for skilled labor, which can be derived from a unit cost function. Rather than focusing on skilled and unskilled labor, the models in this analysis focus on male and female workers. The firm-level analysis additionally controls for capital stock per output, which is unavailable in the cross-country sector regressions. For more information on the World Bank Enterprise Surveys, see https://www.enterprisesurveys.org/en/data.

12 Export status thus explains one-third (2.5 out of 7.5 percentage points) of the higher female wage share of exporters relative to nonexporters, whereas other firm characteristics and fixed effects explain the other two-thirds. The difference in the female wage share between importers and nonimporters is smaller at roughly 1 percentage point, explaining less than 30 percent of the difference in female wage shares between importers and nonimporters (23.0 percent versus 19.5 percent). The findings hold when excluding female-intensive sectors apparel and computing from the sample.

13 Excluding textiles and apparel as well as metal (with extremely low female wage shares) from the manufacturing sample yields a much smaller positive increase of 1.8 percentage points. Doubling exports in nonapparel, nonmetal manufacturing sectors in the sample would raise the female wage share from the current share of 22.6 percent to 24.5 percent.

14 The findings suggest that a firm's export status explains roughly half of the difference in the female labor share (4.4 out of 8.9 percentage points), and other factors explain the other half. Similarly, a firm's import status explains about 40 percent of the difference in the female labor share (1.9 out of 4.7 percentage points). The results are in line with Shepherd (2018).

15 Not controlling for additional firm-level characteristics and fixed effects, which is shown later and in the section titled "How trade affects women producers and business owners."

16 This finding does not necessarily contradict studies relating trade to a skill premium at the firm level (for example, ILO and WTO 2017). The latter perspective focuses on an exporting firm's skill intensity relative to other firms in the same sector, because exporters are more productive and attract more-skilled labor, but not relative to other sectors. A country's sectoral specialization is still determined by its comparative advantage, which in a developing country context tends to be low-skilled labor.

17 In two recent applications the World Bank Group has analyzed the implications of tariff liberalization reforms in Pakistan and Sri Lanka. The results suggest that trade policy reforms would increase imports by 6 percent, exports by 10.6 percent, and GDP by 0.2 percent. The textile and apparel industries would benefit the most through access to cheaper imported inputs, resulting in gains in competitiveness and increased exports. This result would in turn increase the demand for female labor because the gender composition of workers in both sectors significantly favors women. The model simulations suggest that job creation would increase by 20 percent and 12 percent, respectively, in textiles and wearing apparel by 2023 in the combined scenario as compared to the baseline. Similarly, the tariff liberalization scenario in Sri Lanka would also lead to an expansion of employment in textiles and wearing apparel where women represent more than half of the workforce, unlike other sectors in 2016. The expected increases in employment amount to 12 percent and 11 percent, respectively, by 2028 in the para-tariff scenario, and 13 percent and 11 percent in the full reform scenario (see World Bank, forthcoming).

18 For more information on the World Values Survey, see http://www.worldvaluessurvey.org/WVSDocumentationWV6.jsp.

19 Kongar (2006) shows in an unpublished article that women with low wages suffered disproportionate job losses in U.S. manufacturing because of rising imports. Consequently, the average wage of remaining employed women increased, which explained the narrowing of the gender wage gap.

20 In the United States, female labor participation decreased in those industries that where highly exposed to import penetration from Mexico after establishing NAFTA (Sauré and Zoabi 2014).

21 The level of capital intensity of a firm—that is, the use of more machines relative to other factors of production such as labor to produce a certain good—is also negatively correlated with average wages, implying that capital is a substitute for female labor. Older and larger firms are linked to a higher average wage rate.

22 This analysis tests for the gender wage gap indirectly, by correlating the female labor share with a firm's average wage rates. A negative correlation implies the existence of a gender wage gap. Although this type of analysis can be performed only with firm-level data, it cannot control for worker characteristics, which might also explain part of the gender wage gap. See annex 1C for the methodology.

23 These findings are in line with the literature on FDI spillovers, which suggests that foreign investors can help domestic firms upgrade their technological capabilities directly through sharing of production techniques and product design and assisting with technology acquisition (Paus and Gallagher 2008), and indirectly through personnel training, advance payment, leasing of machinery, provision of inputs, help with quality assurance, and organization of product lines (Crespo and Fontoura 2007; Javorcik 2008; Lall 1980).

24 Majority-female-owned firms have female ownership of at least 50 percent (conversely, majority-male-owned firms have male ownership of at least 50 percent).

25 The gender gap is smaller when looking at management rather than firm ownership. Firms with a female top manager differ from firms with a male top manager only in some characteristics. They are less likely to participate in GVCs, are smaller in firm size, pay lower wages, and are less productive. Female-managed services firms are additionally younger and less likely to have their own website or to use email. The findings imply that gender inequalities in firm performance and rights are more pronounced when it comes to firm ownership.

26 This result is in line with WTO 2019.

27 First, female-headship combines women who have never married, women who are widowed or divorced, and some women who are married. A related concern is that the headship concept risks conflating gender gaps with differences caused by demographic composition. For example, many female-headed households contain children but not adult males, whereas most male-headed households contain adult women and children. Second, self-reported household headship reflects social norms and views about who is understood as the head of the household—for example, the main breadwinner, the main decision maker, the oldest man, and so on. These norms may vary across countries, within countries, or across income groups, and might privilege one sex over the other (World Bank 2018).

28 Using semiparametric restrictions on individual preferences within a collective model, one can identify how total household resources are divided up among household members by observing how each family member's expenditures on a single private good like clothing vary with income and family size (Dunbar, Lewbel, and Pendakur 2013).

29 Results hold after accounting for differences in education and wealth among the households surveyed.

30 In the absence of individual consumption-level data, Casale (2012) proposes to study the distributional effects of indirect or consumption taxes in South Africa by classifying households as being more female or more male according to demographic and economic attributes (for example, households headed by a woman or in which only women are employed).

31 This result is in line with the analysis of Jensen (2012), which finds that business process outsourcing employment opportunities in India raised educational attainment of girls and led to delayed marriage and fertility.

32 In the case of Bangladesh, the educational requirements of the garment sector are higher than those of other sectors; managers prefer educated workers who are better at tasks like keeping records or learning new work from a pattern. The study also found that trade had a bigger impact on girls than on boys. This outcome is explained by the high levels of female employment in this sector (approximately 80 percent of the garment factory workers in Bangladesh are female).

33 However, the districts that relied heavily on employment in protected industries before liberalization did not experience as large an increase in schooling or decline in child labor. The data suggest that the relationship between district exposure to trade reforms and schooling was driven by the poverty impact of declining tariffs. Another study also suggests that tariff reductions in India raised male and female labor supply and in turn increased maternal labor supply and improved schooling probability for children (Marchand, Rees, and Riezman 2013).

34 Much of the information in this annex comes from Rocha and Winkler 2019.

References

Aitken, B., G. H. Hanson, and A. E. Harrison. 1997. "Spillovers, Foreign Investment, and Export Behavior." *Journal of International Economics* 43 (1–2): 103–32.

Anukriti, S., and T. J. Kumler. 2019. "Women's Worth: Trade, Female Income, and Fertility in India." *Economic Development and Cultural Change* 67 (3): 687–724.

Autor, D., D. Dorn, and G. Hanson. 2018. "When Work Disappears: Manufacturing Decline and the Falling Marriage-Market Value of Young Men."*American Economic Review: Insights* 1 (2): 161–78.

Atkin, David. 2016. "Endogenous Skill Acquisition and Export Manufacturing in Mexico." *American Economic Review* 106 (8): 2046–85.

Becker, G. 1957. *The Economics of Discrimination.* Chicago: The University of Chicago Press.

———. 1960. "An Economic Analysis of Fertility." In *Demographic and Economic Change in Developed Countries,* edited by G. Becker. Princeton, NJ: Princeton University Press.

Ben Yahmed, S. 2017. "Gender Wage Discrimination and Trade Openness. Prejudiced Employers in an Open Industry." ZEW Discussion Paper No. 17-047, ZEW–Leibniz Centre for European Economic Research, Mannheim.

Ben Yahmed, S., and P. Bombarda. 2018. "Gender, Informal Employment and Trade Liberalization in Mexico." ZEW Discussion Paper No. 18-028, ZEW–Leibniz Centre for European Economic Research, Mannheim.

Berik, G., Y. van der Meulen Rodgers, and J. E. Zveglich. 2004. "International Trade and Gender Wage Discrimination: Evidence from East Asia." *Review of Development Economics* 8 (2): 237–54.

Bernard, A. B., and J. B. Jensen. 1999. "Exceptional Exporter Performance: Cause, Effect or Both?" *Journal of International Economics* 47 (1): 1–25.

Black, S., and E. Brainerd. 2004. "Importing Equality? The Impact of Globalization on Gender Discrimination." *Industrial and Labor Relations Review* 57 (4): 540–59.

Bøler, E. A., B. Javorcik, and K. H. Ulltveit-Moe. 2018. "Working across Time Zones: Exporters and the Gender Wage Gap." *Journal of International Economics* 111 (March): 122–33.

Borin, A., and M. Mancini. 2015. "Follow the Value Added: Bilateral Gross Export Accounting." Bank of Italy Working Paper No. 1026, Bank of Italy, Rome.

Brown, R. S., and L. R. Christensen. 1981. "Estimating Elasticities of Substitution in a Model of Partial Static Equilibrium: An Application to U.S. Agriculture, 1947–1974." In *Modeling and Measuring Natural Resource Substitution,* edited by E. R. Berndt and B. C. Field, 209–29. Cambridge, MA: MIT Press.

Brussevich, M. 2018. "Does Trade Liberalization Narrow the Gender Wage Gap? The Role of Sectoral Mobility." *European Economic Review* 109 (March): 305–33.

Busse, M., and C. Spielmann. 2006. "Gender Inequality and Trade." *Review of International Economics* 14 (3): 362–79.

Bussolo, M., and R. E. De Hoyos, eds. 2009. *Gender Aspects of the Trade and Poverty Nexus: A Macro-Micro Approach.* Washington, DC: World Bank.

Casale, D. 2012. "Indirect Taxation and Gender Equity: Evidence from South Africa." *Feminist Economics* 18 (3): 25–54.

Chen, Z., Y. Ge, H. Lai, and C. Wan. 2013. "Globalization and Gender Wage Inequality in China." *World Development* 44 (April): 256–66.

Clerides, S. K., S. Lach, and J. R. Tybout. 1998. "Is Learning by Exporting Important? Micro-dynamic Evidence from Colombia, Mexico, and Morocco." *Quarterly Journal of Economics* 113 (3): 903–47.

Cozzi, G., M. Francesconi, S. Lundberg, N. Mantovan, and R. M. Sauer. 2018. "Advancing the Economics of Gender: New Insights and a Roadmap for the Future." *European Economic Review* 109: 1–8.

Crespo, N., and M. Fontoura. 2007. "Determinant Factors of FDI Spillovers—What Do We Really Know?" *World Development* 35 (3): 410–25.

Darity, W., and R. Williams. 1985. "Peddlers Forever? Culture, Competition, and Discrimination." *American Economic Review* 75 (2): 256–61.

Depetris-Chauvin, N. D., and G. Porto. Forthcoming. "The Gender Bias of Trade Policy in Developing Countries." Working Paper, World Bank, Washington, DC.

Der Boghossian, A. 2019. "Trade Policies Supporting Women's Economic Empowerment: Trends in WTO Members." Staff Working Paper ERSD-2019-07, World Trade Organization, Geneva.

Do, Q.-T., A. A. Levchenko, and C. Raddatz. 2016. "Comparative Advantage, International Trade, and Fertility." *Journal of Development Economics* 119 (March): 48–66.

Dolan, C. S. 2005. "Benevolent Intent? The Development Encounter in Kenya's Horticulture Industry." *Journal of Asian and African Studies* 40 (6): 411–37.

Dunbar, G. R., A. Lewbel, and K. Pendakur. 2013. "Children's Resources in Collective Households: Identification, Estimation, and an Application to Child Poverty in Malawi." *American Economic Review* 103 (1): 438–71.

Ederington, J., J. Minier, and K. R. Troske. 2009. "Where the Girls Are: Trade and Labor Market Segregation in Colombia." IZA Discussion Paper No. 4131, Institute for the Study of Labor, Bonn.

Edmonds, E. V., N. Pavcnik, and P. Topalova. 2010. "Trade Adjustment and Human Capital Investments: Evidence from Indian Tariff Reform." *American Economic Journal: Applied Economics* 2 (4): 42–75.

FAO (Food and Agriculture Organization of the United Nations). 2011. *The State of Food and Agriculture 2010–2011*. Rome: FAO.

Feenstra, R. C., and G. H. Hanson. 1995. "Foreign Investment, Outsourcing and Relative Wages." NBER Working Paper No. 5121, National Bureau of Economic Research, Cambridge, MA.

———. 1997. "Foreign Direct Investment and Relative Wages: Evidence from Mexico's Maquiladoras." *Journal of International Economics* 42 (3–4): 371–93.

Fontana, M. 2009. "The Gender Effects of Trade Liberalization in Developing Countries: A Review of the Literature." In *Gender Aspects of the Trade and Poverty Nexus. A Macro-Micro Approach*, edited by M. Bussolo and R. E. De Hoyos, 25–50. Washington, DC: World Bank.

Gaddis, I., and J. Pieters. 2017. "The Gendered Labor Market Impacts of Trade Liberalization: Evidence from Brazil." *Journal of Human Resources* 52 (2): 457–90.

Greenaway, D., and R. Kneller. 2008. "Exporting, Productivity, and Agglomeration." *European Economic Review* 52 (5): 919–39.

Greenhill, B., L. Mosley, and A. Prakash. 2009. "Trade-Based Diffusion of Labor Rights: A Panel Study, 1986–2002." *American Political Science Review* 103 (4): 669–90.

Heath, R., and A. M. Mobarak. 2015. "Manufacturing Growth and the Lives of Bangladeshi Women." *Journal of Development Economics* 115 (C): 1–15.

Horrell, S., and P. Krishnan. 2007. "Poverty and Productivity in Female-Headed Households in Zimbabwe." *Journal of Development Studies* 43 (8): 1351–80.

ILO (International Labour Office). 2006. *Handbook on Decent Work in the Informal Economy in Cambodia*. Informal Economy, Poverty and Employment, Cambodia, Series Number 1, Bangkok, ILO.

———. 2013. "Resolution 1: Resolution Concerning Statistics of Work, Employment and Labour Underutilization." ICLS Resolution from the 19th International Conference of Labour Statisticians, Geneva, ILO. https://www.ilo.org/wcmsp5/groups/public/—dgreports/—stat/documents/normativeinstrument/wcms_230304.pdf.

———. 2018. *Women and Men in the Informal Economy: A Statistical Picture*, Third Edition. Geneva: ILO.

ILO and WTO (International Labour Office and World Trade Organization). 2017. *Investing in Skills for Inclusive Trade*. Geneva: ILO and WTO.

Javorcik, B. 2008. "Can Survey Evidence Shed Light on Spillovers from Foreign Direct Investment?" *World Bank Research Observer* 23 (2): 139–59.

Janse van Rensburg, C., C. Bezuidenhout, M. Matthee, and V. Stolzenburg. 2019. "Exporters and the Gender Wage Gap: Evidence from South Africa." Paper presented at the Conference on Closing the Gender Gaps, Geneva, December 7, 2018.

Jensen, R. T. 2012. "Do Labor Market Opportunities Affect Young Women's Work and Family Decisions? Experimental Evidence from India." *Quarterly Journal of Economics* 127 (2): 753–92.

Juhn, C., G. Ujhelyi, and C. Villegas-Sanchez. 2014. "Men, Women, and Machines: How Trade Impacts Gender Inequality." *Journal of Development Economics* 106 (January): 179–93.

Kazandjian, R., L. Kolovich, K. Kochhar, and M. Newiak. 2019. "Gender Equality and Economic Diversification." *Social Sciences* 8 (4): 118.

Keller, W., and H. Utar. 2018. "Globalization, Gender, and the Family." NBER Working Paper No. 25247, National Bureau of Economic Research, Cambridge, MA.

Kilic, T., A. Palacios-Lopez, and M. Goldstein. 2013. "Caught in a Productivity Trap: A Distributional Perspective on Gender Differences in Malawian Agriculture." Policy Research Working Paper 6381, World Bank, Washington, DC.

Kinkingninhoun-Medagbe, F. M., A. Diagne, F. Simtowe, A. R. Agboh-Noameshie, and P. Y. Adegbola. 2010. "Gender Discrimination and Its Impact on Income, Productivity, and Technical Efficiency: Evidence from Benin." *Agriculture and Human Values* 27 (1): 57–69.

Kis-Katos, K., J. Pieters, and R. Sparrow. 2018. "Globalization and Social Change: Gender-Specific Effects of Trade Liberalization in Indonesia." *IMF Economic Review* 66 (4): 763–93.

Kongar, E. 2006. "Importing Equality or Exporting Jobs? Competition and Gender Wage and Employment Differentials in U.S. Manufacturing." Working Paper No. 436, Levy Economics Institute of Bard College, Annandale-on-Hudson, NY.

Lahey, K. 2018. "Gender, Taxation and Equality in Developing Countries:

Issues and Policy Recommendations." Discussion Paper, UN Women.

Lall, S. 1980. "Vertical Inter-firm Linkages in LDCs: An Empirical Study." *Oxford Bulletin of Economics and Statistics* 42 (3): 203–26.

Majlesi, K. 2016. "Labor Market Opportunities and Women's Decision Making Power within Households." *Journal of Development Economics* 119 (March): 34–47.

Marchand, B. U., R. Rees, and R. G. Riezman. 2013. "Globalization, Gender and Development: The Effect of Parental Labor Supply on Child Schooling." *Review of Economics of the Household* 11 (2): 151–73.

Minten, B., D. Stifel, and S. Tamru. 2014. "Structural Transformation of Cereal Markets in Ethiopia." *Journal of Development Studies* 50 (5): 611–29.

Moazzem, K. G., and M. A. Radia. 2018. "'Data Universe' of Bangladesh's RMG Enterprises: Key Features and Limitations." Centre for Policy Dialogue, Dhaka.

Nano, E., G. Nayyar, S. Rubínová, and V. Stolzenburg. 2019. "The Impact of Service Sector Liberalization on Education: Evidence from India." Presentation at IMF-WB-WTO Conference, June 25. https://www.wto.org/english/res_e/reser_e/s5_d_enriconanowto_imf_wb_india_250619.pdf.

Neumayer, E., and I. De Soysa. 2011. "Globalization and the Empowerment of Women: An Analysis of Spatial Dependence via Trade and Foreign Direct Investment." *World Development* 39 (7): 1065–75.

Oostendorp, R. H. 2009. "Globalization and the Gender Wage Gap." *World Bank Economic Review* 23 (1): 141–61.

Otobe, N. 2015. *Export-Led Development, Employment and Gender in the Era of Globalization.* Employment Working Paper No. 197. Geneva: International Labour Organization.

Palacios-López, A., and R. López. 2015. "The Gender Gap in Agricultural Productivity: The Role of Market Imperfections." *Journal of Development Studies* 51 (9): 1175–92.

Paus, E., and K. Gallagher. 2008. "Missing Links: Foreign Investment and Industrial Development in Costa Rica and Mexico." *Studies of Comparative International Development* 43 (1): 53–80.

Prakash, A., and M. Potoski. 2007. "Investing Up: FDI and the Cross-Country Diffusion of ISO 14001 Management Systems." *International Studies Quarterly* 51 (3): 723–44.

Qian, N. 2008. "Missing Women and the Price of Tea in China: The Effect of Sex-Specific Earnings on Sex Imbalance." *Quarterly Journal of Economics* 123 (3): 1251–85.

Rashid, S., N. Tefera, N. Minot, and G. Ayele. 2013. "Fertilizer in Ethiopia: An Assessment of Policies, Value Chain, and Profitability." IFPRI Discussion Paper 01304, International Food Policy Research Institute, Washington, DC.

Roberts, M. J., and J. R. Tybout. 1997. "The Decision to Export in Colombia: An Empirical Model of Entry with Sunk Costs." *American Economic Review* 87 (4): 545–64.

Rocha, N., and D. Winkler. 2019. "Trade and Female Labor Participation: Stylized Facts Using a Global Dataset." Policy Research Working Paper 9098, World Bank, Washington, DC.

Sauré, P., and H. Zoabi. 2014. "International Trade, the Gender Wage Gap and Female Labor Force Participation." *Journal of Development Economics* 111 (November): 17–33.

Schultz, T. P. 2007. "Does the Liberalization of Trade Advance Gender Equality, in

Schooling and Health?" In *The Future of Globalization: Explorations in Light of Recent Turbulence*, edited by E. Zedillo, 178–208. London: Routledge.

Shepherd, B. 2018. "Global Value Chains and Women's Labor: Firm-Level Evidence." Working Paper DTC-2018-6, Developing Trade Consultants.

Siddiqui, R. 2009. "Modeling Gender Effects of Pakistan's Trade Liberalization." *Feminist Economics* 15 (3): 287–321.

Tejani, S., and W. Milberg. 2016. "Global Defeminization? Industrial Upgrading and Manufacturing Employment in Developing Countries." *Feminist Economics* 22 (2): 24–54.

Tian, X., X. Yu, and S. Klasen. 2018. "Gender Discrimination in China Revisited: A Perspective from Family Welfare." *Journal of Chinese Economic and Business Studies* 16 (1): 95–115.

UNICEF (United Nations Children's Fund). 2007. *The State of the World's Children 2007: Women and Children—The Double Dividend of Gender Equality*. New York: UNICEF.

Wang, Z. 2018. "Bringing the State Back In: Explaining Women's Economic Empowerment in an Era of Globalization." *Political Studies* 66 (4): 1043–66.

Williams, R. 1987. "Capital, Competition, and Discrimination: A Reconsideration of Racial Earnings Inequality." *Review of Radical Political Economics* 19 (2): 1–15.

World Bank. 2011. *World Development Report 2012: Gender Equality and Development*. Washington, DC: World Bank.

———. 2018. *Poverty and Shared Prosperity 2018: Piecing Together the Poverty Puzzle*. Washington, DC: World Bank.

———. 2019. *World Development Report 2020: Trading for Development in the Age of Global Value Chains*. Washington, DC: World Bank.

———. Forthcoming. "Africa Continental Free Trade Area: Economic and Distributional Effects." World Bank, Washington, DC.

World Economic Forum. 2017. *The Global Gender Gap Report 2017*. Geneva: World Economic Forum.

WTO (World Trade Organization). 2019. *World Trade Report 2019: The Future of Services Trade*. Geneva: WTO.

Chapter 2

HOW CONSTRAINTS AND OPPORTUNITIES SHAPE *WOMEN'S* ROLES IN TRADE

Key messages

- Compared to men, women face many constraints that restrict their ability to trade and to realize the benefits of trade. Some of these barriers are directly related to the way that goods and services cross international borders, such as higher trading costs and discrimination that women can face at border crossings. But "beyond-the-border" constraints are equally important. For example, women's limited access to education explains, in part, why female employment is concentrated in low-skill sectors such as textiles. Female entrepreneurs also have more difficulty than men in obtaining finance, especially for riskier activities like trade. Ingrained gender bias for domestic tasks such as child rearing limits women's flexibility and mobility. These limitations can severely reduce women's access to trade-related employment and services.

- Three global trends present new and powerful opportunities for women to grow their presence in 21st-century trade and better reap its benefits:

  » First, servicification describes the growing role of services in the global economy and trade. The share of services in gross domestic product and employment has been rising since the 1940s as workers move out of agriculture and manufacturing. Even within agriculture and manufacturing, an increasing amount of value-added output is generated by services tasks, from design to marketing and distribution. The result has been increased female labor force participation because services employ, with few exceptions, a higher share of women than does agriculture or manufacturing; and it coincides with more and more services being traded across borders, bringing greater opportunities for women workers to benefit from trade.

  » Second, the rise of global value chains, beginning in the early 1990s, has brought with it an increasing fragmentation of production. Goods that used to be produced in a single establishment are now assembled using parts and components made in factories spread out across the world. This development has positive implications for women workers because it has raised the demand for female skills, such as in the textile sector. It has also improved the access of micro, small, and medium enterprises—many of which are owned or managed by women—to foreign markets by integrating them into the supply chains of larger firms. Women workers also benefit from the increase in foreign direct investment and from regional value chains that can increase small-scale traders' profits.

» Third, digital technologies can magnify women's gains from trade by facilitating their access to finance and education, increasing demand for women's skills, and removing trade barriers as well as time and mobility constraints. This trend also benefits women consumers and decision makers. For instance, new technologies generate a more transparent and faster shopping process, especially for imports.

Introduction

Women stand to gain from increased trade, but they face obstacles that prevent or hinder them from accessing those opportunities. These constraints help explain why women work in certain sectors, own and run certain types of businesses, consume certain types of goods, or make certain decisions within households—as detailed in chapter 1. The growing role of services in the global economy and trade (hereafter *servicification*), the rise of global value chains (GVCs), and the adoption of new technologies create new and powerful opportunities for women to trade more and to better reap trade's benefits. By examining these trends through a gender lens, it is possible to illustrate how women can grasp a bigger share of the gains from trade.

This chapter first examines the trade-relevant constraints that women encounter throughout their lives and then analyzes the new opportunities that have arisen for women.

Credit: ©Jacob Lund/ Shutterstock.com. Used with permission; further permission required for reuse.

Barriers reducing *women's* share in the gains from trade

Women struggle with many trade-relevant constraints that either do not apply to men or apply to them to a lesser degree (figure 2.1). These obstacles affect women in the workplace, as consumers, and as decision makers.

Some of these barriers are directly related to the way that goods and services cross international borders, such as higher trading costs and discrimination that women can face at border crossings. But "beyond-the-border" constraints are equally important. For example, women's limited access to education explains, in part, why female employment is concentrated in low-skill sectors such as textiles. Female entrepreneurs also have more difficulty than men in obtaining finance, especially for riskier activities like trade. Ingrained gender bias for domestic tasks such as child rearing limits women's flexibility and mobility. These limitations can severely reduce women's access to trade-related employment and services. The negative impacts of border and beyond-the-border barriers on women in their different roles are exacerbated in countries with high levels of conflict and fragility (see box 2.1).

Box 2.1 Women traders are likely to be more affected by conflict and violence

Fragility, conflict, and violence reduce the gains from trade. They often directly hinder the ability to trade across (and within) borders and can lead traders to make suboptimal production and investment decisions (World Bank Group and WTO 2015). Trade openness can reduce the risk of conflict and support postconflict economic growth and stability. In the aftermath of conflict, trade allows countries to reconnect with the world and to access goods and services that are critical for their economic and social development. Trade also generates solidarity between communities as people from different ethnicities and backgrounds exchange with each other across borders (World Bank 2015). In contexts where trading activities see a significant involvement of women (such as agricultural cross-border trade in Sub-Saharan Africa or the textile and garments industry in South Asia), the preventive effect of trade on conflict and violence can also act as an insurance mechanism against higher risks of gender-based violence, which are often linked to fragility.

Fragility, conflict, and violence affect women and men differently, especially in the case of small-scale cross-border trade. In various fragile countries across Sub-Saharan Africa, such trade is a major source of livelihoods for many women, who often complete numerous journeys across a given border daily (Brenton et al. 2014). Sudden border closures following conflict often stop business activities for those women, with severe consequences for their ability to meet basic household needs. Although reliable data may not be readily available, anecdotal evidence suggests that, for instance, the closure of the Garoua-Boulaï border (Cameroon-Central African Republic) following an attack by rebel groups in December 2017 caused major disruptions to local cross-border trade, severely affecting women (Gaskell et al. 2018). Estimates of the economic impact of the 2014 Ebola outbreak—which was also followed by various border closures in Guinea, Liberia, and Sierra Leone—suggest that the epidemic caused a 10 percent loss in economic activity overall and that its consequences were especially negative for the livelihoods of small-scale traders, among whom women were disproportionately affected (World Bank Group 2016).

Fragility, conflict, and violence also exacerbate some of the constraints that women traders face relative to men. For instance, gender gaps in education and skills can be widened by the breakdown of the education system during conflict and subsequent brain drain. In Liberia prolonged years of conflict led to higher female illiteracy rates and a larger proportion of women lacking basic business skills and often finding themselves in low-productivity jobs. The current generation of women entrepreneurs lacks many of the basic skills needed to successfully operate a business (IFC 2014).

Higher trading costs for women than for men

Economic policies can have unintended consequences for gender equality, often making it more challenging for women to access opportunities. These consequences are influenced by the types of jobs women have, the industries they are concentrated in, and gender differences in consumption.

Trade policy can affect women in all their roles. As workers and producers of goods and services, women are affected both by foreign trade policy that restricts their access to foreign markets and by domestic trade policy that shelters them from foreign competition but restricts access to imported materials. Export competitiveness is determined by the ability to move goods and services across borders rapidly, cheaply, and, above all, predictably. But traders face a number of challenges when moving products across

Figure 2.1 Constraints affecting women in trade are diverse

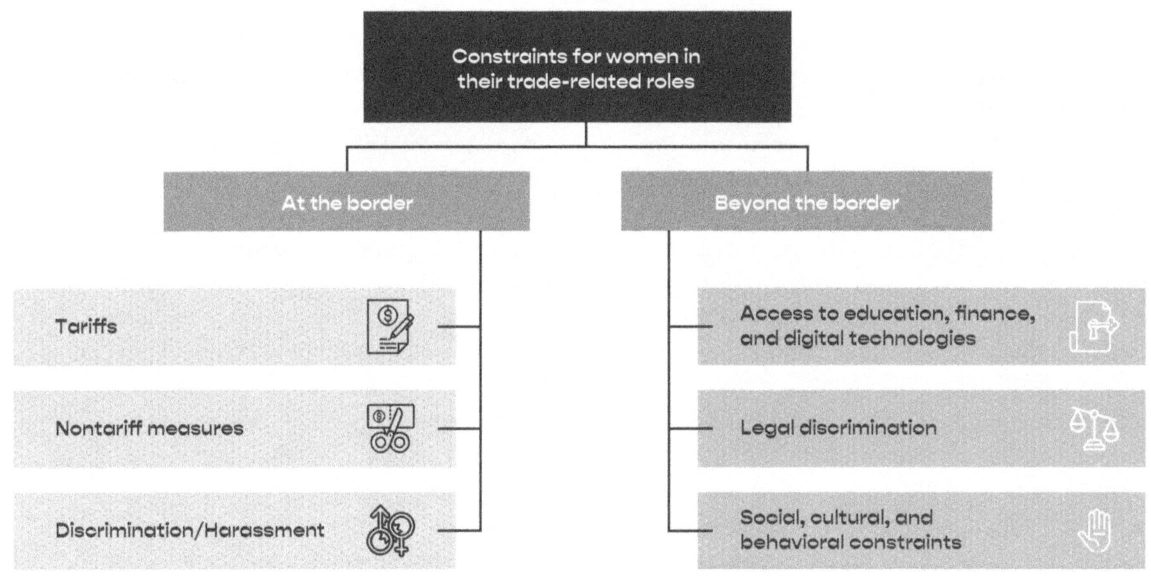

Source: Original figure for this publication.

borders. These difficulties are accentuated for women and can be traditional trade barriers such as tariffs and nontariff measures (NTMs), burdensome customs requirements and red tape, poor infrastructure, and even physical security. Finally, women as consumers are affected by domestic trade policy through its impact on prices of goods and services.

Women as workers are overrepresented in sectors that have high trade barriers

Women's employment tends to be concentrated in sectors that suffer from high trade costs. Sectors that employ more women have lower market access abroad in both developed and developing countries. In India, women exporters have faced persistently higher average tariff barriers in foreign markets compared to men (Mendoza, Nayyar, and Piermartini 2018). In 2012, goods produced by women faced an average tariff of 13 percent, whereas those produced by men faced a tariff of 7.8 percent, a 67 percent lower average tariff. This gap in tariffs faced by Indian women exporters is, to a large extent, driven by women's high employment share in agriculture. In developed countries such as Germany and the United States, women face on average 25 percent and 15 percent higher tariffs than men, respectively. In those countries, the gap is driven by women's high employment in sectors such as food processing, textile, and footwear industries.

One reason for the gender tariff gap in merchandise exports is that sectors employing relatively more low-wage workers tend to face higher tariffs, and women are overrepresented among low-wage workers (box 2.2). This may be the result of a coordination problem between countries when it comes to trade policy. Each country applies high tariffs on sectors employing low-wage workers to shield them from foreign competition; however, because low-wage workers tend to work in the same sectors everywhere, it also means that these sectors face less market access

Conditions of access to international markets are key to ensure that trade is inclusive, including for women. Recent empirical evidence shows, however, that women-produced goods continue to be subject to higher tariffs than men-produced goods.

Table B2.2.1 shows that, in India, women workers consistently face higher tariffs across all wage deciles, except for the highest decile where men face tariffs that are on average 1.0 percentage point higher than those faced by women. The difference for each wage decile is not particularly pronounced, varying between 0.3 and 5.0 percentage points. The number of women workers in the higher-income deciles is much smaller, however, than the number of men. In the 10th income decile, for example, women account for only 6 percent of the respondents (this pattern is also captured in table B2.2.2 for Germany and the United States). This disparity, combined with the fact that tariffs are higher for lower wage deciles, results in a much higher average gap between tariffs faced by Indian men and women (6 percentage points). Similar patterns hold for Germany and the United States. Hence, the gender gap in tariffs on merchandise exports is largely driven by women workers being predominantly employed in low-wage jobs that tend to face higher tariffs in international markets.

In addition, products produced by poor workers face a greater number of nontariff measures (NTMs) (Mendoza, Nayyar, and Piermartini 2018). On average, the poorest (income deciles 1 and 2) face some 200 different types of NTMs whereas workers belonging to the top income decile face only 127. Unlike tariffs, which consistently decline across the income deciles, the total numbers of NTMs for the poorer five deciles are not significantly different.

Table B2.2.1 Tariff faced in top destination markets, by gender and wage decile

	India, 2012			Germany, 2015			United States, 2015		
Income decile	Men	Women	Difference	Men	Women	Difference	Men	Women	Difference
1	20.4	21.7	-1.3	5.82	8.42	-2.60+	5.68	5.73	-0.05
2	22.2	22.6	-0.4	5.56	8.58	-3.02+	5.79	7.11	-1.32+
3	19.9	21.5	-1.6+	7.45	8.18	-0.73	5.34	6.32	-0.98
4	19.9	20.2	-0.3	6.99	7.92	-0.93+	4.26	5.63	-1.37+
5	18.1	21.7	-3.6+	6.39	6.72	-0.33	4.72	4.76	-0.04
6	15.8	18.2	-2.4+	5.64	5.05	0.59	4.3	3.96	0.33
7	14.7	19.7	-5.0+	5.67	4.36	1.31	4.71	4.35	0.36
8	12.0	15.1	-3.1+	4.83	4.53	0.30	3.89	3.49	0.40
9	7.8	8.6	-0.8	4.51	5.01	-0.49	3.69	3.48	0.21
10	4.6	3.6	1.0+	4.31	4.68	-0.37	3.23	2.78	0.45

Source: Mendoza, Nayyar, and Piermartini 2018; World Trade Organization calculations based on German Socio-economic Panel (SOEP) and Panel Study of Income Dynamics (PSID) databases matched with applied tariff rates from the World Integrated Trade Solution (WITS) database.
Note: The sign + denotes that the difference between the average tariff faced by men and by women is statistically significant (based on a t-test).

Table B2.2.2 Distribution of women and men, by income

	Germany, 2015		United States, 2015	
Income decile	Men	Women	Men	Women
1	8.0	16.1	7.6	12.8
2	5.9	10.8	7.1	12.6
3	5.6	14.9	9.2	14.2
4	8.3	13.1	7.2	9.4
5	9.5	10.4	11.1	12.7
6	11.3	9.4	8.3	8.0
7	11.7	8.6	11.3	10.6
8	11.9	6.9	10.6	7.7
9	12.8	6.2	12.2	7.6
10	15.1	3.5	15.3	4.4

Source: World Trade Organization calculations based on German Socio-economic Panel (SOEP) and Panel Study of Income Dynamics (PSID) databases matched with applied tariff rates from World Integrated Trade Solution (WITS) database.

In contrast, there is a significant jump from the 5th to the 6th decile, from the 7th to the 8th decile and from the 9th to the 10th decile. As with tariffs, this distribution of NTMs across income deciles implies a higher incidence on women workers who are overrepresented at the bottom of the income distribution. An important reason behind this result is that many women work in agriculture, a sector that faces high tariffs abroad as well as many NTMs related to production and hygiene standards. In addition, it is subject to subsidization in many developed countries, which further limits market access.

abroad. As a result, potentially positive effects of domestic protection for low-wage workers are counterbalanced by the negative effects of reduced access to foreign markets (Mendoza, Nayyar, and Piermartini 2018).

Sectors that employ more women face higher tariffs on the inputs they import. World Trade Organization calculations find a large positive correlation of 0.79 between input tariffs and female employment shares (figure 2.2). The sector with the highest female employment share, food and beverages, faces average import tariffs on inputs more than twice as high as the sector with the lowest share, mining. The high input tariffs are partly a result of the high tariffs on female-intensive sectors discussed above because each sector sources most of its inputs from within that sector. Cross-industry links also contribute to this phenomenon because some sectors that employ more women source more inputs from other female-intensive sectors. An obvious example in this regard is the heavy reliance of the textile sector on inputs from the agricultural sector. This type of relationship leads to a diffusion of high tariff barriers across female-intensive sectors. As a result, female-intensive sectors face high tariffs on both their inputs and their outputs.

Finally, in many countries women work predominantly in services sectors that are less trade-intensive, such as hospitality, education, or health (figure 2.3). These sectors face much higher barriers to trade than manufacturing sectors where most of the male labor force is employed. This factor can limit the gains that the ongoing servicification of economies generates for women (see the section titled "Opportunities for women in trade through servicification" later in the chapter).

As noted previously, in most countries, women face higher barriers to trade than men

Figure 2.2 Sectors that employ more women face higher input tariffs

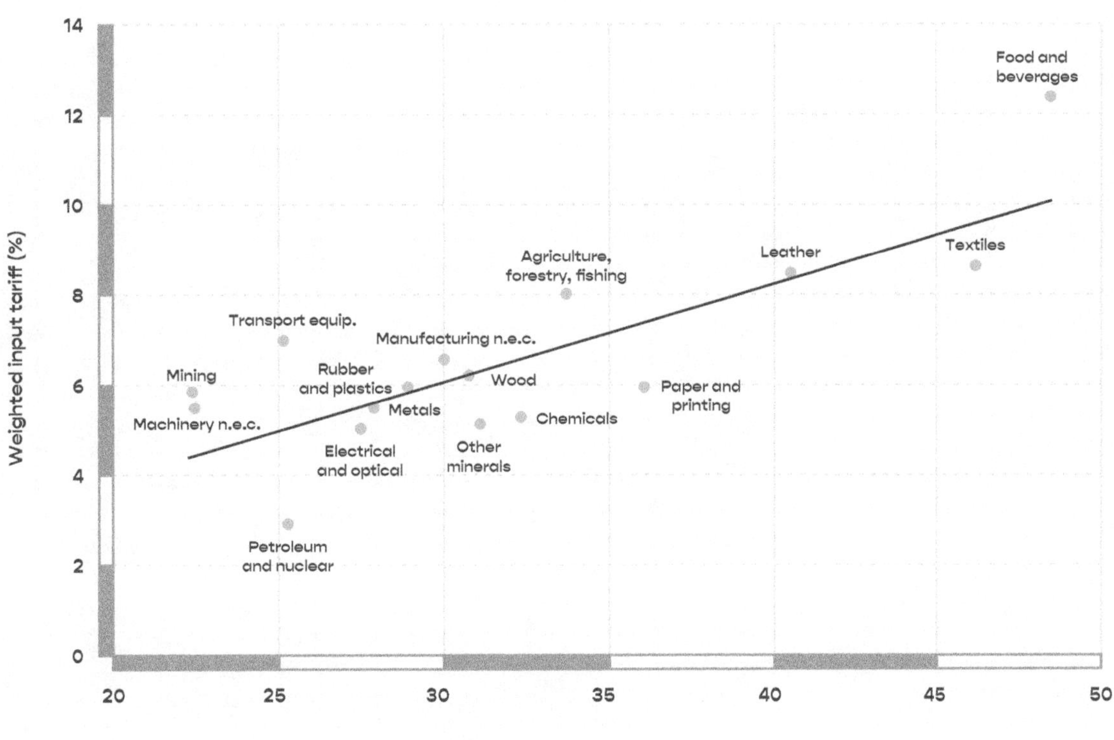

Source: World Trade Organization (WTO) Secretariat calculations based on Asian Development Bank multiregional input-output tables, WTO-Integrated Data Base tariff data, and World Bank Household Surveys for the most recent available years.
Note: Weighted input tariffs are calculated as a weighted average of sectoral tariffs with the weights being the share of inputs a sector provides in total inputs. n.e.c = not elsewhere classified.

do (figure 2.4). These obstacles comprise not only policy barriers but also the importance of face-to-face contact, among other frictions that make foreign services sales more difficult than domestic ones. The need for face-to-face interactions for services like hairdressing or counseling, also referred to as proximity burden (Francois and Hoekman 2010), makes cross-border supply of many services impossible and requires the service provider's presence in the importing country, either through investing in a commercial presence or through traveling to the importing country. Both these modes of services face high trade barriers, which tend to be even steeper for women, who often lack the access to finance needed for foreign direct investment (FDI) and tend to be less mobile.[1] It is important to add in this context that technological advancement continues to alleviate the proximity burden, turning services into an opportunity for women in trade (see "Opportunities for women in trade through digital technology" later in this chapter).

NTMs are more burdensome for women-owned exporting businesses

Product standards and certification procedures, burdensome customs and bureaucratic procedures, and obtaining import licenses are examples of NTMs that make it costly for firms to export and import. The burdens of NTMs are multiplied in the context of GVCs, which involve back-and-forth trade and cross-border just-in-time

Figure 2.3 On average, women work in services sectors that are less trade-intensive

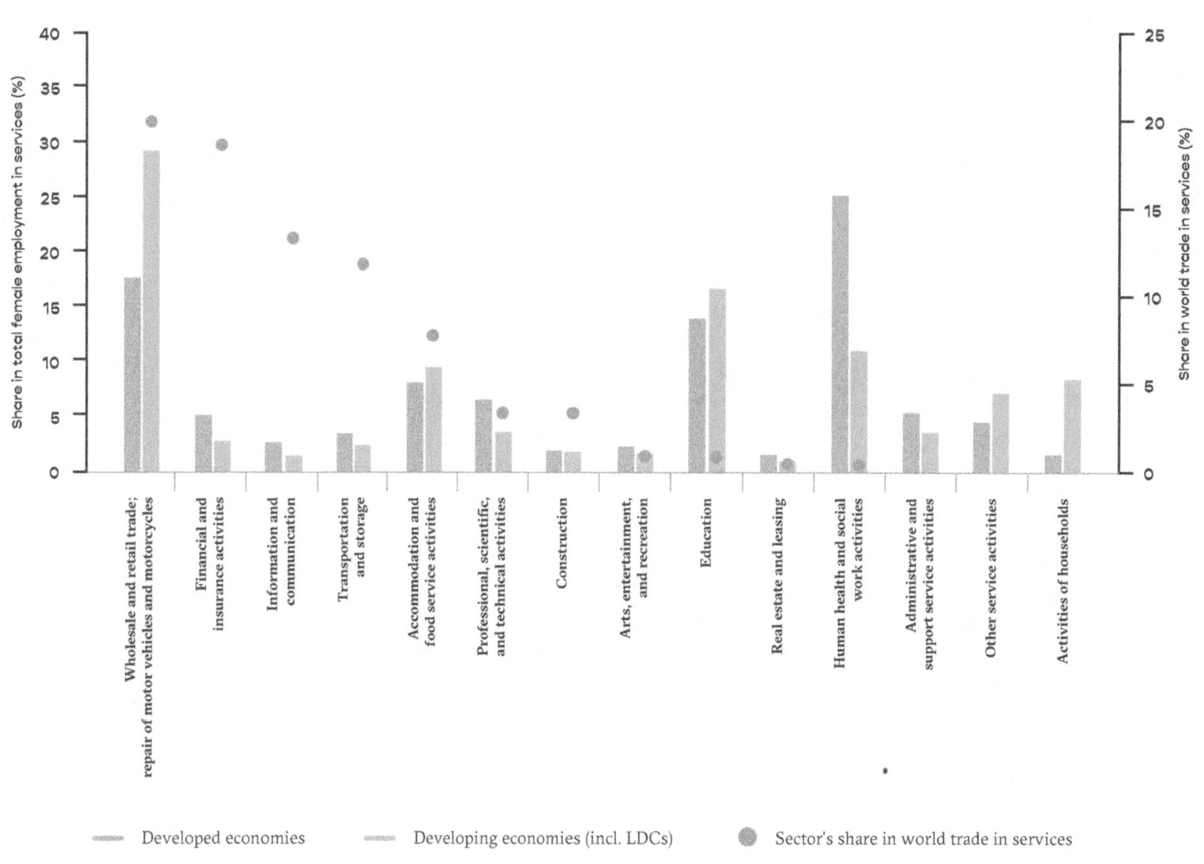

Source: WTO 2019.

Note: The sector's share in world trade takes into account all four modes of services supply as defined in the World Trade Organization General Agreement on Trade in Services (GATS), that is cross-border (mode 1), consumption abroad (mode 2), commercial presence (mode 3), and presence of natural persons (mode 4). Note that wholesale and retail trade appears as an outlier to the general observation that women work predominantly in less traded sectors. To merge trade and employment data, however, it is necessary to combine wholesale trade and retail trade into one sector. Women work on average more in retail than wholesale trade, but the latter is significantly more trade-intensive. In addition, more granular information suggests that women work in and own on average smaller establishments that trade less, but this fact is hidden by displaying only sector averages. Therefore, the actual tradability of the sector would actually be lower if only female employment and ownership were taken into account. LDC = least-developed country.

production (see the section "Opportunities for women in trade through GVCs" later in this chapter). Because NTMs often represent a fixed cost of trading, their costs are more prohibitive for small and medium enterprises (SMEs) than for large companies with high turnover, which can easily recoup such costs. Small exporters also lack specialized teams to handle the trading process and, because they export infrequently or in small batches, are particularly exposed to costs derived from cumbersome and lengthy administrative procedures (World Bank Group and WTO 2018). Combined with the fact that women are more likely to own and run SMEs than large firms and that they often export and import a smaller amount of goods, this pattern also suggests that NTMs affect women entrepreneurs more severely than men.

The difference in terms of barriers to trade between SMEs and large firms is illustrated in figure 2.5, which shows the main perceived obstacles to trade in manufacturing and services based on a survey of U.S. firms

Figure 2.4 On average, women face an export cost 13 percent higher than men's cost

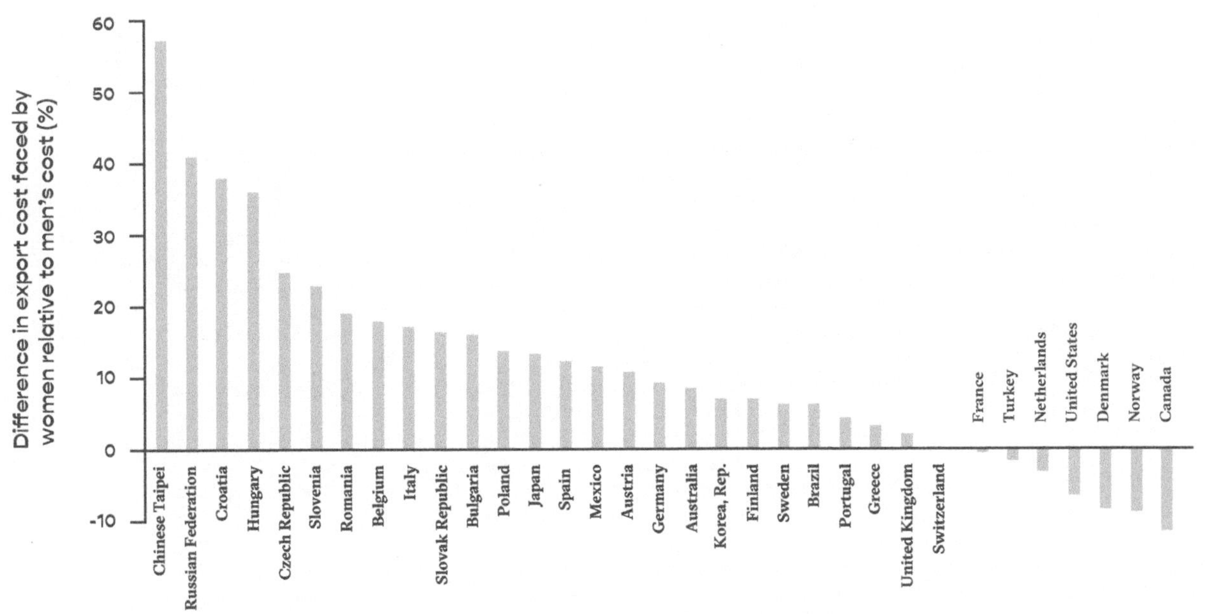

Source: World Trade Organization (WTO) Secretariat calculations.
Note: Calculations are based on bilateral trade cost estimates for 2016 from the WTO's Trade Cost Project and International Labour Organization statistics on employment by sex and economic activity. Trade costs are estimated with a sector-level gravity model specification proposed in Egger et al. (2018) using an experimental multiregional input-output database from the Asian Development Bank. First, the coefficients on country-pair dummies are obtained from a fully saturated gravity model with appropriate parameter constraints. Second, these estimates are transformed using a sectoral elasticity of substitution estimated by Egger et al. (2018).

Figure 2.5 Customs procedures and regulations are more burdensome for small firms

a. Manufacturing firms

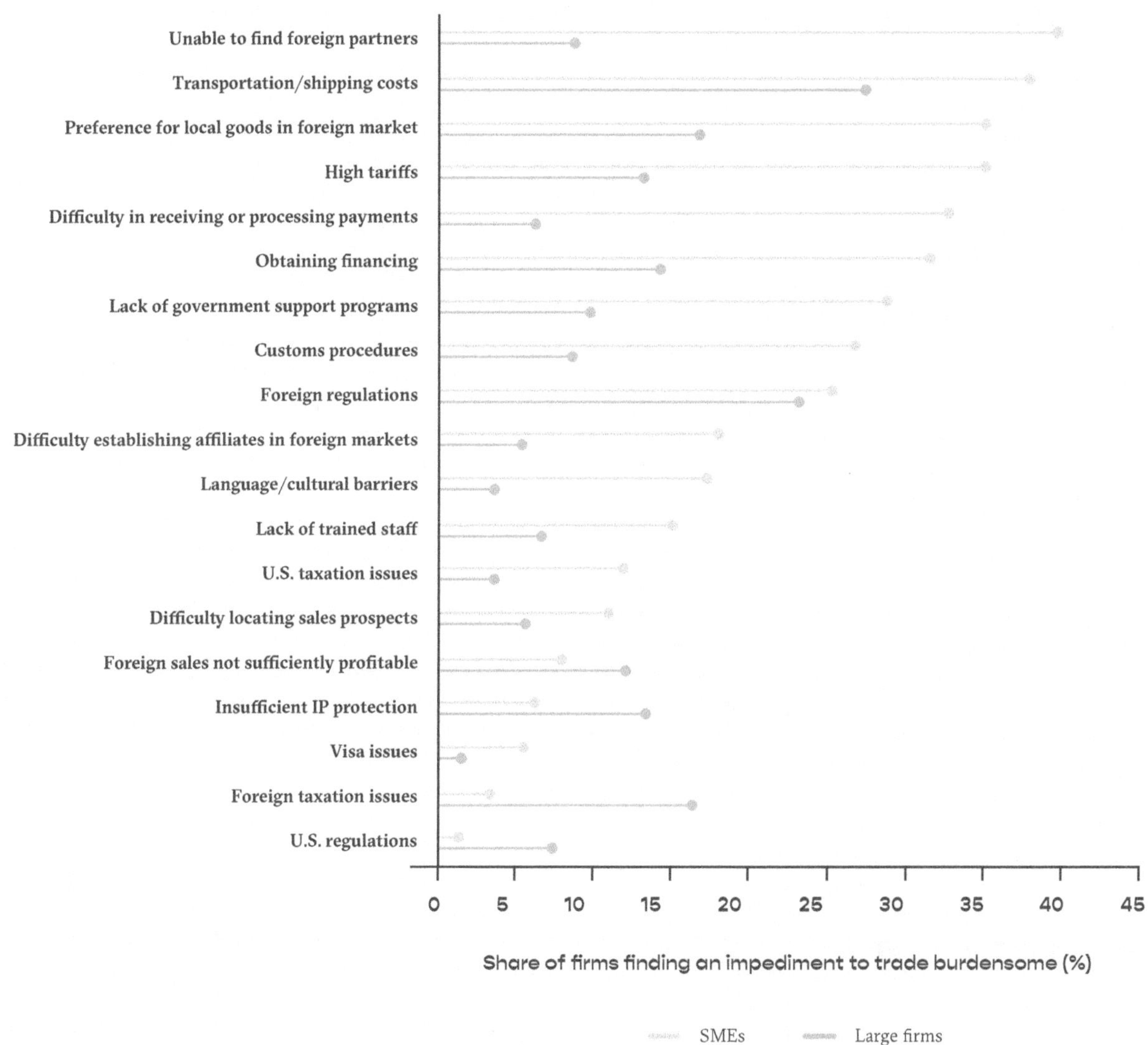

(WTO 2016). In manufacturing, these obstacles are mainly customs procedures and foreign regulations. For instance, almost 30 percent of SMEs find customs procedures burdensome whereas this is the case for less than 10 percent of large firms. In services, the obstacles are related to domestic regulations but also to the establishment of foreign affiliates and obtaining visas—policies related to the supply of services through commercial presence (mode 3) and presence of natural persons (mode 4) (see figure 2.3).

These findings are corroborated from business surveys in developing countries that were conducted as part of the Fourth Global Review of Aid for Trade (OECD and WTO 2013). Table 2.1 shows the top-five perceived constraints to entering, establishing, or moving up value chains for SMEs in developing countries as well as for businesses already integrated into value chains in agri-food, information and communication technology (ICT), and textiles and apparel. SMEs in these sectors consider certification costs, customs paperwork, and

b. Services firms

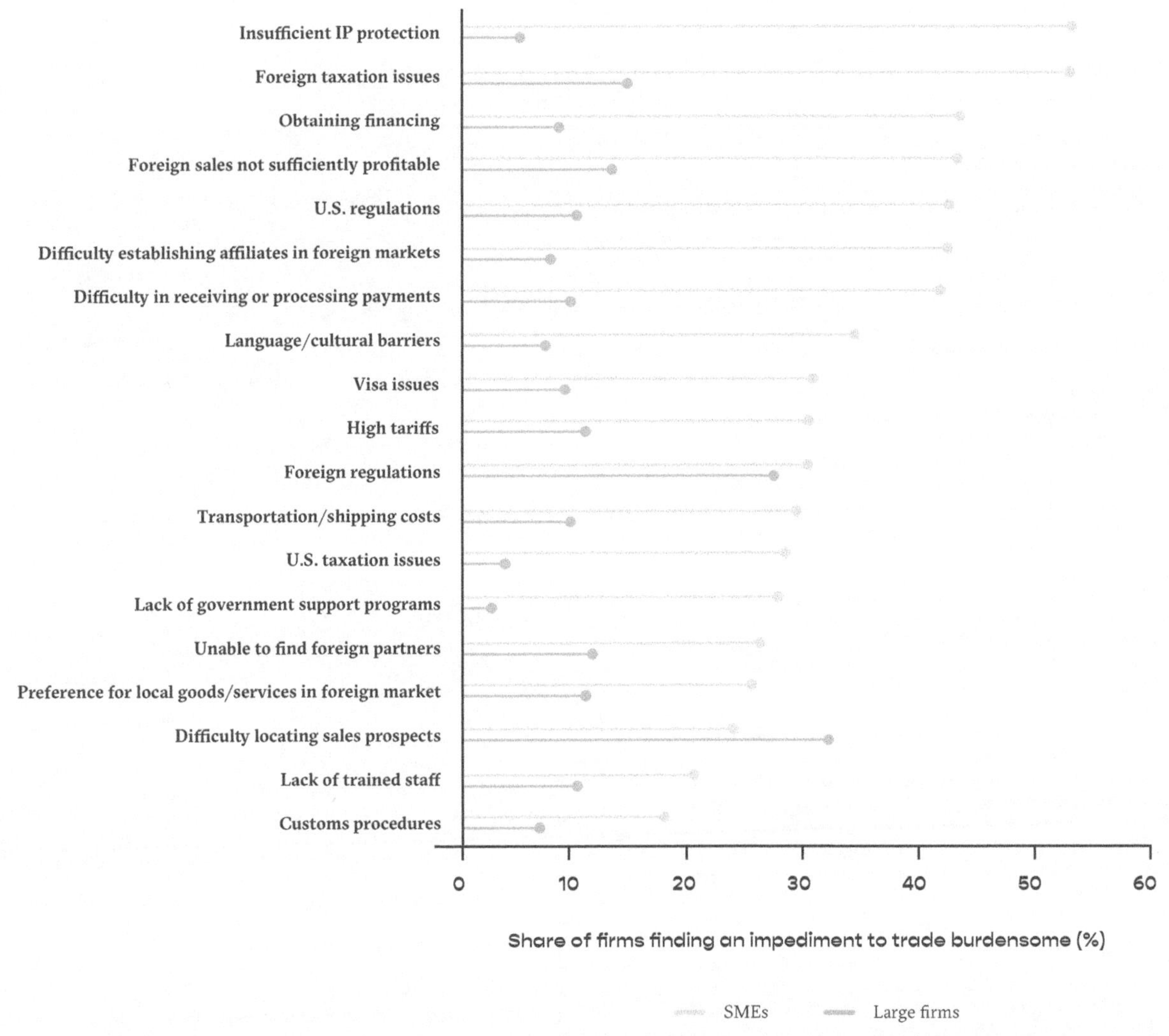

Source: WTO 2016.
Note: The results are based on a U.S. International Trade Commission survey of more than 8,400 U.S. firms. Firms with between 0 and 499 employees in the United States are categorized as SMEs; those with 500 or more employees are categorized as large firms. Responding firms rated the severity of 19 impediments on a 1-to-5 scale, with 1 indicating no burden and 5 indicating a severe burden. The figures show the shares of SMEs and large firms that replied 4 or 5, thus rating an impediment as burdensome. IP = intellectual property; SME = small and medium enterprise.

the lack of transparency in the regulatory environment to be especially burdensome.

Finally, survey evidence from Pakistan suggests that, although the types of NTMs reported as burdensome by women entrepreneurs are similar to those reported by men-owned companies, women are more affected (ITC and World Bank Group 2020). Overall, 66 percent of women-owned exporting companies report facing difficulties with NTMs, compared to 51 percent of men-owned firms. These difficulties are due to either regulations being too strict or complex to comply with or related procedural obstacles making compliance to given regulations difficult (box 2.3).

Table 2.1 Access to finance and transportation costs are important perceived constraints for SMEs in developing countries

Agriculture	Information and communication technology	Textiles and apparel
Access to business finance	Access to trade finance	Access to trade finance
Transportation costs	Lack of transparency in regulatory environment	Customs paperwork or delays
Certification costs	Unreliable and/or low band Internet access	Shipping costs and delays
Access to trade finance	Inadequate national telecommunications networks	Supply chain governance issues (e.g., anticompetitive practices)
Customs paperwork and delays	Customs paperwork or delays	Other border agency paperwork or delays

Source: WTO 2016.
Note: The table is based on a 122-question survey that was completed by 524 firms and business associations in developing countries, presenting the binding constraints these firms face in entering, establishing, or moving up value chains. In addition, 173 lead firms, mostly from Organisation for Economic Co-operation and Development countries, also completed the questionnaire to highlight the obstacles they face in integrating developing-country firms into their value chain. SME = small and medium enterprise.

Women consumers may be more vulnerable to the impact of import tariffs

Evidence from the United States suggests that women consumers face higher tariffs. In 2015, products specifically consumed by women had a higher tariff burden (Gailes et al. 2018) because of the combination of higher applied tariffs and greater spending on imported goods by women consumers. First, the average applied tariff rates on women-specific products are higher than the average applied tariff rates on men-specific products. This difference is predominantly driven by apparel, which is responsible for about 75 percent of the total tariff burden on U.S. households. Second, U.S. consumers spend twice as much money on women's clothing than on men's clothing, and the vast majority of this clothing is imported. The study finds that the tariff burden for U.S. households on women's apparel was US$2.77 billion more than on men's clothing, and this gender gap grew about 11 percent in real terms between 2006 and 2016.

Female-headed households would benefit more than male-headed households from the removal of import tariffs in most developing countries. Similar to the U.S. situation and as discussed in chapter 1, the import tariff burden falls disproportionately more on female-headed households (Depetris-Chauvin and Porto, forthcoming). It is difficult to draw inferences on gender inequality from differences observed on the basis of the gender of the household head, which in turn highlights the need for better data—in this context, consumption data collected at the individual rather than at the household level.

Nontariff measures (NTMs) are important barriers to trade and often have differential effects across firms of different size. A business survey in Pakistan by the International Trade Centre (ITC) identifies the key regulatory and procedural obstacles to trade faced by Pakistani exporters and importers. Overall, ITC interviewed representatives from about 1,200 Pakistani companies on hurdles they face when exporting or importing. The following analysis presents the key hurdles faced by businesses that are managed or owned by women.

Female employment and company ownership are concentrated in a few sectors. Almost half of the women-owned or women-managed companies are in the textiles and clothing sectors (45 percent) followed by fresh and processed foods (27 percent). Another 10 percent of the companies are from the miscellaneous manufacturing sector exporting products such as handicrafts (figure B2.3.1).

More than half (54 percent) of the NTM-related difficulties faced by women-owned or women-managed businesses are due to Pakistani export regulations, which men-led businesses cite as much less problematic. These measures include Pakistani inspection regulations, export restrictions, and difficulties with tax rebates on exported products (figure B2.3.2). Exporters find Pakistani inspection requirements and customs clearance burdensome; the most commonly cited problems are arbitrary behavior of customs officers, reckless handling of goods during inspection, unnecessary delay during inspection, demands for bribes or other informal payments, and the need to submit a large number of different documents. Concerning imports, almost half of the issues relate to advance payment restrictions.

Figure B2.3.1 Pakistani women-led companies engage mainly in the textiles and food industries

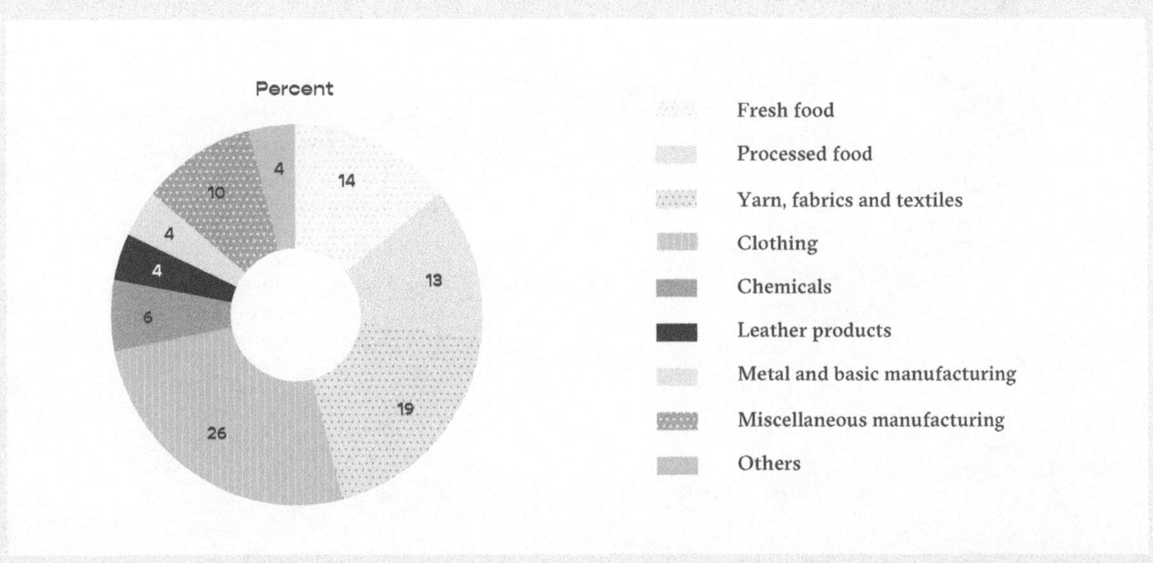

Source: ITC and World Bank Group 2020.
Note: Women-led companies are those with majority women ownership or management.

Figure B2.3.2 Pakistani export-related measures and conformity assessment procedures are the main impediments faced by women-led firms

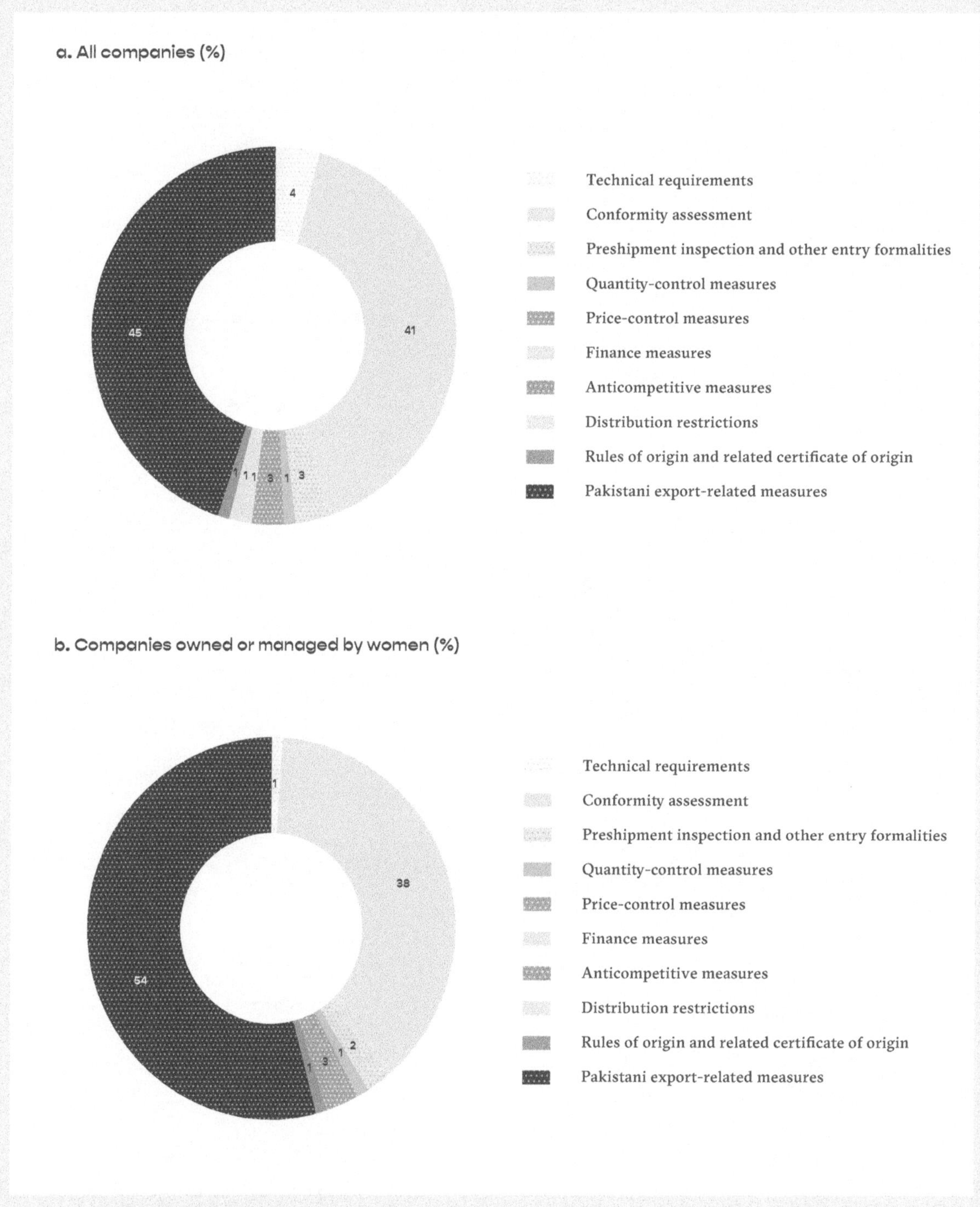

Source: ITC and World Bank Group 2020.
Note: Women-led companies are those with majority women ownership or management.

In addition to problems with domestic regulations, women-led businesses face most of the difficulties with conformity assessment requirements (38 percent), such as product testing and certification. In fact, exporters face more problems proving compliance with regulations than actually achieving that compliance. This finding is consistent with survey results from other developing countries: it is more challenging to prove that a product meets given criteria than to satisfy the criteria themselves because of the high costs and administrative hurdles related to the conformity assessment. Factors such as limited infrastructure and lack of well-trained staff have also contributed to various problems of quality compliance in Pakistan.

The adverse effects of limited access to finance, skills, and digital technologies for women in trade

Many domestic constraints hold women back from participating fully in trade as well. These challenges include inequities in accessing finance, education, and digital infrastructure; higher risk of job replacement; and persistent gender discrimination and gaps in the education and skills needed for the digital age. These beyond-the-border constraints disadvantage women by limiting their access to resources that would help them play a bigger role in trade.

Women have limited access to finance

It is more difficult for women than men to access finance in both developing and developed countries. Access to finance refers to the ability to access formal, basic financial services, such as holding bank accounts or at least having access to nonbank, microcredit institutions that allow customers to make formal payments, deposit money, and apply for loans. Without this access, women face greater difficulties in collecting and saving income and in growing their businesses.

As a result, women in their different roles have less access to the various gains from trade. Women entrepreneurs face difficulties financing import and export transactions, especially because trade is perceived to be more risky than domestic transactions. If they are liquidity-constrained, women consumers cannot benefit from imports in the same fashion as men, and women workers and decision makers can finance less training and education for themselves or their children to obtain the skills demanded by trading firms.

Women face barriers even with basic financial instruments

International surveys show that women-led businesses have a lower probability of obtaining credit and are charged a higher interest rate for loans once approved (Muravyev, Schäfer, and Talavera 2009). They are also 30 percent more likely to need a guarantor even when all other observable criteria but gender are identical (Brock and De Haas 2019). In addition, women-led businesses generally raise less formal and informal venture capital than men-led businesses (Carter et al. 2003). Even microfinance institutions, many of which explicitly target underfinanced individuals, have been found to maintain and even exacerbate the gender gap in the loans they approve and the amount they disburse (Brana 2013).

The International Finance Corporation estimates that as many as 70 percent of women-owned SMEs in developing countries are unserved or underserved by financial institutions, resulting in a total credit gap of US$287 billion, which is 30 percent of the total credit gap for SMEs.

Gender differences in access to and use of financial services can have direct negative ramifications for the whole economy (Aterido, Beck, and Iacovone 2013) because barriers to finance reduce an efficient capital allocation and aggravate income inequalities (Beck, Demirgüç-Kunt, and Levine 2007).

Evidence based on measures of financial inclusion by gender shows that women's access to basic financial services was 7 percentage points behind that of men globally in 2014, and 9 percentage points behind that of men in developing countries (World Bank 2014a). Over 1 billion women did not use or have access to the financial system. Furthermore, developing economies had 200 million more male than female cell phone owners. Without equal access to mobile technology, women are excluded from secure and convenient digital payment systems, which have been a major means of accessing nonbank payments, particularly in developing countries. This lack of access limits the extent to which the adoption of digital technologies can provide benefits for women (see "Opportunities for women in trade through digital technology" later in this chapter).

Women's financial inclusion has kept pace with men's in recent years, although there are few signs that women are bridging the gender gap (Demirgüç-Kunt et al. 2017). For example, from 2014 to 2017 men's ownership of bank accounts grew from 60 percent to 67 percent, whereas women's ownership grew likewise from 52 percent to 59 percent. This general trend masks, however, gains made in India and in some African economies. The gender gap in India fell by 14 percentage points (from 20 percent to 6 percent) over the three years, in part because of government-driven efforts aimed at helping women obtain basic bank accounts.

Limited access to finance puts trade credit out of reach for women entrepreneurs

Trade finance is a narrower concept than finance. It refers to specialized financial products, such as letters of credit, for mitigating risks involved in international trade transactions. Most often, access to basic finance is a precondition of eligibility for trade finance products. Because international trade carries more perceived risk than that of domestic trade, the requirements by financial institutions on clients in terms of creditworthiness, due diligence information, collateral, and financials are typically higher than for access to basic bank services.

Available survey data reveal that, although 100 percent of women-led firms requesting trade finance have access to formal finance (such as a bank account), only 18 percent of them receive sufficient trade finance (table 2.2) (ADB 2016). Women-owned firms requesting trade finance tend to be smaller than median surveyed firms. They are also more dependent on trade finance for their ability to trade, but their requests are more likely to be rejected by a financial institution. They are also more likely to use digital financial solutions. Moreover, women-owned firms face 50 percent more rejections for their trade finance requests than men-owned firms. Once rejected, women-owned firms are more likely to seek out alternative financing than are enterprises led by men (41 percent versus 35 percent) (ADB 2017).

Women have limited access to education

Large and persistent gender wage gaps exist in all economies. Part of this persistent trend is that women tend to work and run businesses in sectors and occupations that command relatively lower wages than their male-intensive counterparts. This tendency is partly explained by gender differences in education, which limit women's access to higher-paying professions, many of which are concentrated in tradable sectors.

Women in lower-income countries face more education constraints

Women are frequently excluded from the benefits of trade because they lack the skills or education required, particularly in developing countries. Although women have become more educated and have substantially narrowed the difference in educational attainment

Table 2.2 Women-led firms face higher rejection rates for trade finance

	Women-led firms	Men-led firms
Median number of employees	11 (55% women)	16 (37% women)
Rejection rates for trade finance (self-reported) (%)	21	14
Dependence on trade finance (for trade) (%)	50	43
Likelihood to seek alternatives (%)	41	35
Proportion using digital finance (%)	26	6

Source: ADB 2016.

compared to men, the small average gap masks major differences across income groups (figure 2.6). On the one hand, females have higher completion rates than males in upper-middle-income and high-income countries. In low-income countries, on the other hand, the male completion rate is almost twice as high as the female rate, and in lower-middle-income countries it is 16 percent higher.

Women in low-income and lower-middle-income countries face barriers in access to education for a variety of reasons. Evidence suggests that, when parents cannot finance the schooling costs for all their children, they tend to keep girls out of school. When labor market opportunities for women in many developing economies remain poor, the opportunity cost of schooling is perceived to outweigh potential returns to education. In contrast, evidence from India shows that with increased returns to education comes a corresponding increase in educational attainment of girls. Similarly, reducing the cost of schooling through conditional cash transfers has been shown to close educational gender gaps in several countries. Increased connectivity between villages and schools has also been shown to reduce educational gender gaps because girls are considered to face a higher safety risk on their way to school (Edmonds, Pavcnik, and Topalova 2010; Fiszbein et al. 2009; Jensen 2012; Muralidharan and Prakash 2017; Song, Appleton, and Knight 2006).

Women are underrepresented in science, technology, engineering, and mathematics fields

In high-income and upper-middle-income countries, educational gender gaps are visible in discipline-specific enrollment rates, despite a narrowing of the gender gap overall. Women tend to be severely underrepresented in the STEM (science, technology, engineering, and math) subjects, despite evidence that no gender-specific differences exist in STEM grades between female and male fourth-graders in 47 countries (OECD 2017). Whereas the female share of graduates from all bachelor's programs in most Organisation for Economic Co-operation and Development (OECD) countries is above 50 percent, it is only 31 percent in STEM fields.

Survey evidence from Europe reports that girls tend to lose interest in STEM fields around

Figure 2.6 Women's upper-secondary completion rates are lower than men's in low-income and lower-middle-income countries

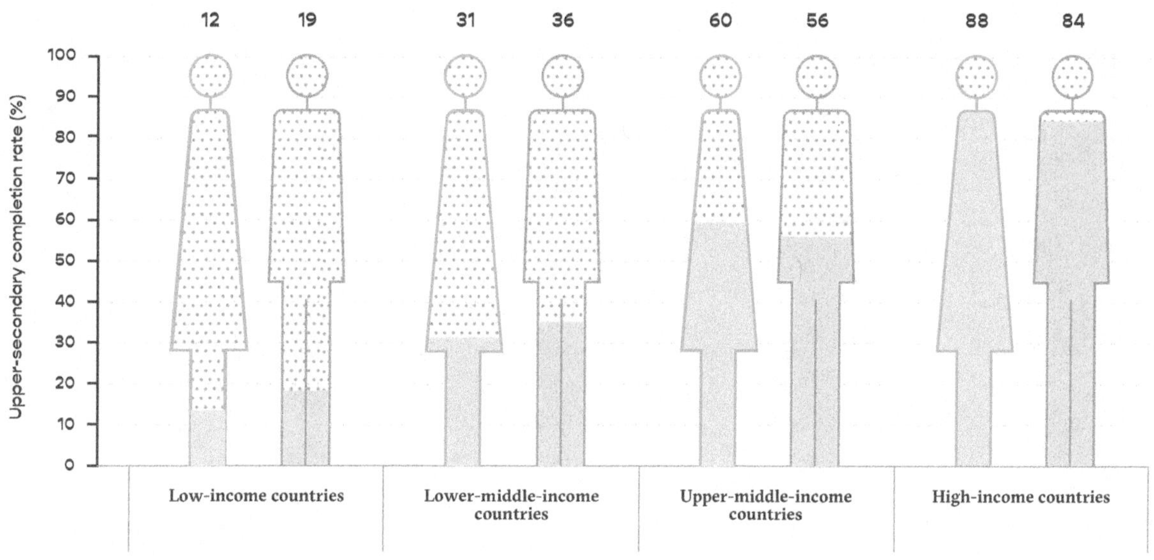

Source: World Trade Organization Secretariat calculations based on World Inequality Database on Education, United Nations Educational, Scientific, and Cultural Organization Institute for Statistics.
Note: Percentage of people aged 20–29 years who have completed upper-secondary school based on latest year for which data are available.

the age of 15 because they lack encouragement and mentorship, access to practical experience, and role models. This finding is also reflected in a study of 65 developed and developing countries, which found that girls have considerably less self-confidence than boys with respect to their skills in mathematics or science and that less than 5 percent of girls contemplate pursuing a career in engineering and computing (Microsoft 2017; OECD 2015).

Educational gender gaps prevent women workers from accessing the gains from trade

Educational constraints for women reduce their potential wages and job opportunities from new trade opportunities in both developing and developed countries. Women's gains from trade are reliant largely on their outsize share of employment in low-skill occupations, such as the garment and apparel industries. Without increases in their educational and skill levels, women cannot increase their share in higher-productivity trading firms that pay more. These constraints also limit women's abilities to benefit from upgrading in GVCs (see the section, "Opportunities for women in trade through GVCs," later in this chapter).

Women's opportunities are limited for several reasons. First, many of the most productive tradable sectors are skill-intensive. Access to international markets may require knowledge of a different language, different regulations, and different market conditions. Data from Norway and South Africa suggest that trading firms hire relatively more skilled women relative to men when compared to domestic firms (Bøler, Javorcik, and Ulltveit-Moe 2018; Janse van Rensburg et al., forthcoming), which means that trading firms expect more education and skills from women workers than from men. Second, trade seems to reward specific types of skills. The most trade-intensive sectors are also relatively intensive in STEM employment so that female barriers to STEM studies become a barrier to their participation in trade (figure 2.7).[2]

Figure 2.7 Trade-intensive sectors employ more workers with STEM backgrounds

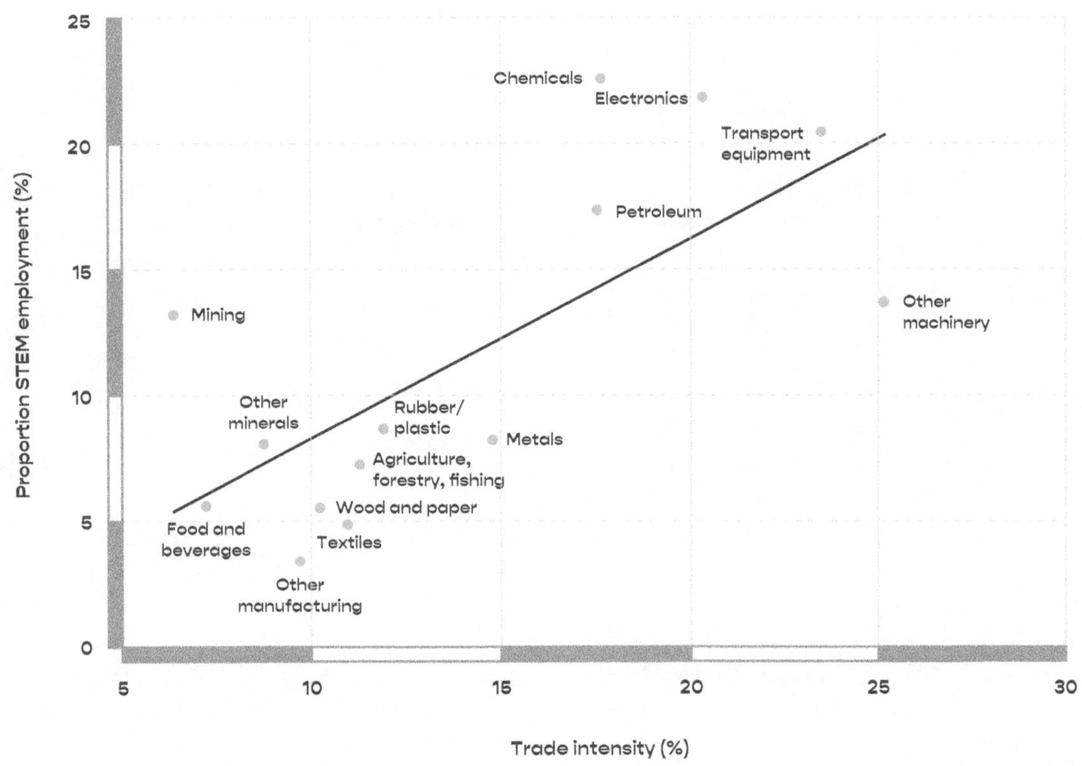

Source: World Trade Organization Secretariat calculations based on the American Community Survey for 2017 and Organisation for Economic Co-operation and Development Trade in Value Added (TiVA) data for 2015.
Note: STEM (science, technology, education, and math) employment is calculated following O*NET definitions (see https://www.onetonline.org/). Trade intensity is calculated as gross exports as a proportion of gross output by 2-digit sector.

Third, trade may promote specialization in relatively skill-intensive production stages as well as skill-biased technological upgrading (Burstein and Vogel 2017; Bustos 2011; Feenstra and Hanson 1995). Fourth, trade causes some sectors and firms to contract with new import competition and others to grow thanks to new markets. Thus, trade benefits workers who can adjust and move easily across firms or sectors. This ability, however, is most pronounced in workers with more education (Ruppert Bulmer et al. 2014). Hence, barriers to education reduce women's share in the gains from trade.[3]

Women have limited access to digital technology

The rise of digital technologies promises to help women's access to trade. The section, "Opportunities for women in trade through digital technology," later in this chapter highlights how the various new technologies make it easier for women to benefit from trade. It shows, for instance, how technology can improve women entrepreneur's access to external finance, and how it can ease the time burden of women workers or small-scale agricultural traders who have to handle both domestic duties and work. Despite these potential benefits, women have less access to digital technologies than men. Recent estimates by the International Telecommunication Union reveal that the digital gender gap is persistent and tends to get wider over time. For instance, the Internet user gender divide increased from 11 percent in 2013 to 12 percent 2016, with more than 250 million fewer women than men now online at the global level (ITU 2016).

Although this digital gender divide is prominent globally, its extent varies significantly across countries—ranging from 2.3 percent in developed economies to 7.6 percent in developing countries. The rate of female online presence has reached 80 percent in developed economies, but it stands below the world average in developing countries at 37.4 percent. Least-developed countries lag even further behind—with less than 13 percent of women online (figure 2.8). The lack of women's online empowerment in these countries could further hamper their attempts to participate more actively in the digital economy and in trade.

The gender gap is also visible in statistics on the use of mobile phones. The latest estimates suggest that 184 million fewer women than men own a mobile phone across low- and middle-income countries, in part because of costs and social norms (map 2.1). Even when women own a mobile phone, they are far less likely than men to use it, especially when it comes to more transformational services like mobile Internet and mobile money services (GSMA 2018). This finding does not necessarily apply to female business owners or managers; evidence suggests that firms in developing economies with female top managers use ICT tools and services as intensively as—or in some instances even more intensively than—firms with male top managers (ADB 2019).

Legal barriers to women's participation in trade

Many laws and regulations directly discriminate against women, preventing them from entering the workforce, starting a business, or making decisions for the household (figure 2.9). Even in very open and advanced economies, laws have limited women's economic participation until recently. For instance, in many developed countries

Figure 2.8 The digital gender divide persists

a. Internet penetration, by region

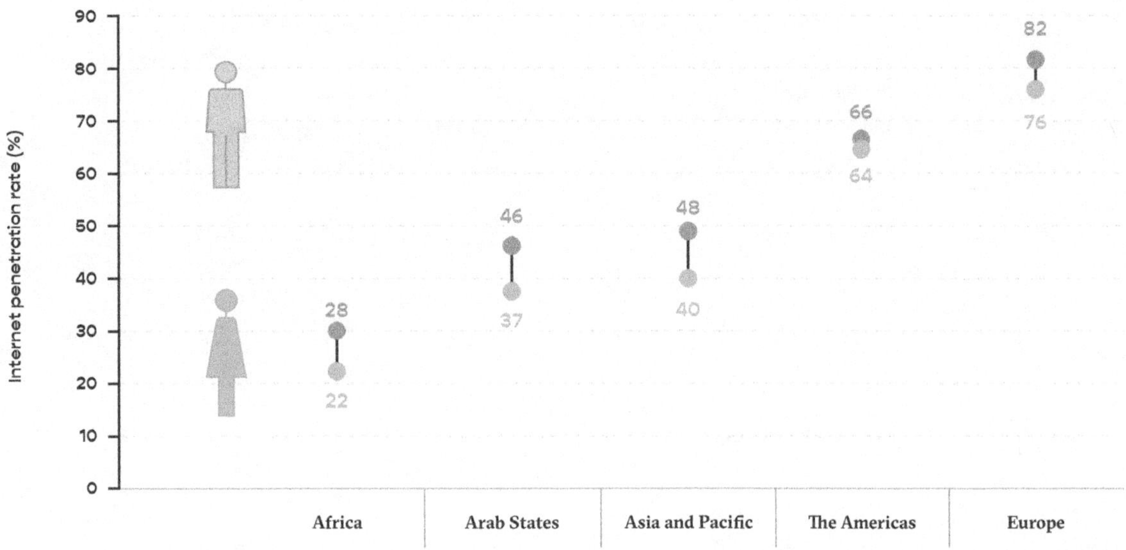

b. Internet penetration, by level of development

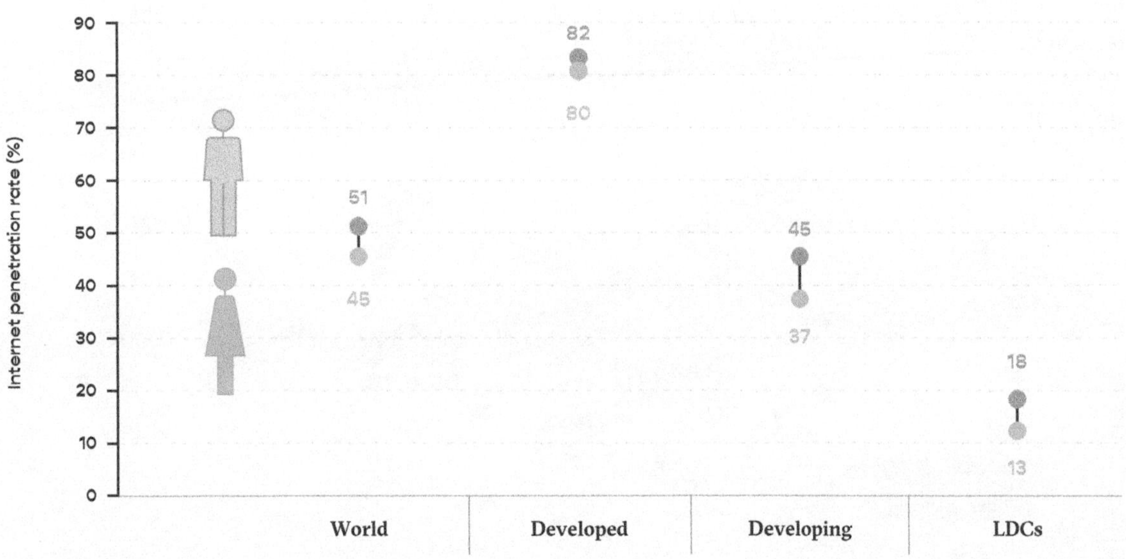

Source: ITU 2016.
Note: Penetration rates in this figure refer to the number of women and men who use the Internet, as a percentage of the respective total female and male populations. LDC = least-developed country.

women were not allowed to work without their husband's consent until the 1960s or 1970s.

Legal gender differences matter for women's economic participation. The question is how the wider legal framework may affect women's economic choices and their engagement in trade, as entrepreneurs and employees in trade-related industries but also as decision makers in the household. In economies where the law provides equality of opportunity, more women work, and they are better paid (figure 2.10).

Many laws place basic constraints on women's legal decision-making abilities, which can hinder their economic opportunities from trade. Among the restrictions women still face are the following:

- Restrictions in setting up a business
  - » In some countries, women still cannot open a bank account in the same way as men.
  - » Some economies impose additional legal or administrative hurdles on a woman registering a business, such as the requirement to provide her husband's name when registering a business, whereas a man is not required to provide such information about his wife (World Bank Group 2018a).
  - » When applying for a national identification card, women are required to present additional permission or documentation not required for men.
- Restrictions on mobility

Map 2.1 The gender gap in mobile ownership is particularly high in Africa and South Asia

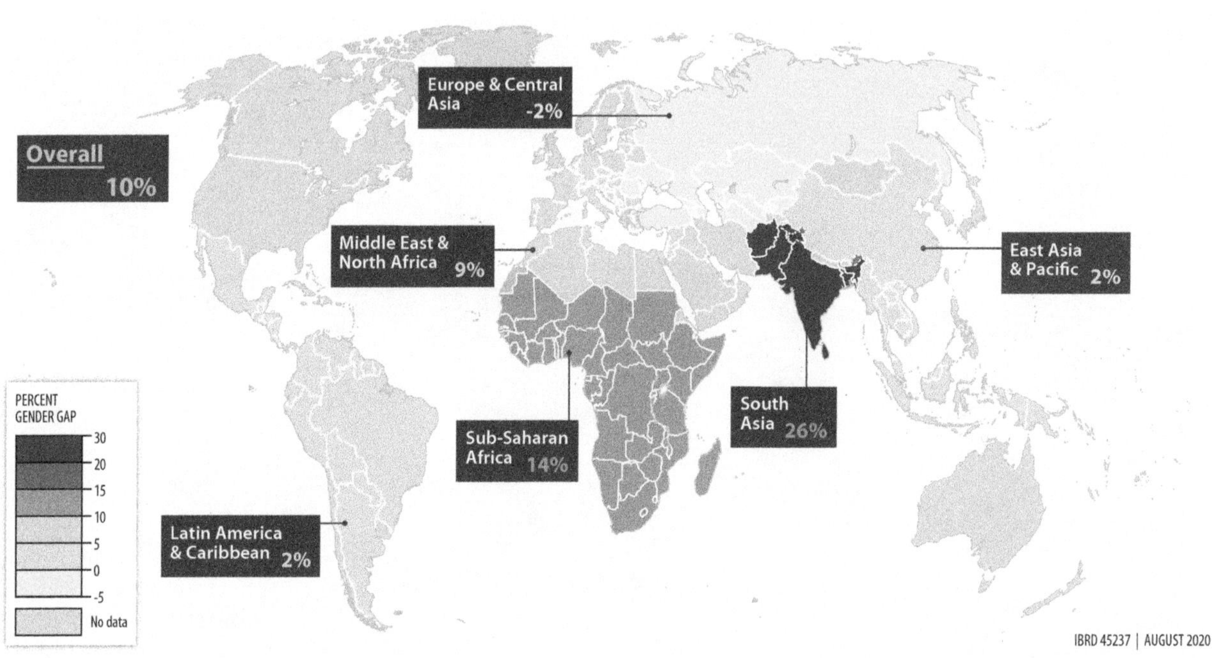

Source: GSMA 2018.
Note: The gender gap refers to how less likely a woman is than a man to have mobile access, which is defined as a person having sole or main use of a SIM card (or a mobile phone that does not require a SIM) and using it at least once a month. Data based on survey results and modeled data for adults aged 18+.

Credit: © sirtravelalot/ Shutterstock.com. Used with permission; further permission required for reuse.

Figure 2.9 Laws affect women throughout their working lives

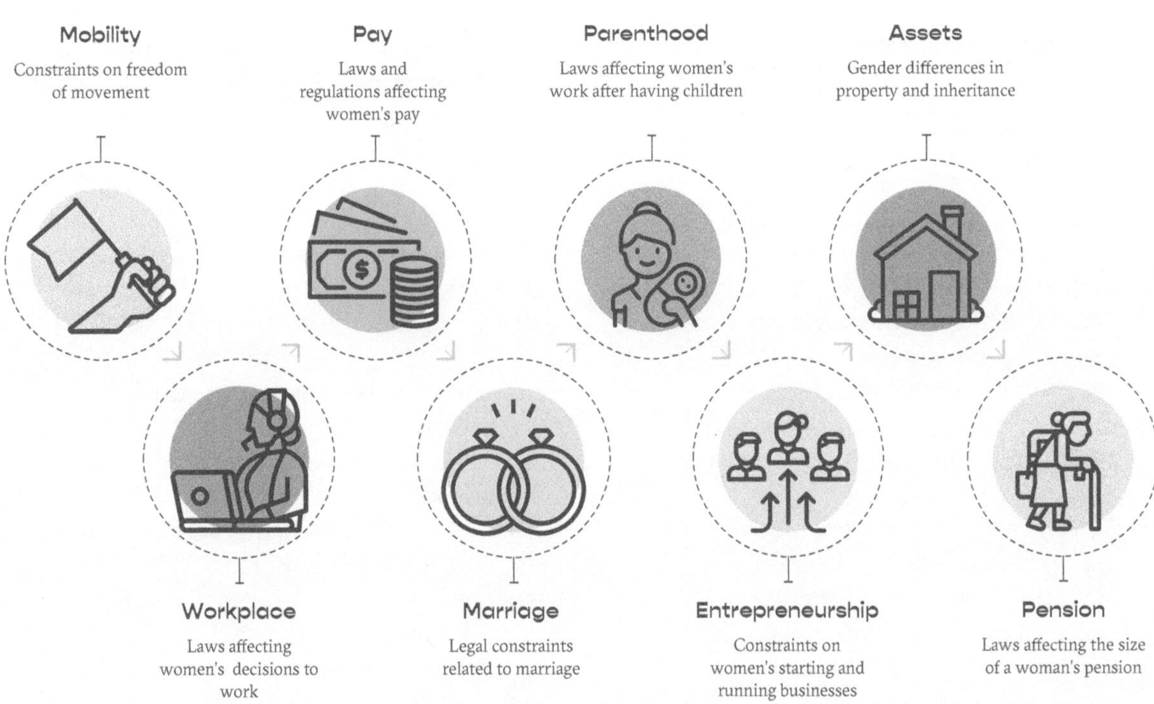

Source: World Bank Group 2018a.

- Certain laws can restrict, and in some cases prevent, a woman's mobility by requiring her to obtain permission from a husband or guardian to travel. Six economies globally prevent women from traveling outside the country in the same way as men.
- In many developing economies, women cannot apply for a passport in the same way as men. In some legal traditions, women do not have their own passport, but they are entered on their husband's passport and travel under the same document.
- Several economies restrict a woman's ability to leave the marital home, for example, by requiring that she have permission from her husband to do so. Additionally, some economies legally restrict a woman's decision about whether to work outside the home. In some economies worldwide, laws require a woman to get permission from her husband to work outside the home, or she can face consequences under the law if her work is against the family's interest.

- Restrictions on working in trade-related sectors
  - In many economies, women are still barred from freely choosing their occupation because of legal restrictions. Such restrictions can prevent women from working in trade-related sectors or firms. Restrictions can apply to women's employment in specific industries, such as mining, manufacturing, construction, energy, agriculture, water, and transportation.
  - Laws can also limit women's work at night or in certain jobs deemed hazardous, arduous, or morally inappropriate for women. Such laws prevent women from taking shift work or interacting with customers and suppliers in distant time zones.

- Restrictions on property rights
  - Women, more often than men, lack conventional collateral such as land because of inheritance systems and family laws that disfavor women when allocating assets. For example, in many economies sons and daughters do not have equal rights to inherit assets from their parents; and many economies limit the inheritance rights of widows. These systems can severely affect women's access to property.
  - In some countries, men and women do not have equal ownership rights to immovable property because of gender differences in the allocation of marital property or legal restrictions on property ownership for women.
  - In some economies, spouses do not have equal administrative authority over assets during marriage, which can limit women's ability to benefit from trade as workers, consumers, or decision makers. For example, women are less likely to hold leadership positions in business when their property rights are not guaranteed (figure 2.11).

Where women face more hurdles than men, business and trade activities become more difficult. For example, women are less likely to borrow from a financial institution in economies where processes for getting a national identity card differ by gender (World Bank Group 2018a). Such legal differences can significantly affect a woman's engagement in international business and trade. Mobility is important to enable women workers and entrepreneurs to access markets and can affect women traders more than home-based entrepreneurs. Access to finance is critical for women traders who are planning to start or grow their business. Another important factor in determining a woman's access to property is the legal treatment of spousal assets. Equally critical is removing the husband's sole control over property.

Figure 2.10 With greater equality of opportunity, more women work, and they receive higher wages

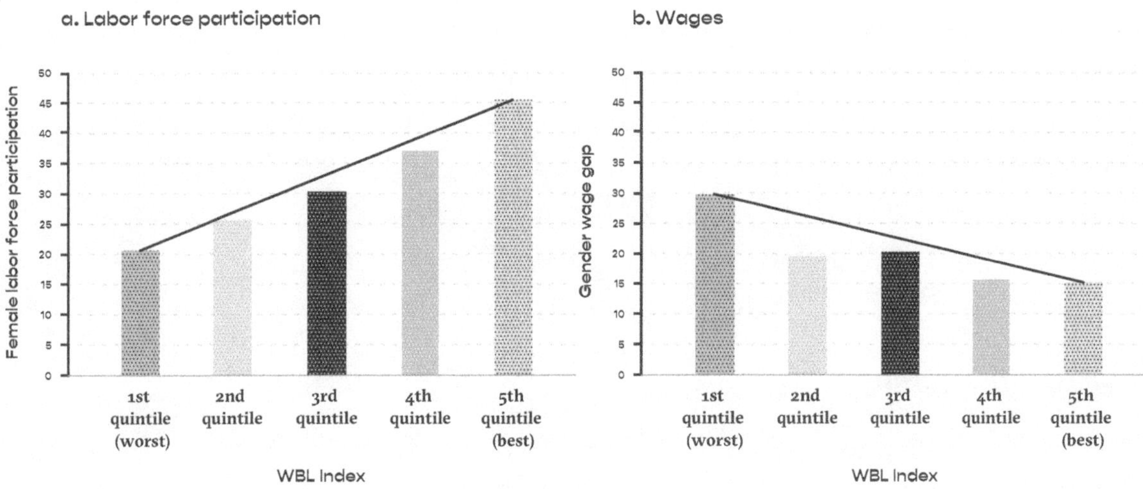

Source: Women, Business and the Law (WBL) and World Development Indicators databases; World Economic Forum.
Note: The positive relationships between the 10-year average WBL index and the ratio of female-to-male labor force participation rate, and between the 10-year average WBL index and the ratio of female-to-male estimated earned income are statistically significant at the 1 percent level after controlling for the log of gross national income per capita. These relationships remain statistically significant at the 1 percent level even after controlling for the ratio of female-to-male gross enrollment in secondary education, the ratio of female-to-male population, total urban population (percent), and total fertility rate (births per woman). Sources for the control variables include the World Development Indicators database. Regression analyses are based on 161 and 138 economies for which data are available, respectively. These statistical relationships should not be interpreted as causal.

Social, cultural, and behavioral constraints to women's participation in trade

Even if all discriminatory laws and practices were addressed overnight, women would still face challenges to playing a more active role as traders. Many of the barriers that prevent them from accessing the benefits of trade are rooted in social, cultural, and behavioral phenomena that legal and regulatory reforms can affect only over time.

Society puts an unfair burden on women

An important reason for women's relatively lower share in the gains from trade is that established traditions and norms impose constraints on women that are in conflict with the requirements of trading firms, such as irregular hours or business travel.

Social and cultural norms constrain the flexibility, skills, mobility, and networks of women producers

In most societies gender differences are partly due to an uneven distribution of household work and childcare, which restricts women's available time for paid work. Because women spend more time on domestic duties, they have less time to spend on paid work, especially when they have children and a partner (figure 2.12).

These differences in time use are driven both by women's indicated preferences and by binding social norms, although the latter might obviously drive the former (Fagan 2001; World Bank 2012). The differences can be based on historical developments, which implies that they are difficult to adjust in the short run. For instance, agricultural practices, in particular the use of the plow, have been found to have led to low female labor participation and cultural norms in some societies that can still be observed today—even in emigrants from these societies living abroad (Alesina, Giuliano, and Nunn 2013). As a result of differences in time use, women as workers

Figure 2.11 Women are less likely to hold leadership positions in business when they lack property rights

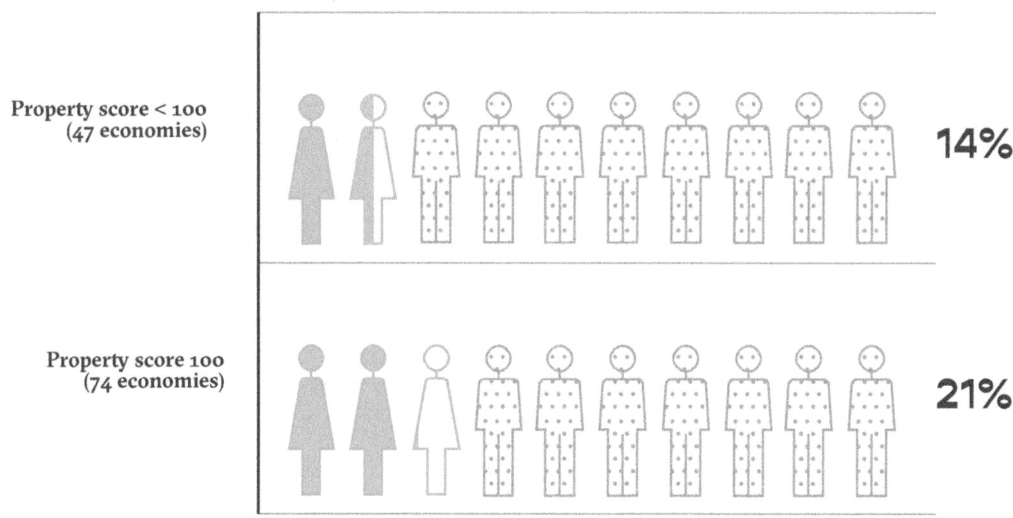

Source: Women, Business and the Law and Enterprise Surveys databases; World Development Indicators and Barro-Lee Educational Attainment databases.
Note: The difference in the percentages illustrated is statistically significant at the 10 percent level after controlling for the log of gross national income per capita (2015), the ratio of female-to-male (mean) years of education (ages 25+) (2015), the proportion of seats held by women in national parliaments (2016), and the rule of law (2016). Regression analysis is based on 121 economies for which data are available. This statistical relationship should not be interpreted as causal.

are likely to enjoy lower gains from trade compared to their male counterparts.

As discussed in chapter 1, trading often requires greater time use than nontrading occupations. Women—perceived to have dual commitments to work and family—are often perceived by employers as less reliable and less committed to their work than men. This disadvantage is exacerbated by trade liberalization that, by fostering competition, usually brings higher demands for working hours and travel from exporting firms. It can also limit women's access to trade-intensive sectors. For instance, evidence from the Kenyan tourism industry indicates that the camping accommodation industry that generates high profits due to foreign customers is almost exclusively male-operated, because the remote locations of these camps are a detriment to women who have responsibilities at home and are expected to stay close to their families (Homewood et al. 2009).

Another area where norms can hurt women is in the area of education. Part of the gender gap with respect to studying technical subjects (see the earlier section on women's limited access to education) might be due to parental attitudes (Microsoft 2017). Surveys reveal that parents have higher expectations for boys than for girls to eventually work in STEM jobs, independent of the performance of their children. Teacher biases and gender norms can also contribute to different enrollment rates in STEM education. A study of elementary schools in Israel found that girls performed better than boys when graded anonymously but worse when teachers knew the name of the children. It also found that girls who were falsely graded were much less likely to pursue advanced STEM courses later in life. A study with Dutch data found that girls are less likely to pursue STEM careers when their friends have more traditional gender norms. A series of other studies has shown that math score gaps narrow or disappear in more equal societies (Guiso et al. 2008; Lavy 2008; Lavy and Sand 2018; Pope and Sydnor 2010; van der Vleuten, Steinmetz, and van de Werfhorst 2019).

Figure 2.12 Women spend considerably less time than men on paid work

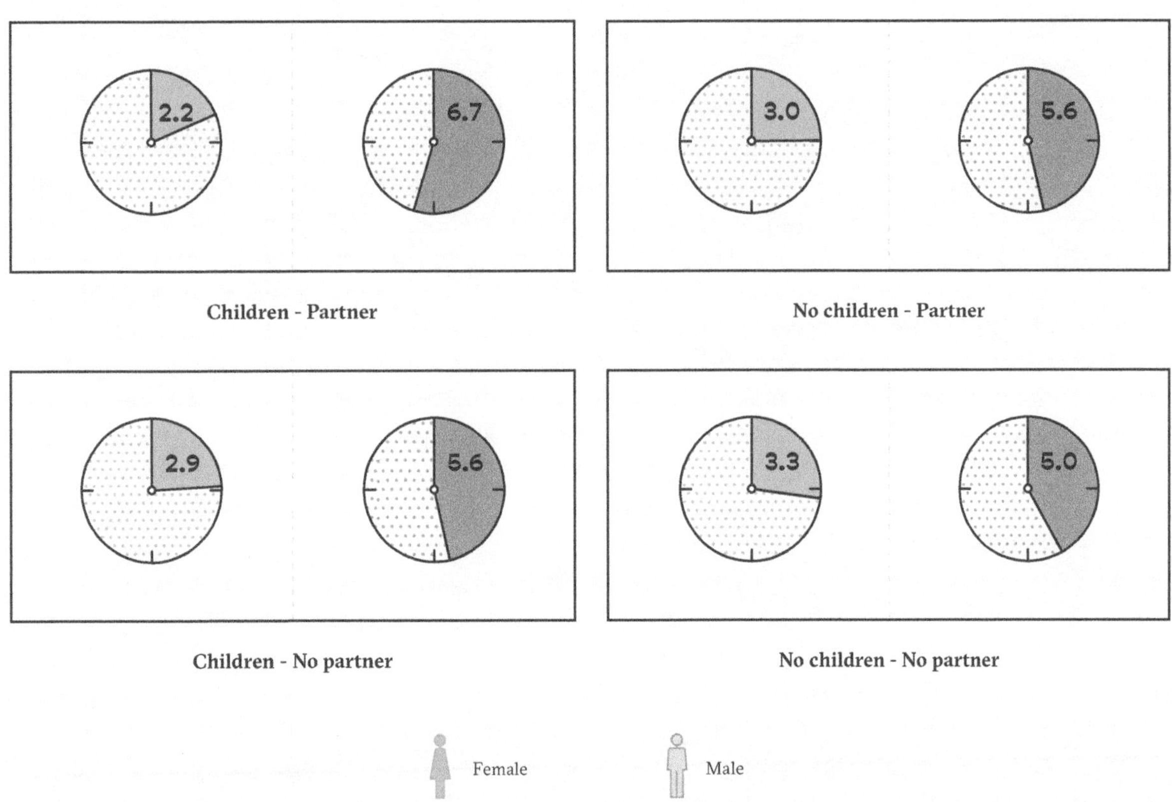

Source: Rubiano-Matulevich and Viollaz 2019.
Note: Based on harmonized time use and household surveys from 19 countries from the period 2006–14.

Sectoral and geographical mobility is key for workers to benefit from trade liberalization because shrinking and growing industries tend to be located in different regions. Social norms often limit gender mobility across sectors by branding as masculine some trade-intensive sectors such as transport (Brussevich 2018). Survey data from Ghana show that women are significantly less likely than men to move for economic reasons (box 2.4). Similarly, evidence based on German Socio-economic Panel data shows that family migration patterns in "traditional" couples are dominated by men's job characteristics, whereas such gendered roles are not present in "egalitarian" couples—defined using the husband's share of housework done on a typical Sunday (Jürges 2006).

Finally, women often do not have the same access as men to professional and social networks that can support the growth and competitiveness of their businesses. Because they have limited access to contacts in the market, and to role models, women tend to be excluded from traditional male-dominated distribution networks. As a result, their contact with the "business culture," which serves as a foundation for many trading relationships, is often limited. Analysis of male- and female-owned firms suggests that male-owned firms are more likely to find customers through traditional networks of contacts, whereas female-owned firms are forced to find other means. In a recruitment drive in Malawi, men's strong tendency to refer other men for jobs created a significant gender differential in access to labor market outcomes (Beaman, Niall, and Magruder 2017).

Women also use their networks differently (World Bank Group 2019).[4] Women's business networks are mostly composed of other women and are smaller than those of men. They command fewer resources than men's and include more strong family and kin relationships that are less valuable than new connections in creating business opportunities. A major reason for these differences in network usage is that women are more time constrained because of their dual role as caretakers and entrepreneurs, which can prevent them from traveling longer distances to reach markets that offer better prices or from attending network meetings.

Harassment and violence create a significant burden for women producers

The experience or fear of harassment deters women from working, setting up a business, and trading. Over one-third of women worldwide have experienced physical or sexual violence from an intimate partner or sexual violence from a nonpartner (WHO 2013).

Fear of or exposure to harassment has been shown to limit women's access to markets and cross-border trading (World Bank 2011). Traders at border crossings are particularly prone to harassment because they are subject to physical checks by border agents and other officials in positions of authority. Evidence from Cambodia and the Lao People's Democratic Republic suggests that women pay higher border taxes and are more likely to be controlled

Box 2.4 Women's geographical mobility is more limited than men's

Geographical mobility is one important element of labor market adjustments. Physical and economic mobility often go hand in hand: individuals often move to a different town, region, or country to find better economic opportunities. A recent study used survey data from the 2017 Ghana Living Standard Survey to examine whether men and women differ in their likelihood to migrate to other regions of Ghana or out of the country (Orkoh and Stolzenburg 2020). It found that, although men and women are equally likely to migrate, men are much more likely to move for economic reasons—confirming similar results obtained from other African economies (FAO 2017). Women by contrast move predominantly for social reasons such as marriage. This finding is supported by both indicated reasons for migration and indirect evidence.

For instance, when asked about their migration motives, women indicate marriage six times more often than men (figure B2.4.1). A 15 percent to 20 percent gender gap also exists when it comes to migrating to take care of family or relatives. In contrast, men said they moved for reasons related to work 3.5 times more often than women. These indicated motives for migration are reflected in migration outcomes. Men are about 1.5 times more likely to work or look for work after migrating than women. They also send higher and more frequent remittances, which signals a better financial situation.

These differences in geographical mobility imply that men are better able to benefit from trade. Though direct causation is difficult to establish, cultural norms and legal constraints that exist in several countries are closely correlated with these patterns (see the section in the main text on legal barriers). In any case, the evidence shows that geographical mobility constitutes a further barrier for women when it comes to making the most of the economic benefits generated by trade.

Figure B2.4.1 Women are more likely to migrate for social reasons, whereas men migrate for economic reasons

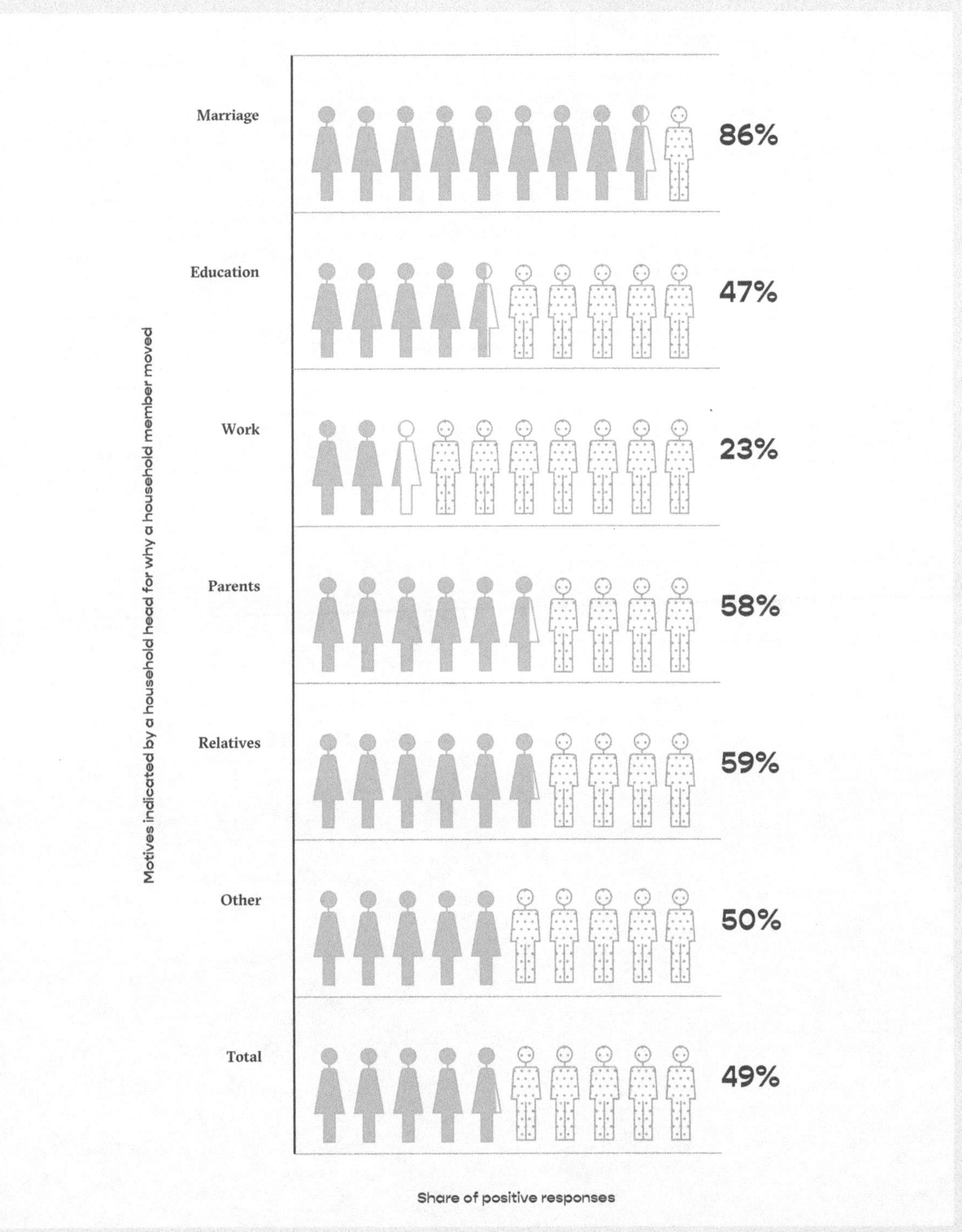

Source: Orkoh and Stolzenburg 2020, based on data from the 2017 Ghana Living Standard Survey.

by quarantine services than male traders—and not because of a greater likelihood of illegal behavior (Seror, Record, and Clarke 2018). Similarly, women involved in small-scale cross-border trade in the Great Lakes Region of Africa are often subject to extortion, physical harassment, and other forms of abuse (Brenton et al. 2011).[5] These constraints raise costs for traders and create an unpredictable and insecure trading environment.

Because of an insufficient, inefficient, and unsafe environment for handling and processing goods and people, the potential for small-scale cross-border trade to increase income and job creation while simultaneously reducing poverty is not being fully realized. These constraints raise costs for traders and create an unpredictable and insecure trading environment. Weak governance, including lack of transparency and weak controls for monitoring and preventing abuse and corruption, means that these traders are often subject to extortion, physical harassment, and other forms of abuse (Brenton et al. 2011).

Harassment in the form of differential treatment for public service delivery and public safety also restricts women-led trade. Survey evidence from women-owned tourism firms in Ghana shows that these firms face greater challenges than men-led firms. For example, to obtain a water connection, women-owned firms had to wait three times as long as their male counterparts, and 78 percent of women-owned firms reported that an informal gift was requested or expected for the provision of the service, compared to only 13 percent for male-owned firms. To obtain a telephone connection, women had to wait nearly four times as long as men and 66 percent of women reported that an informal gift was expected. Fifty percent of all women-owned businesses reported being victims of theft, compared to 17 percent for male-owned firms (Twining-Ward 2019).

Harassment can also prevent women from entering certain male-dominated and trade-related sectors. Women traders are particularly vulnerable to sexual harassment because of irregular work hours required to work in tradable sectors and the need to constantly establish new client relationships. A study on tourism GVCs found that in some instances women were able to sell their goods, such as handicrafts, to hotels only if the women established romantic relationships with key hotel intermediaries (Staritz and Reis 2013).

(Perceived) characteristics hold back women entrepreneurs

Behavioral characteristics and persistent stereotypes hold women back from trading. Such characteristics are most frequently the result of an environment that assigns

Credit: © vickydoc/ Shutterstock.com. Used with permission; further permission required for reuse.

different roles and values to men and women (Booth 2009). Implicit stereotypes are found as early as in elementary-aged girls who exhibit low self-esteem with respect to their math skills (Steffens, Jelenec, and Noack 2010). Such implicit stereotypes can affect women's careers more than explicit gender-math stereotypes of teachers or parents or actual math ability, especially in competitive environments such as trade (Bordalo et al. 2019; Kiefer and Sekaquaptewa 2007).

Stereotypes and biases disadvantage women entrepreneurs

A large literature from the field of behavioral economics points to women being on average more risk-averse than men—although the significance and quality of this evidence have recently been challenged (Eckel and Grossman 2008; Fellner and Maciejovsky 2007; Nelson 2018). Independently of whether women are actually more risk-averse, empirical evidence suggests that they are perceived as such, for instance by financial advisers when it comes to preparing credit offers (Nelson 2018). As highlighted in the section "Women have limited access to finance," earlier in this chapter, female entrepreneurs on average suffer from lower access to capital, in both developed and developing countries. Implicit biases and stereotypes can explain part of this gender gap in finance (Beck, Behr, and Madestam 2011). For instance, the type of questions posed by venture capital firms to male and female entrepreneurs tend to be different: both male and female venture capitalists are more likely to ask women about the potential for losses and men about the potential for gains. This bias has important consequences for the likelihood that entrepreneurs will obtain funding as well as for the size of funding, favoring men-led startups over women-led ones (Kanze et al. 2017).

The gender gap in treatment due to implicit biases and differential assessments has also been found in job advertising and recruitment (Gaucher, Friesen, and Kay 2011), education, employment and retention of women in STEM jobs (Jackson, Hillard, and Schneider 2014), entry to academia, and mentoring and hiring choices (Milkman, Akinola, and Chugh 2015; Moss-Racusin et al. 2012). This gap is likely to contribute to occupational segregation and keeps women out of trade-intensive firms or sectors.

The same finding applies to biases about women's capabilities as confirmed by several survey analyses. Women often face gender discrimination through gender-biased misconceptions including that women are less suitable for entrepreneurship, are less able to work under pressure or on a team, lack up-to-date knowledge and skills, lack innovative attitudes, exhibit more risk aversion

in seeking finance, have less time for learning and networking, or have less physical strength (APWINC 2018; Homewood, Chenevix Trench, and Kristjanson 2009; ITC 2017). Such biased views represent obstacles that negatively affect the credibility of women-owned or women-managed firms and hinder their ability to raise start-up funds, attract clients or business partners, and ultimately export.

An illustrative example is the tourism sector in Kenya. For Kenya, the sector generated over US$1.6 billion in 2016, contributing 8.3 percent of gross domestic product and directly supporting 451,000 jobs. Although women are well represented in the labor force in Kenya (62.3 percent labor participation in 2017 according to the World Development Indicators), there are very few women in the tourism industry. For example, out of 31 category A tour operators, the major providers of excursion services, only 2 are female-owned and led. Similarly, Kenya has no female gold-certified tour guides and only six female silver-certified guides, which relates to the perception that women do not possess the physical strength to lead trekking excursions and operate off-road vehicles (Homewood, Chenevix Trench, and Kristjanson 2009).

Certain gender-specific characteristics constrain women entrepreneurs

Overconfidence in men may lead them to be on average more competitive than women, according to observational and laboratory studies (Niederle and Vesterlund 2011). Experimental evidence from Kenya suggests for instance that women are less than half as likely to participate in a competition than men, no matter whether the stakes associated with winning are low or high (World Bank Group 2019). This reticence has been found to negatively affect women's educational achievements as well as to produce gender occupational segregation in which women are less represented in the most competitive sectors (Kleinjans 2009).

Women, conversely, have been found to be more cooperative and inequality-averse (Carlsson, Daruvala, and Johansson-Stenman 2005; Croson and Gneezy 2009; Eckel and Grossman 1998). These qualities may give them certain advantages in building durable firm-to-firm relationships, which are at the core of modern GVCs (World Bank 2019). Women's greater concern for fairness and reciprocity, however, might negatively affect women-led firms in negotiations about how to distribute profits along the value chain. Women-led micro, small, and medium enterprises (MSMEs), when negotiating to supply large multinationals, might receive a smaller share of profits than possible if their managers are too cooperative.

Men are also more likely than women to take decisions with uncertain outcomes—such as undertaking acquisitions, making investment decisions, issuing debt, or accessing foreign markets (Barber and Odean 2001; Felton, Gibson, and Sanbonmatsu 2003; Huang and Kisgen 2013). This characteristic can disadvantage women, particularly entrepreneurs, because, as mentioned above, trade is considered more uncertain than domestic activity. For instance, evidence from the U.S. stock market shows that industries more exposed to trade policy uncertainty are characterized by a higher risk premium, hence enjoying higher stock returns (Bianconi, Esposito, and Sammon 2019).

New opportunities for *women* to benefit from trade

Women stand to benefit from several trends that have the potential to increase their share in the gains from trade and lessen the constraints. Servicification, the rise of GVCs, and the adoption of new technologies offer immense untapped potential because all have elements that work in women's favor and offer ways for them to increase their participation in trade. Although these three key trade opportunities can further empower women economically, women can also benefit from greater participation in trade in traditional areas, particularly agriculture. As discussed in chapter 1, women represent a large share of agricultural workers in many developing and least-developed countries. More open agricultural markets can therefore have a large impact on women's empowerment (box 2.5).

Opportunities for women in trade through servicification

Services play an increasingly greater role in employment, economic output, and trade in countries at all development levels. In fact, they now create most jobs globally and they do so earlier in the development process (Ghani and O'Connell 2014; Rodrik 2016). This trend can be referred to as *servicification*. It shows itself in employment statistics where the share of services in employment has increased steadily over the last 40 years in all regions (figure 2.13). Moreover, this trend is not limited to the services sector itself. Services also contribute a growing share of value added to the production and trade of agricultural and manufacturing goods (figure 2.14). In some regions the value added generated by services exceeds 50 percent.

This change can be traced back to several factors. The value of goods increasingly depends on the software within them, which has given rise to a wide array of new services, such as online gaming or the sharing economy, that make up a growing share of global consumption baskets. Technological change has increased the quality and accessibility of services through digital means. Weather and climate services, for instance, are important factors for agricultural productivity. Aging populations and the demands they place on health-related services are another important factor in the rise of services. The U.S. Bureau

Box 2.5 Trade can benefit agricultural development and help close the gender productivity gap

Trade plays a key role for agricultural development. Providing women farmers equal opportunities in the sector can help close the gender productivity gap in the following four ways:

1. **Providing access to markets for outputs and increasing returns to farmers.** Trade connects farmers to overseas markets and to regional value chains that deliver food from surplus production areas in one country to consumers in food deficit areas (such as cities) in another country. Trade increases the returns to agricultural products that the country has an advantage in producing and raises the economic cost of discrimination that leads to lower yields for women farmers. Improved market access and

higher prices through trade can increase the returns to farmers from investing to increase yields to applying modern seeds and increased use of fertilizers.

2. **Improving access to key inputs and technology** (seeds, fertilizers, pesticides, machinery, and knowledge/advice). Trade can reduce the cost and increase the quality and the variety of key inputs. Often the successful use of higher-yield seeds, such as hybrid varieties, requires increasing use of specialized fertilizers and hence significant up-front investments by farmers. By increasing input costs, trade barriers can exacerbate the gender gap in access to seeds, fertilizers, and machinery by making them unaffordable for women—who have more limited access to finance. Reducing the cost of these investments through greater competition in input markets may be of particular benefit to women.

3. **Increasing competition among providers of critical services** to rural communities and, in particular, finance, transport and logistics, and wholesale services. Lack of competition in these critical services can mean that the potential benefits from trade are denied to rural communities and to smallholder farmers. A recurring issue in the ability of women farmers to increase their productivity and to diversify into higher-value crops is direct access to credit and insurance. Typically, tackling this issue requires new products and especially better service delivery models to address the constraints faced by women in accessing finance (Fletschner and Kenney 2014).

   Opening services to foreign competition can provide a mechanism for bringing in new products and approaches to service delivery while regional integration can provide a larger market to attract foreign direct investment. For example, because women farmers have lower productivity, they are particularly at risk from adverse weather events. Such risks may also constrain them from diversifying into higher-value, higher-return export crops. Weather-indexed insurance can provide a critical role in stabilizing incomes and supporting diversification and may be of particular importance to women as part of a risk management strategy. The provision of weather-indexed insurance becomes more viable if the financial institution is able to offer coverage to farmers over a wide region and has a common and predictable regulatory regime for that area.

4. **Increasing production of high-value-added agricultural products and opportunities for off-farm employment for women.** The increasing commercialization of agriculture in rural areas of poor countries and the shift into agro-processing and higher-value crops is central to poverty reduction in many countries. In some cases, exports—such as cut flowers and horticulture—to rich countries in Europe and the United States have driven this commercialization. It is now being accompanied by rising demand in developing countries for higher-value agricultural products as a result of increasing urbanization and an emerging middle class.

The expansion of high-value, export-oriented agro-industries can bring better opportunities for women as farmers and workers than traditional agricultural work. For example, production of fruits and vegetables is more labor-intensive than production of cereal crops. Because such activities also offer more postharvest opportunities to add value through packing and processing, the number of women employed in the sector has increased substantially (Bamber and Fernandez-Stark 2013). Linked to the growth of agro-processing is the emergence of contract farming or out-grower schemes whereby large firms that seek a consistent quality and volume of supply can provide small-scale farmers with access to inputs and to knowledge that supports higher productivity.

Figure 2.13 The employment share of services has steadily increased, 1970–2010

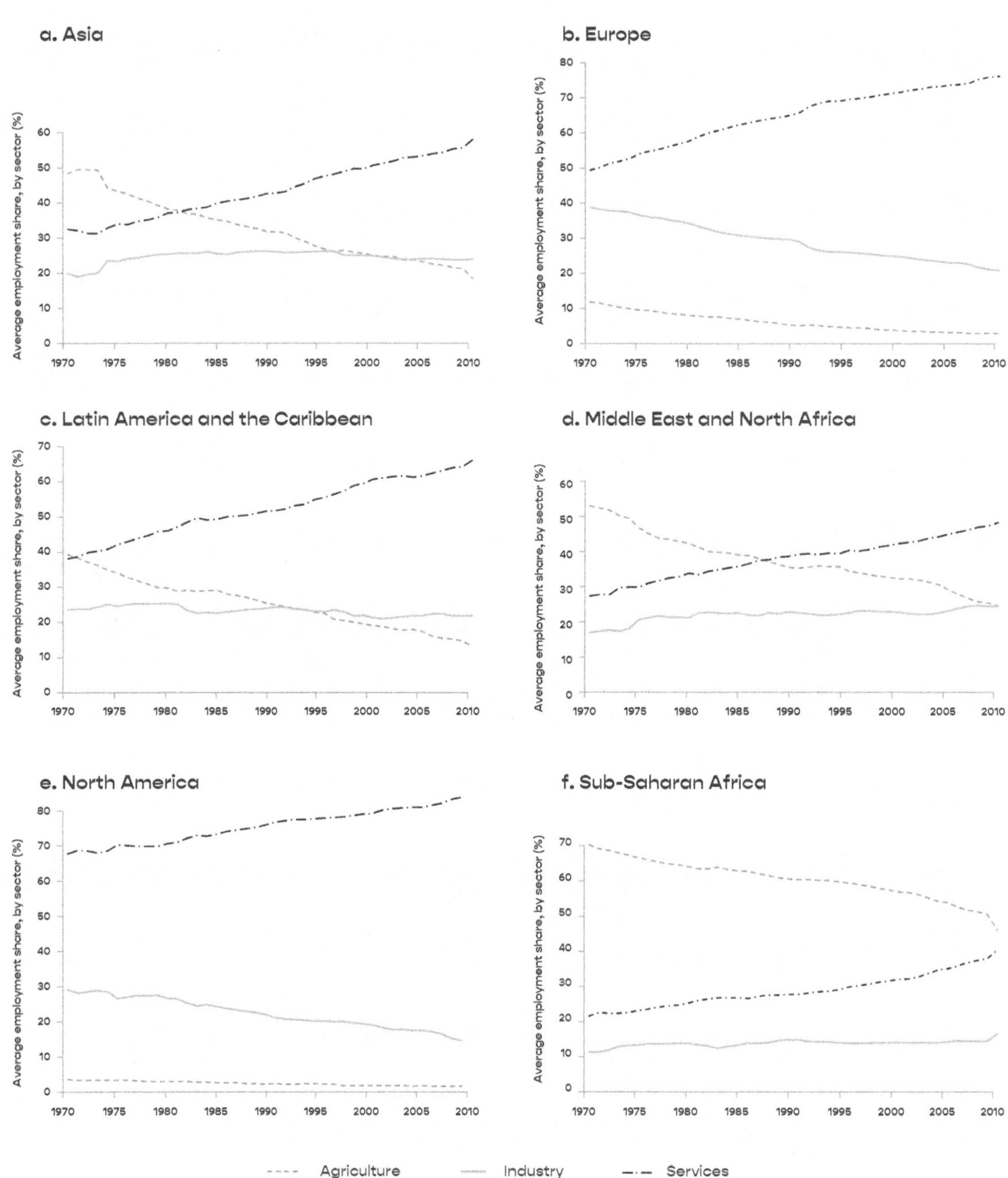

Source: de Vries, Timmer, and de Vries 2015.
Note: This figure covers 40 economies: 10 developed and 30 developing. Agriculture consists of activities in agriculture, hunting, forestry, and fishing. Industry consists of mining and quarrying, manufacturing, construction, and public utilities (electricity, gas, and water). Services consists of the remaining activities.

Figure 2.14 Services contribute a growing share of value added to agricultural and manufacturing goods, 2011–16

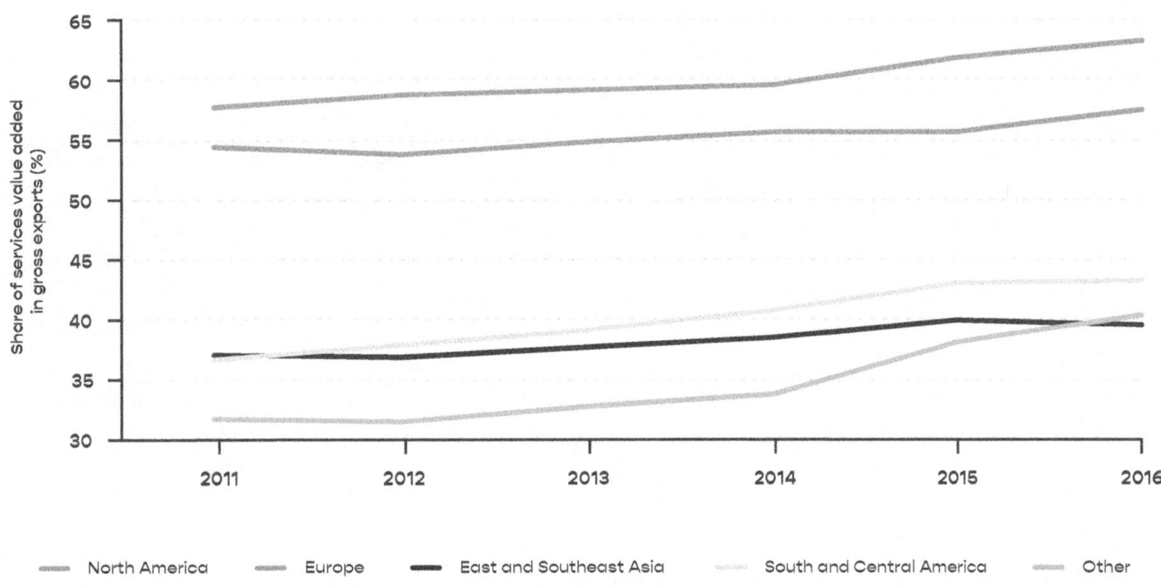

Source: World Trade Organization Secretariat calculations based on the Organisation for Economic Co-operation and Development Trade in Value Added (TiVA) database.

of Labor Statistics forecasts that until 2028 health care will add more jobs than any other sector in the United States.[6] Finally, as household incomes rise, consumption shifts increasingly toward services in developing economies (Sachetti et al. 2019; WTO 2019).

Servicification raises the gains from trade for women as workers

Servicification holds important implications when viewed through a gender lens. The service economy, including services trade and investment, provides an important source of inclusive growth (Ngai and Petrongolo 2017). Many services rely on social or networking skills in which many women excel, whereas these services do not require the physical strength sometimes demanded in agriculture or manufacturing (Cortes, Jaimovich, and Siu 2018). As discussed in chapter 1, the services sector on average employs more women than manufacturing or agriculture, and women continue to increase their share in services employment as they transition from other sectors to services at a faster pace than men.[7] This overall trend has important implications for recovery after the COVID-19 pandemic, during which some services with high women's participation, such as travel and tourism, have been hit hardest. (see box 2.6). Given the high share of services in women's employment, taking services into account in the design of greater inclusive growth policy is crucial.

Higher employment shares of women are not limited to specific sectors within services, such as education or health. In fact, female employment shares are higher in most services sectors in the United States with the exception of infrastructure, manufacturing, and agriculture services (figure 2.15, panel a). Looking at a broader set of mostly developing countries shows that this observation also

The large disruption experienced by the services sector during the COVID-19 pandemic is already having a big impact on women's employment given their relatively high employment share in the sector. Although women's employment is more concentrated than men's in relatively less cyclical sectors, such as education and health care, some service occupations with high female employment shares, such as retail and hospitality and food services, have experienced negative impacts due to social distancing measures and mobility restrictions imposed by governments to combat COVID-19 (Alon et al. 2020). In fact, many women tend to work in activities that require face-to-face interactions, such as health and retail activities, and cannot telecommute (figure B2.6.1) (Adams-Prassl et al. 2020; Avdiu and Nayyar 2020). Computer specialists, financial specialists, architects, and engineers are some of the occupations more prone to teleworking, but they are also activities in which women tend to be less present. The problem is particularly pronounced in developing countries, where fewer women tend to work in occupations that offer the possibility of remote work. Many women have therefore been unable to work and earn a living during the lockdown.

The disruption in the services sector has affected women entrepreneurs as well. Small and medium-sized enterprises (SMEs), many owned by women, account for a large share of service providers. Existing problems facing many SMEs, including limited financial resources and borrowing capacity, are exacerbated by the economic impact of the COVID-19 pandemic. Recent survey evidence confirms that many SMEs in both developed and developing economies have faced limited workforce availability, supply disruptions, and temporary or in some cases permanent business closures during the pandemic.

Figure B2.6.1 Women's occupations require more face-to-face interactions than men's and offer less opportunity for remote work

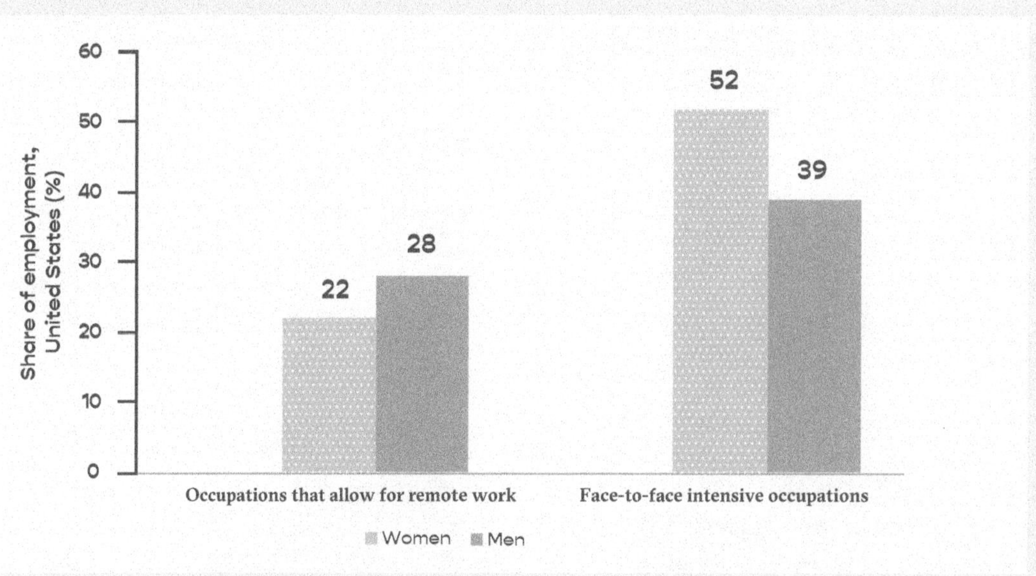

Source: WTO 2020a, using telecommuting data from Alon et al. 2020, face-to-face data from Avdiu and Nayyar 2020, and employment data by occupation from the International Labour Organization Department of Statistics, https://www.ilo.org/stat/lang--en/index.htm.

Box 2.6, continued

The pandemic has severely impeded trade in services that require physical proximity between suppliers and consumers (WTO 2020b). Services that require consumption abroad, such as tourism, or that involve the temporary movement of services suppliers abroad, have been directly affected by international and regional travel restrictions. Women tend to work more than men in services trade requiring physical proximity (figure B2.6.2). The largest trade-related COVID-19 economic costs are likely to be borne by highly traded nonstorable services activities, such as cultural events and tourism. Because of their very nature, these services cannot later offset the economic losses accumulated during the pandemic.

Tourism, in which women make up the largest share of employees, has experienced direct impacts from national and international mobility restrictions adopted to fight COVID-19. As a result, tourism activities have contracted significantly and are expected to experience a longer recovery because of lower consumer confidence and higher likelihood of continuing restrictions on international movement of people (UNWTO 2020). Other sectors that depend on tourism, including food services and handicrafts, have also felt negative impacts. These impacts are particularly challenging for women with low skills or who work informally, especially in economies highly dependent on tourism and offering limited job opportunities in other sectors.

The COVID-19 crisis has led consumers and suppliers to move and expand their online activities (Petro 2020). Whereas online shopping for some products, such as clothing, has declined, online purchases of groceries, essentials, and health and safety products have increased significantly during the partial or complete lockdowns (Nielsen 2020). Electronic commerce has offered an important way to mitigate the impact of the crisis in distribution and retail services sectors. Other services, such as education, telecommunication, gaming and audiovisual services, have also expanded their online operations. These changes in consumer behaviors may contribute to a long-term shift toward online services. Limited information technology skills, however, can prevent women entrepreneurs and workers, particularly in developing economies, from fully applying digital technologies to mitigate the adverse economic effects of the pandemic.

Figure B2.6.2 Women tend to be employed in services sectors that face larger trade disruption

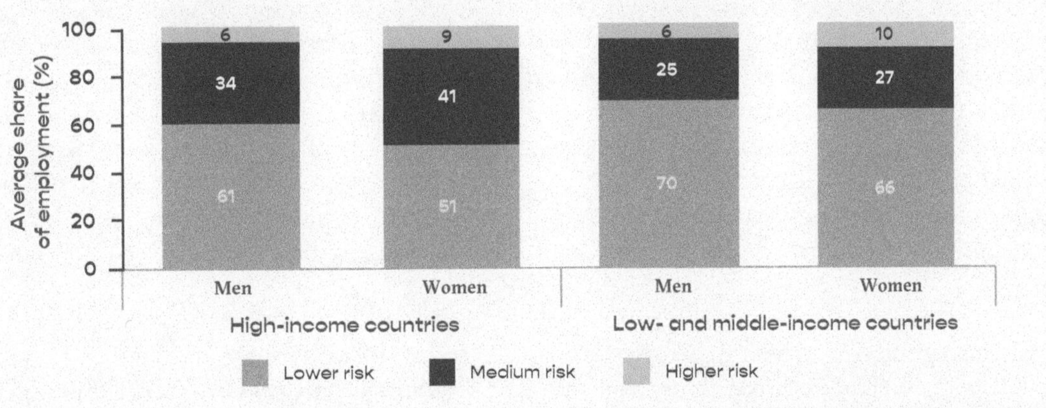

Source: WTO 2020a, using Trade in Services data by Mode of Supply (TISMOS), https://www.wto.org/english/res_e/statis_e/trade_datasets_e.htm.
Note: The services trade disruption risk index ranks services sectors according to potential exposure to travel restrictions and distancing measures. Services largely traded via movement of consumers abroad (mode 2) or whose supply requires the movement of services suppliers abroad (mode 4) are ranked as high-risk sectors. Services supplied across borders by information technologies (mode 1) are ranked as relatively low-risk sectors. Recreation and events are considered medium risk although they are traded mainly through commercial presence (mode 3) because their consumption is often limited by distancing measures.

Figure 2.15 Female employment shares in manufacturing and agriculture are lower than in most services

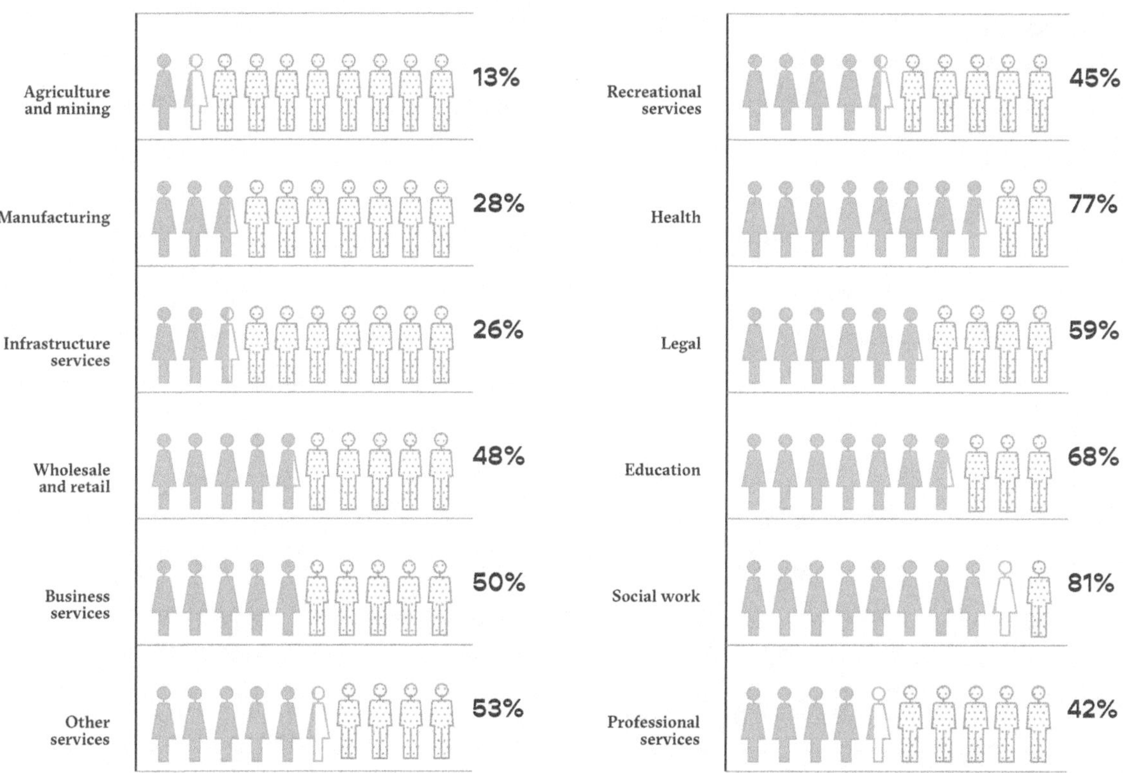

applies to these economies (figure 2.15, panel b). Relatively high-skill and trade-intensive sectors such as finance or business services exhibit higher female employment shares than the average agricultural or manufacturing industry. In contrast to traditional gender stereotypes, women occupy increasingly high-skill positions within services. In OECD economies, women accounted for 46.5 percent of doctors in 2015 (figure 2.16)

Trade in services has been growing faster than trade in goods (figure 2.17). Since 2005, the average growth of services trade was about 1 percentage point—or 17 percent higher than the average growth of trade in goods. This growth increases the access of women workers to trade. Servicification is partly driven by changing demographics that increase the demand for health-related services in developed countries and education-related services in developing countries. In addition, it is driven by technological advancements that require new skills, further boosting demand for education-related services. As a result, the growth in services trade is particularly rapid in these two sectors that have high shares of female employment but have traditionally been less traded (WTO 2019).

Servicification also expands access to the gains from trade to women outside of the services sector. As the value of manufacturing and agricultural goods increasingly depends on services inputs, tasks within manufacturing firms have shifted away from physically demanding tasks (that are typically male-intensive) to more creative and abstract tasks.

b. Women's employment in selected countries, 2016

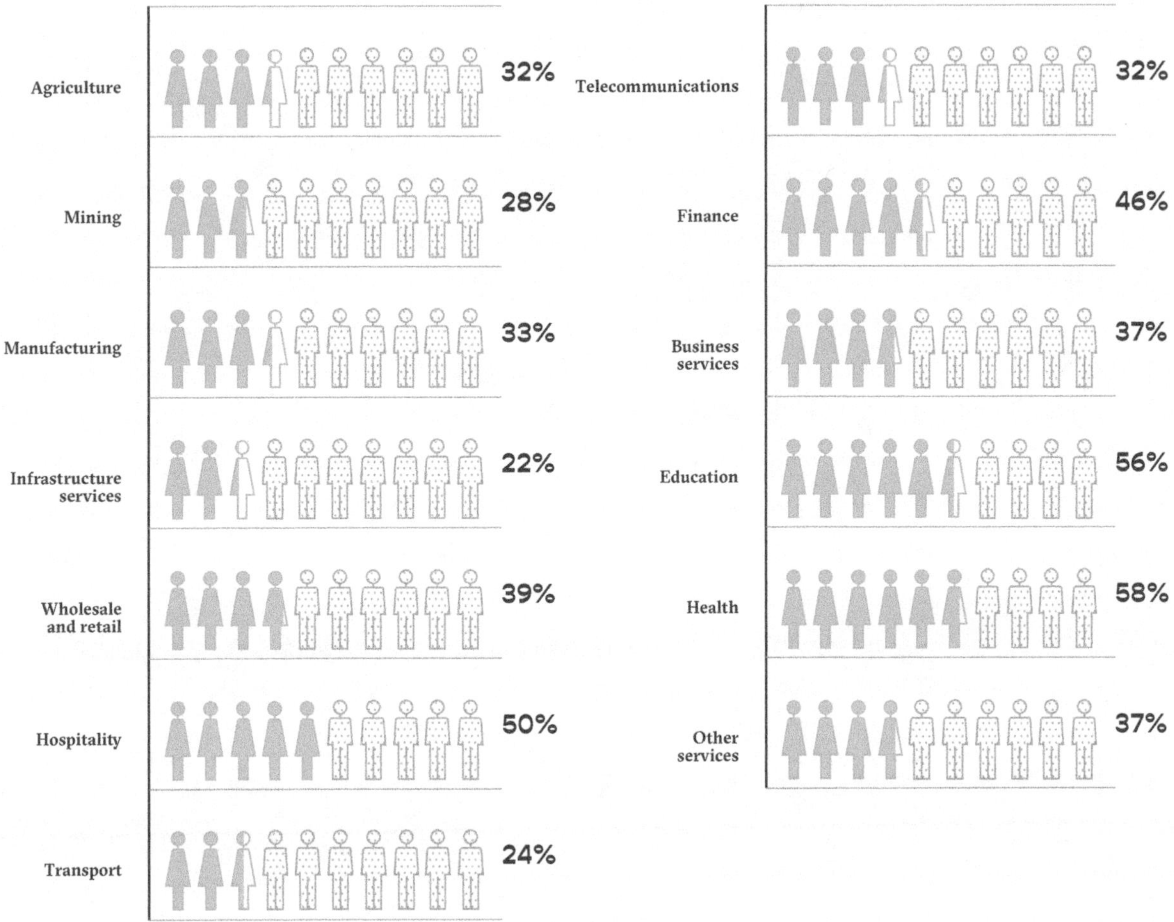

Source: World Trade Organization Secretariat calculations based on the 2016 American Community Survey for the United States (panel a) and World Bank Household Surveys for various available years for a set of 72 available countries (panel b).
Note: Because of differences in the underlying industry classification, the industries are not identically defined across the two panels even where their names would suggest so.

Servicification boosts female entrepreneurship

Although the leadership role of women in business remains generally low around the world, recent empirical work suggests that the picture looks more promising in services than in manufacturing. The share of female-owned and female-managed firms is on average higher in services than in manufacturing, a trend that holds across all regions of the world (figure 2.18) (WTO 2019). The share of female-owned and female-managed firms has risen as the cost of discrimination increases and as countries progressively address gender inequalities (Lan and Shepherd 2018). The greater share of such firms in the services sector is likely due to lower entry barriers for women in services than in manufacturing. Within services, the average share of female-managed firms is highest in retail trade, followed by tourism, transport, and ICT-related services. The share of female-managed firms is lowest in construction services.

Figure 2.16 Women account for a large and growing share of doctors in OECD countries, 2000 versus 2015

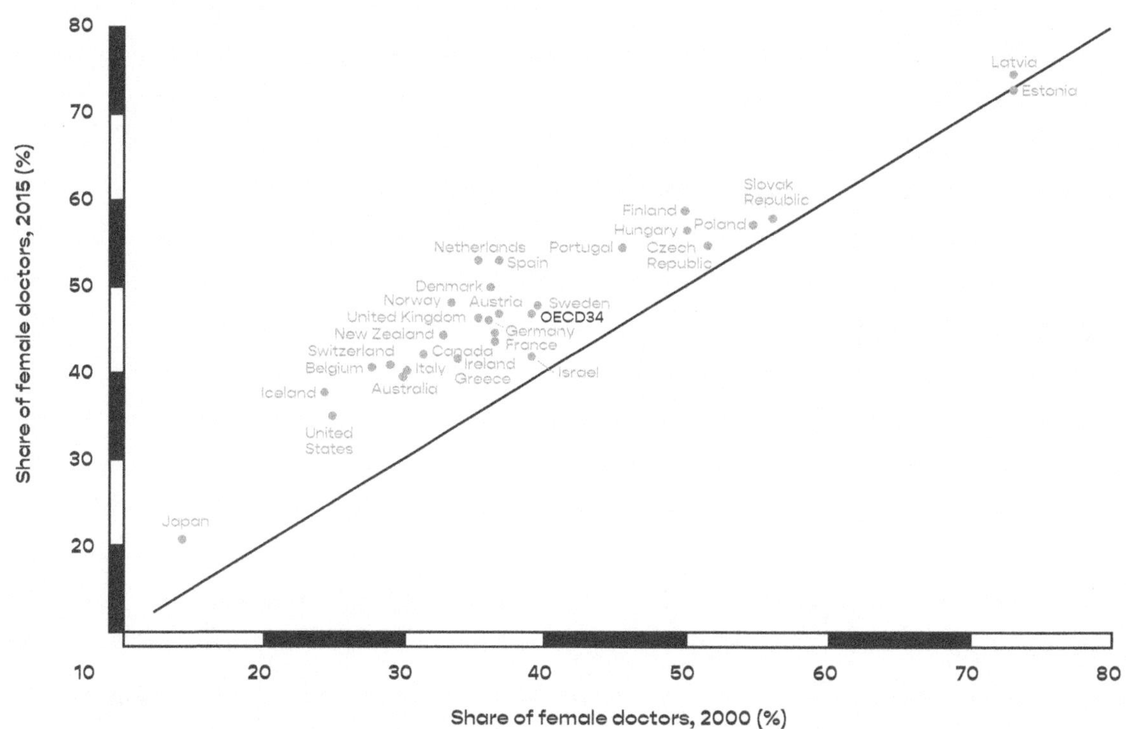

Source: Organisation for Economic Co-operation and Development (OECD) health statistics 2017.

Figure 2.17 Trade in services has been growing faster than trade in goods

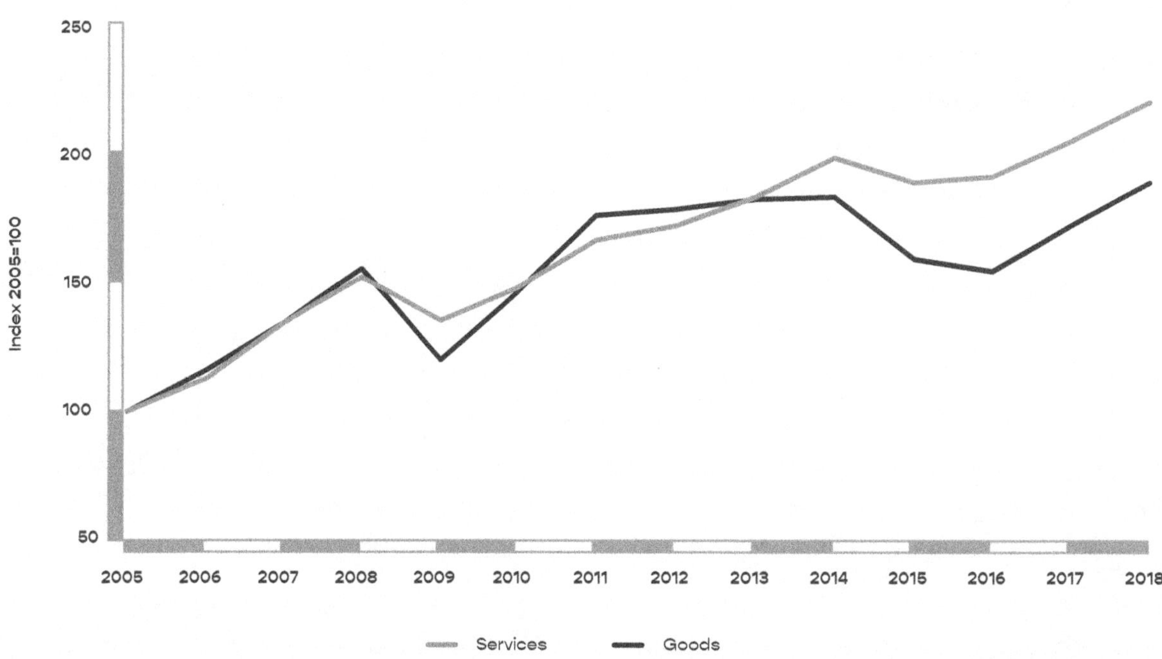

Source: WTO 2019.
Note: World trade is calculated as the average of world exports and world imports.

Figure 2.18 The share of female-managed firms is higher in services than in manufacturing

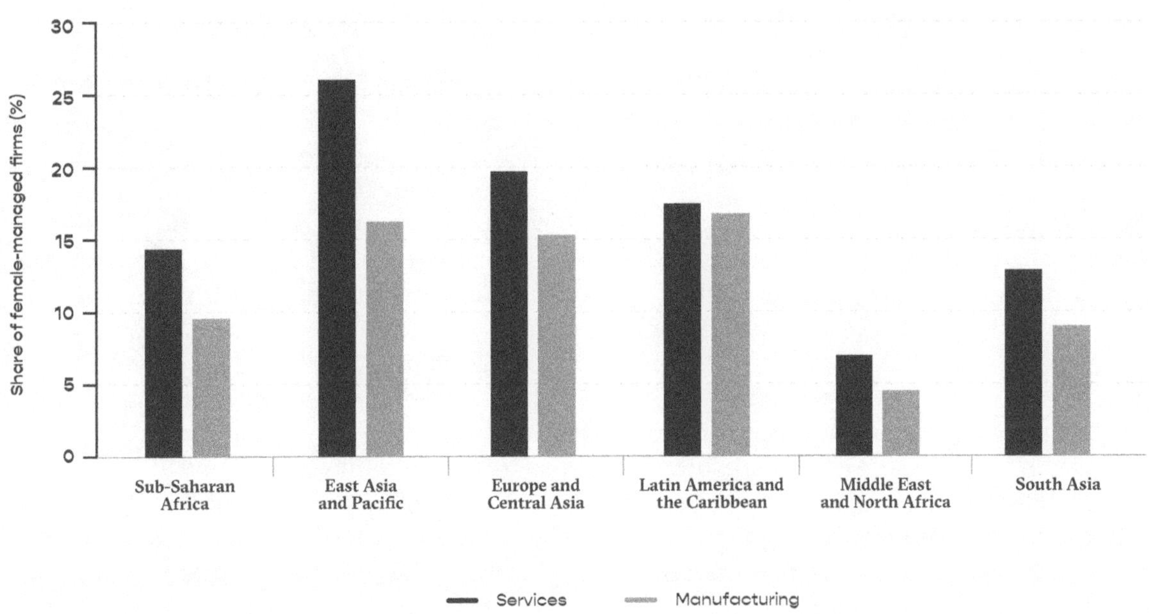

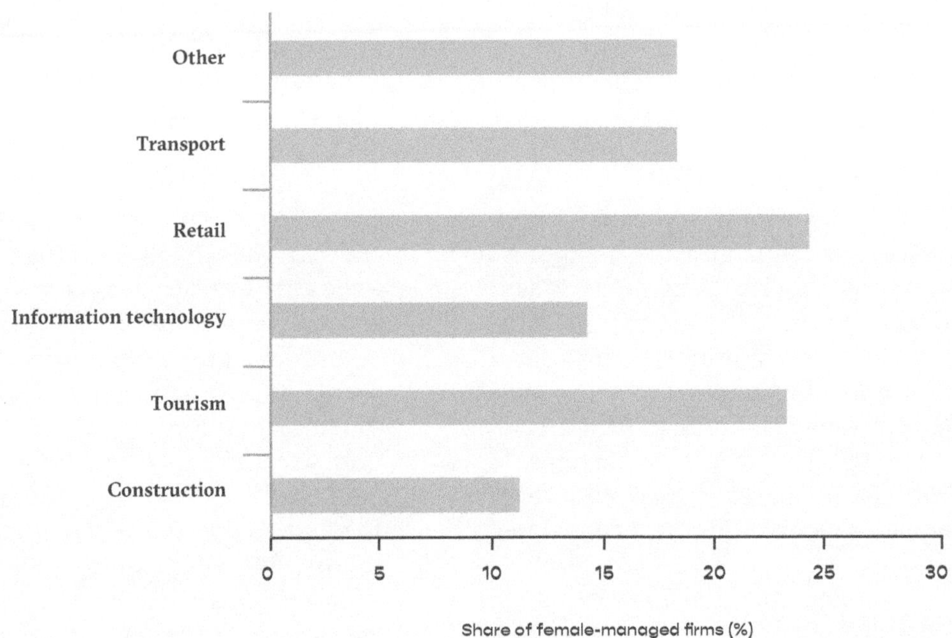

Source: Lan and Shepherd 2018, and based on World Bank Enterprise Surveys.

The relatively higher share of trade of women-owned firms in services compared to goods can be explained by the lower capital and collateral requirements to start a business venture in services compared to manufacturing. The cost of funding and storing inventory is lower in most service industries. The predominance of MSMEs in services therefore broadly favors female ownership because firms owned by women tend to be smaller than firms owned by men.

Because the gender gap in exporting is smaller in services than in manufacturing, structural change from manufacturing to services should benefit women entrepreneurs relatively more. In addition, firm size tends to be less important for exporting in services than in manufacturing, according to evidence from French MSMEs. As a result, the constraints that cause female-owned firms to be smaller than male-owned firms tend to be less restrictive in services than in manufacturing (Carranza, Dhakal, and Love 2018; Coste and Dihel 2013; Lan and Shepherd 2018; Lejárraga et al. 2014; WTO 2019).

Servicification and services trade benefit women consumers and decision makers

Trade and investment liberalization in services can improve and enlarge access to imports of a host of lower-priced and higher-quality producer services, such as transportation, energy, telecommunications, finance, health, and education. This access is likely to benefit women consumers more than men because it can help them overcome the barriers discussed earlier in the chapter with respect to access to finance or digital technologies.

Greater competition in the finance industry increases credit access at competitive rates. Improved transportation and infrastructure services can benefit women who have less access to private transportation and are often located further away from markets, including women farmers located in rural areas. The benefits also apply to consumer services. Entry of foreign retailers has been shown to generate large welfare gains for the average household, predominantly driven by a reduction in the cost of living. Because female-headed households tend to spend a larger share of their income on food and retail items (see the discussion earlier in the chapter), they are likely to benefit more from imports of consumer services (Atkin, Faber, and Gonzalez-Navarro 2018).

Moreover, the positive effects of formal employment created by trade in services extend beyond just financial earnings. By increasing the economic activity and financial independence of women, services trade has the potential to give women a greater voice in economic decision making within the household. Evidence from India shows that women not only faced better employment prospects but also increased their educational attainment and delayed marriage and childbirth as a result of job opportunities in the business process outsourcing industry and services liberalization more generally (Jensen 2012; Nano et al. 2019).

Opportunities for women in trade through GVCs

GVCs have become a major feature of the global economy and offer women distinct opportunities to participate in international trade. Value chains encompass all the people and activities involved in the production of a good or service and its supply, distribution, and postsales activities. These activities often take place in different stages that span countries across the globe, made possible by advances in information, communication, and transport as well as by falling barriers to trade.

The first phase of GVC development in the 1990s was accompanied by high levels of female participation, leading to theories of feminization of trade. The second phase, however, was accompanied by much lower female participation. Understanding what has driven these divergent trends is critical to better understand the policy responses needed to ensure that GVC participation continues to provide opportunities for

Figure 2.19 GVC firms employ more women than do non-GVC firms

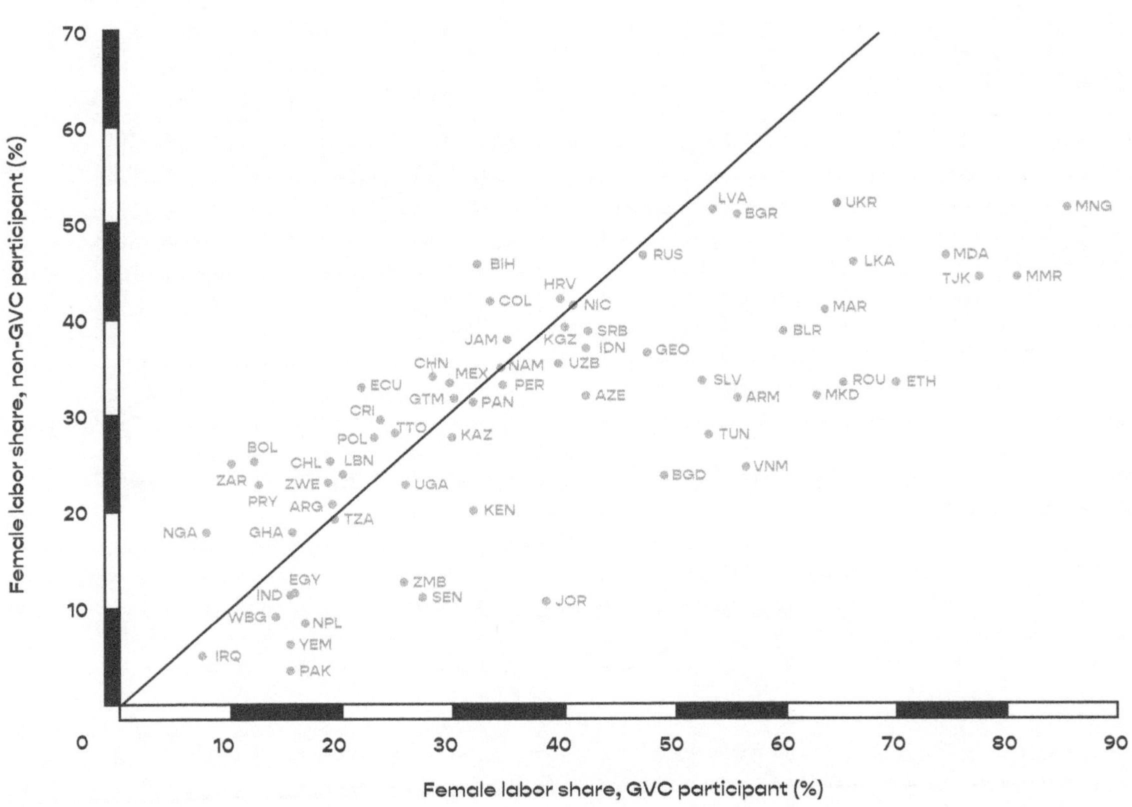

Source: Rocha and Winkler 2019, using data from World Bank Enterprise Surveys.
Note: Each dot represents a country-year observation. The x axis plots the employment-weighted share of female workers in total workers within firms that both export and import (GVC participant) within each country-year. The y axis plots the employment-weighted share of female workers in total workers within firms that do not export and import (nonparticipant). For a list of country codes go to https://www.iso.org/obp/ui/#search/code/.

women. It will also help governments design policies to ensure women's resilience in a world after COVID-19, during which female workers have been more vulnerable to the pandemic's shock on GVCs (see box 2.7).

GVCs raise women workers' employment and wages

The first wave of GVC participation, focused on light manufacturing and agricultural sectors, appears to have boosted female employment in developing countries. Companies tapped into large pools of previously unemployed women workers (Barrientos 2014; Kucera and Tejani 2014; Pickles and Godfrey 2012; Seguino 2000). For many women in developing economies, GVC industries provided them with their first opportunity to move from informal work to waged employment (Dolan and Sorby 2003; Maertens and Swinnen 2009; Pickles and Godfrey 2012).

Apparel production, horticulture, and floriculture GVCs have been major job creators, with women accounting for 60 to 80 percent of the workforce in the apparel industry alone (Barrientos 2014; Christian, Evers,

COVID-19 led to a strong trade drop in manufacturing sectors associated with high participation in global value chains

The current COVID-19 pandemic has led to a dual supply and demand shock across the globe affecting production, consumption, and trade, as governments impose quarantine and social distancing measures to reduce the spread of the coronavirus. Factory closings in China initially led to a drop in the supply of export goods, accompanied by a demand shock in large consumer markets. Consumers have lowered their spending if they lost their jobs, have reduced incomes, or are uncertain about the stability of their jobs and incomes (Muellbauer 2020). In March 2020, U.S. personal consumption expenditures declined by 7.5 percent from the previous month (U.S. Bureau of Economic Analysis).

Figure B2.7.1 Declines of U.S. imports were sharp in many GVC-intensive manufacturing sectors, first quarter 2020

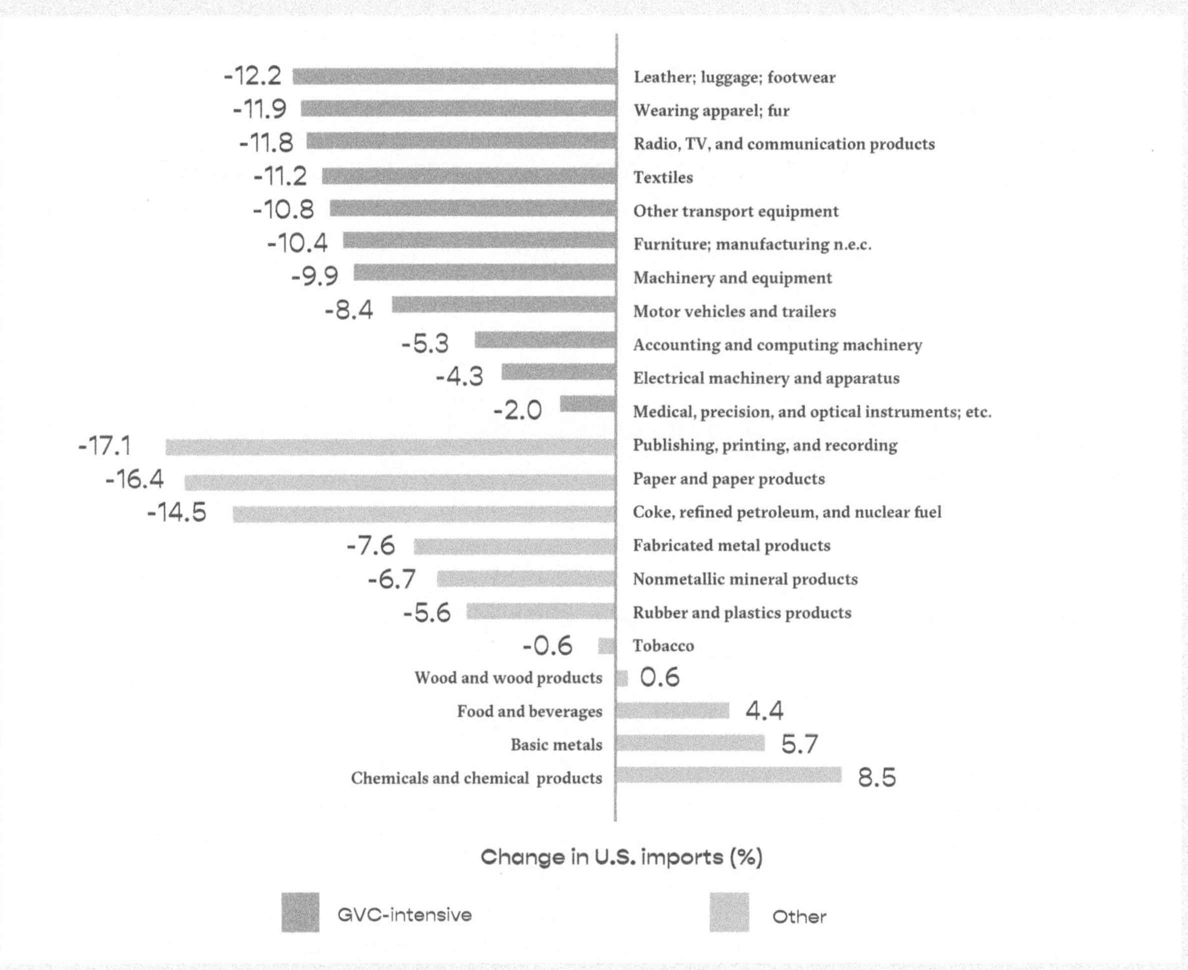

Source: World Bank staff calculations using monthly goods U.S import data from U.S. Census Bureau.
Note: Import growth is computed on the basis of sector's import value between January and March 2020 relative to the value over the same period in 2019. GVC = global value chain; n.e.c. = not elsewhere classified.

The crisis has also affected the demand for consumer goods, often produced in global value chains (GVCs). Although imports to the United States during the first quarter of 2020 dropped across most manufacturing sectors, several GVC-intensive sectors were hit harder (figure B2.7.1). Imports of leather and footwear; apparel; radio, television, and communication products; textiles; transport equipment; furniture; and machinery and equipment all declined by 10 to 12 percent. Several of these manufacturing sectors—particularly apparel, footwear, and electronics—are also characterized by high female labor shares in developing and emerging countries.

The COVID-19 trade shock puts female workers in developing countries at a higher risk

Because women working in GVCs hold a disproportionate share of lower-skill low-wage jobs, they can be particularly vulnerable to trade-related demand and supply shocks. From a demand perspective, the decline in U.S. imports from selected developing and emerging countries was slightly larger in sectors that employ a large share of women in GVC firms (figure B2.7.2); the three most female-intensive sectors—apparel; radio, television, and communication products; and leather and footwear—experienced a sharp drop in U.S. imports from these countries.

From a supply perspective, China's export contraction during the first quarter of 2020 was steep in inputs to the apparel and footwear sectors, which employ a large share of female GVC workers in destination countries (figure B2.7.3). Resulting supply shortages directly affected production by GVC firms in countries upstream and further downstream in the value chain, and ultimately affected female employment. Chinese exports of apparel and fur, leather and shoes, and textiles dropped by between 13 and 22 percent compared to 2019. Both supply and demand shocks hit female workers in apparel, with huge job losses for female apparel workers in Bangladesh and Vietnam already documented (Nilsson and Terazono 2020; Paton 2020).

Figure B2.7.2 U.S. manufacturing imports from selected countries had slightly larger declines in sectors that employ a large share of female GVC workers in the source countries, first quarter 2020

Source: World Bank staff.
Note: Analysis based on U.S. imports from selected countries. The analysis excludes coke and fuel and food and beverages, but the negative correlation still holds when they are included. GVC = global value chain; yoy = year on year.

Figure B2.7.3 Chinese manufacturing exports to selected countries dropped sharply in inputs to the apparel and footwear sectors that employ a large share of female GVC workers in the destination countries, first quarter 2020

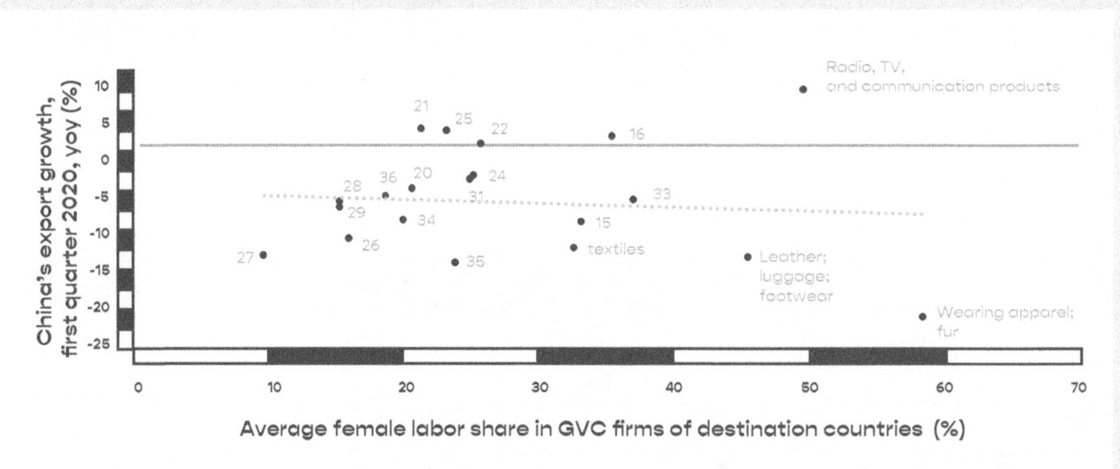

Source: World Bank staff calculations based on monthly Chinese export data from China Customs via World Integrated Trade Solution.
Note: The analysis excludes coke and fuel and food and beverages, but the negative correlation still holds when they are included. Analysis based on Chinese exports to selected countries. GVC = global value chain; yoy = year on year.

Three compounding effects could magnify the potential negative impact of COVID-19 on female workers in GVCs. First, the direct effects of the trade shock can trickle up and down along supply chains and affect more women both within and across countries. Second, declines in trade also affect women working in logistics or other business services embodied in goods and women working in retail distribution in the consumer markets. Finally, women's vulnerability may be exposed more strongly in the longer term if lead firms decide to shift parts of their production closer to larger consumer markets or automate certain labor-saving tasks within supply chains (Seric and Winkler 2020).

and Barrientos 2013; Lopez-Acevedo and Robertson 2016). In many agriculture value chains women are found upstream—working in production, processing, and domestic, small-scale marketing (World Bank Group 2018b). In Papua New Guinea, women engage directly at critical stages of coffee and cocoa production and processing. In fresh produce, women dominate production, harvesting, sorting, packaging, transport to local markets, and, in some instances, the first stages of transport to the roadside or to more distant markets (World Bank 2014b). The apparel and electronics value chains in Vietnam increasingly employ women (see box 2.8). GVC-related employment of women is not limited to manufacturing. All segments of the hotel value chain in Georgia, for instance, have a high level of female participation (World Bank Group 2017).

Firms that are more likely to participate in GVCs show higher female labor intensity. Across the world, firms that both export and import tend to employ more women than firms that do not participate in GVCs (figure 2.19). Foreign-owned firms as well as firms that export or import also have higher female labor shares on average than firms that do not, but the relationship is stronger for GVC participants. More generally, firms that both import and export and are foreign owned tend to have a larger share of female workers (Shepherd and Stone 2012).

GVC-related jobs can also have positive, indirect effects on women as decision makers. In Bangladesh, for example, young women in villages exposed to textile value chains delay marriage and childbirth. In addition, young girls gain an additional 1.5 years of schooling (Heath and Mobarak 2015).

GVC-related FDI often benefits women workers

FDI is a key feature of GVCs. One way that women can benefit from FDI-led GVC development is through improved working conditions. FDI has the potential to narrow gender gaps because foreign firms might implement their domestic corporate culture in acquired companies. If foreign investment inflows originate from countries with lower gender gaps, a transfer of corporate culture and benefit schemes can reduce gender gaps in the receiving country.

Evidence from Japan suggests that foreign affiliates operating in Japan have a higher share of female employees and are more likely to offer flexible working arrangements, telecommuting, and childcare subsidies than their Japanese counterparts (Kodama,

Box 2.8 Female export jobs and earnings in Vietnam

Vietnam has successfully integrated into the global economy and today is one of the economies most open to trade in the world. In addition, the Vietnamese economy has successfully integrated into a number of global value chains (GVCs), most notably automotive, apparel, information and communication technology, and agribusiness. This integration has been important for economic growth, job creation, and poverty alleviation. Vietnam's export growth has also been inclusive for women, in terms of jobs and earnings.

The most female-intensive export activities—measured as the share of female jobs in total export jobs—are services: postal and courier activities, education, and food and beverage services. Women represent more than 65 percent of the jobs supported by these sector's exports. Nearly one-third (28 percent) of export sectors has female job intensities above 50 percent. Land transport, mining of metal ores, and manufacturing of furniture exports are the least female job intensive.

Female employment grew faster than male employment in Vietnamese provinces where GVC participation expanded the most—notably in the apparel and electronics sectors, where assembly of many small parts must be done manually. Within provinces, a 1-percentage-point increase in the share of firms that participate in GVCs is associated with a 3.2 percent increase in female employment and a 2.1 percent increase in male employment (World Bank 2019).

In terms of total employment, the most important export sectors for female employment in 2012 were manufacturing of food products and beverages and wholesale trade (figure B2.8.1). Crop and animal production is also important for unskilled female employment.

Figure B2.8.1 Female employment supports Vietnam's exports

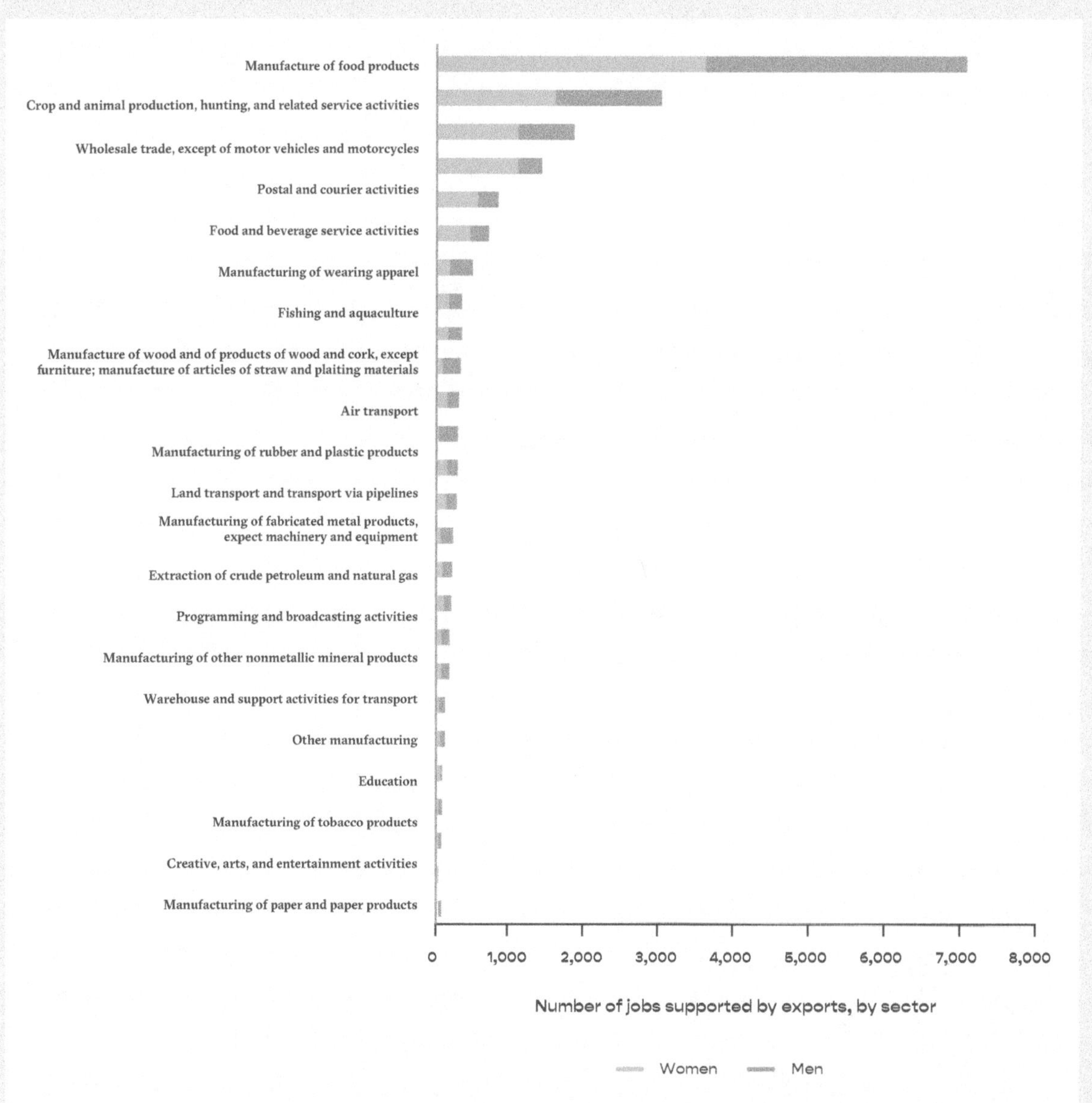

Source: Hollweg 2017, using Vietnam's 2012 Input-Output tables and Labor Force Survey data.
Note: The figure shows 2012 analysis based on International Standard Industrial Classification (ISIC) rev. 4 2-digit codes.

Figure 2.20 SMEs participate significantly in GVCs through indirect exports and large firms

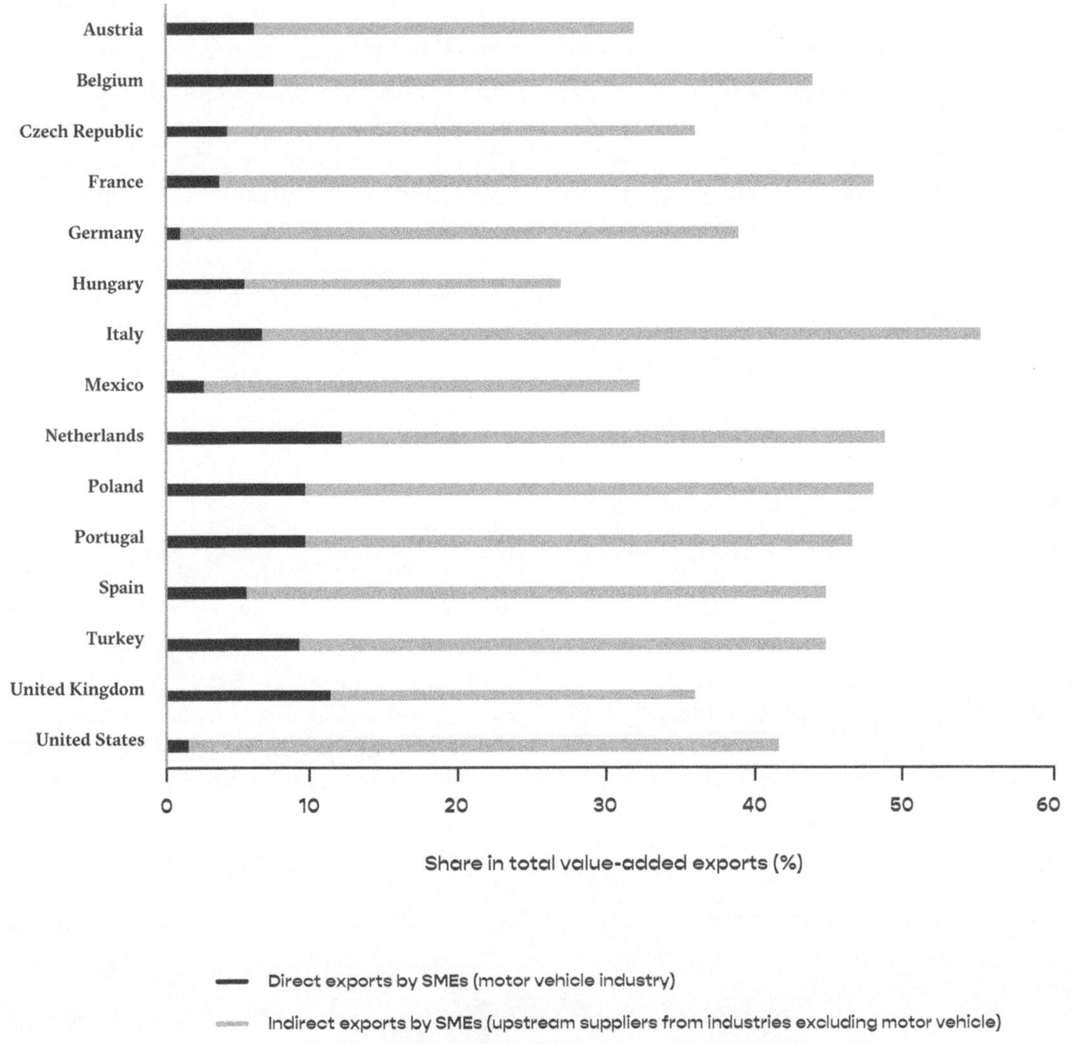

Source: WTO 2016, based on Organization for Economic Co-operation and Development Structural and Demographic Business Statistics database.
Note: Estimates for 2009 based on the motor vehicles industry. SME = small and medium enterprise.

Javorcik, and Abe 2018). Evidence from China further suggests that this effect is driven by foreign affiliates from countries with lower gender gaps and even finds positive spillover effects on firms within the same industry or city (Tang and Zhang 2017). A study on Estonia, however, finds that multinationals, like trading firms, have a larger gender pay gap (Vahter and Masso 2019).

Female small business owners can gain from GVCs

GVCs allow women-owned MSMEs to access foreign markets indirectly by supplying domestic exporters, helping to reduce the fixed costs of exporting. MSMEs account for a large share of economic activity in both developed and developing countries, estimated to account for more than half of all formal employment worldwide (OECD and World Bank Group 2015; WTO 2016). Because women tend to run smaller firms, GVCs can particularly benefit women by integrating MSMEs into supply chains in developed and developing countries.

MSME participation in GVCs takes place mostly through indirect contribution to exports, rather than through exporting directly (figure 2.20) (OECD and World Bank Group 2015). The typical U.S. multinational enterprise buys more than US$3 billion in domestic inputs from more than 6,000 MSMEs—or almost 25 percent of the total input purchased by those firms (Slaughter 2013). Estimates for the United States show that in 2007 the export share of MSMEs increased from approximately 28 percent (in gross exports) to 41 percent (in value-added exports) when such indirect exports are taken into account (USITC 2010).

MSMEs in least-developed countries predominantly operate in the informal economy, and their participation in GVCs is concentrated in the agricultural sector and labor-intensive, very low-value-added manufacturing and services activities, where entry costs are lower. MSMEs in middle- and higher-income countries operate in both the low-value-added end of the spectrum and in higher-skill and specialized niche activities.

GVC integration also helps MSMEs to overcome financial constraints. Because women are more credit constrained, integration is an additional channel through which GVCs can disproportionately benefit women. Recent empirical evidence reveals that Italian SMEs participate in supply chains to overcome liquidity shortages, especially for firms more exposed to bank credit rationing or with weaker relationships with banks. The benefits are even stronger when these SMEs have relationships with large and international trading partners that can provide these SMEs with credit through, for example, delayed payment schemes (Minetti et al. 2019).

GVCs connect small-scale women farmers to foreign markets

By connecting small-scale farmers to regional value chains, agricultural value chains can support gender-inclusive economic development. In agricultural regional value chains in Southern Africa, both male and female employment is mostly informal, with a higher proportion of women engaged in informal employment than male counterparts according to data from Madagascar, South Africa, and Zimbabwe. In many agricultural value chains, women are found upstream working in production, processing, and domestic, small-scale marketing.

Credit: © fizkes/ Shutterstock.com. Used with permission; further permission required for reuse.

Figure 2.21 Women are more likely to be production workers but less likely to own or manage GVC firms

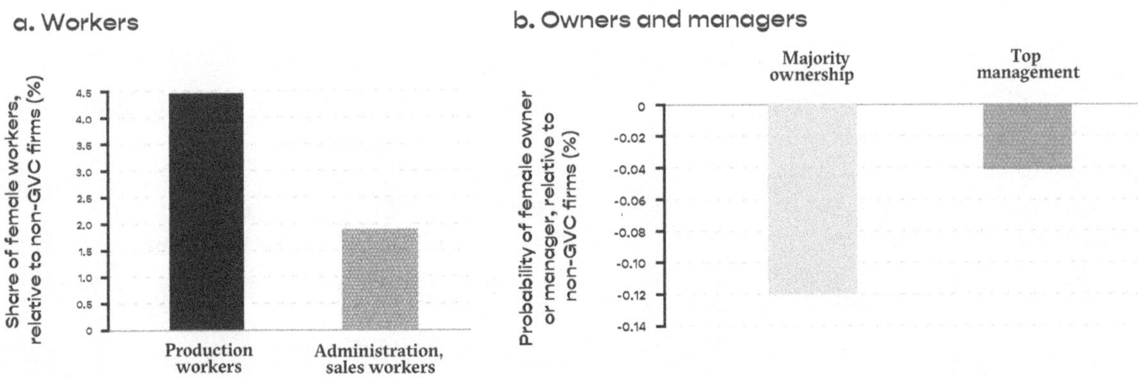

Source: Rocha and Winkler 2019, using data from World Bank Enterprise Surveys.
Note: Exporters are firms with an export share (direct or indirect) of at least 10 percent of total sales. Importers are firms with an imported input share of at least 10 percent of total inputs. GVC (global value chain) participants are firms classified as both an exporter and importer. Panel a plots the coefficient of estimations of the female labor share (production workers, nonproduction workers) on a dummy variable if the firm is a GVC participant controlling for capital intensity, sales, and total factor productivity, as well as country-sector, subnational region, and year fixed effects. Panel b plots the coefficient of estimations of whether a firm is majority-female-owned or has a female top manager on a dummy variable if the firm is a GVC participant controlling for country-sector, subnational region, and year fixed effects.

Value chain integration can play an important role in changing incentives toward cash crop production by providing access to overseas markets and creating relationships with lead firms that improve the availability of inputs, such as higher-yield seeds, fertilizers, and pesticides. Higher-quality inputs support the shift to commercial agriculture, benefitting women who usually have less access to high-quality inputs (see box 2.5). The transition from maize to soybeans in Zambia through the integration into regional value chains in Southern Africa is an example of such an opportunity. Although large-scale farmers were the major producers of soybeans in Zambia during the period 2006–17, small-scale holders, many of whom are women, dramatically increased their production and accounted for about 43 percent of total production in 2017 from less than 5 percent in the mid-2000s.

Upgrading in GVCs can benefit women in GVCs

Many developing countries look to upgrade in GVCs by shifting to high-value-added activities. Given the existing gender gaps within these segments, this shift could have implications for female participation.[8] Gendered analysis generally finds that, as countries upgrade their economies into high-tech and capital-intensive industry segments for the export market, female intensity in employment tends to decline.[9] This pattern reflects how women workers are often located in the upstream and lower-value-added components of value chains. The positive relationship between GVC participation and the female labor share is in production jobs (figure 2.21, panel a), whereas men tend to dominate both employment in the more technical segments and in ownership and management of GVCs (figure 2.21, panel b).

Several factors contribute to this trend. For example, in the case of call centers in the Arab Republic of Egypt, limited access to education, training, promotions, and networks makes it difficult for women to take advantage of rising demand for higher technical skills (Ahmed 2013). Product upgrading into areas that require higher technical skills limits female advancement because of the various constraints women face. Although the concentration of women in Egyptian call centers overall is high, women mostly occupy lower-value activities at a rate of 40 to 69 percent. In more skill-intensive areas of the call center value chain, women's employment share drops to 10 to 38 percent.

The examples of Costa Rica and the Dominican Republic, however, illustrate that this trend does not always need to be the case. Upgrading in the medical devices sector did not hurt female participation and resulted in better-quality jobs. Entry into medical devices and other high-tech industries from low-value sectors such as apparel and agriculture has offered a path to benefit from higher export revenues. Whereas apparel and agriculture are marked by high female intensity, but with low-quality, low-paying jobs, the medical devices GVC allowed for the creation of better jobs for women in export industries with higher salaries and more job security in an industry that receives significantly more export revenues (box 2.9).

Legal discrimination and overall gender inequality are lower in countries that specialize in more sophisticated stages within GVCs (figure 2.22; and see figure 1.3). Although only a correlation, this finding could indicate that upgrading within GVCs leads to higher demand for skilled workers. Gender discrimination therefore becomes more costly because it artificially restricts the supply of skills in the economy.

Box 2.9 Female employment and upgrading in the medical devices global value chain in Costa Rica and the Dominican Republic

The medical devices industry is a high-tech and high-value manufacturing sector that offers well-paid jobs. The workforce consists of skilled and semiskilled workers who hold permanent jobs within firms as opposed to contractual labor arrangements seen in other industries (Bamber and Hamrick 2019). Workforce quality plays a critical role in the industry's globalization, and human capital has been identified in certain cases as the single most important factor driving site selection in the sector (Kimelberg and Nicoll 2012).

The experience of Costa Rica and the Dominican Republic shows how gender dynamics may evolve in this global value chain (GVC). Each is an emerging producer within the industry, although with over a decade of experience. Further, each nation is growing and upgrading into new value chain activities, product categories, or both.

Women account for over half of employment in the sector in both Costa Rica and the Dominican Republic, considerably higher than their participation in the manufacturing sector as a whole and in export processing zones. These predominantly female jobs are also well-paid jobs despite being primarily in production stages. They are sustainable and characterized by long-term, permanent contracts and higher-than-average wages.

Importantly, both countries have maintained high levels of female participation over time alongside considerable export growth and wage growth (figure B2.9.1). At an aggregate level, wages increased 78 percent in Costa Rica (between 2005 and 2011) and in the Dominican Republic by 27 percent for production roles and 30 percent for technical roles (between 2006 and 2016) (calculated in current U.S. dollars). Mean wage increases by early investors in the Dominican Republic were even more pronounced—at 94 percent and 47 percent, respectively. From 2006 to 2016, sector exports from Costa Rica and the Dominican Republic grew at 296 percent and 131 percent, respectively.

Figure B2.9.1 Strong and sustainable female participation in the medical devices GVC

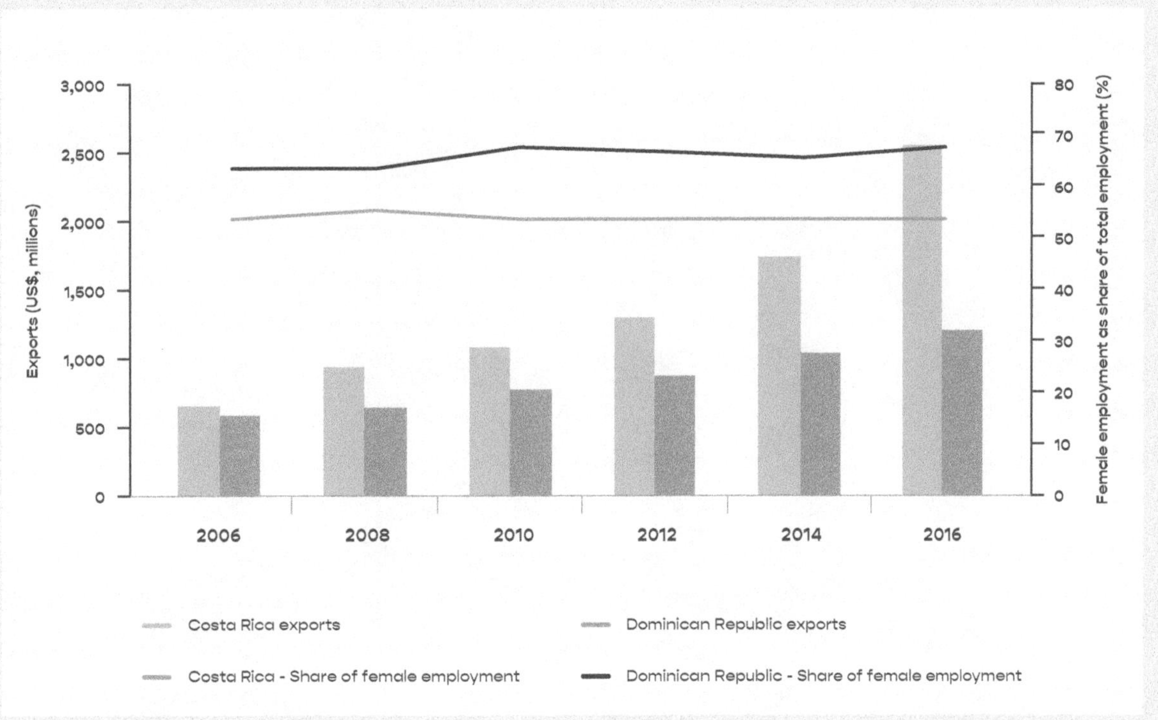

Source: Bamber and Hamrick 2019, using data from CNFZE, PROCOMER, and UN Comtrade.
Note: GVC = global value chain.

Female participation has held steady as the sector upgraded into new, higher-value products, although it differs along value chain segments. Large-scale, multinational assemblers accounted for the largest share of export growth and female job creation, whereas smaller investors and component manufacturers tended to have a comparatively lower female intensity. Specific product categories within these industries vary in their female intensity, with more sophisticated therapeutics offering more opportunities for women than disposable medical devices.

In the case of Costa Rica, firm-level data analysis confirms the increasing female participation as product upgrading took place from disposable devices (for example, catheters) to more sophisticated medical instruments and therapeutic devices. At an aggregate level, female intensity increased as product sophistication increased in 2011—51 percent for disposables compared to 52 percent for instruments and 59 percent for therapeutics.

Gender-sensitive policies in both countries in terms of access to education and supportive maternity leave approaches contributed to ongoing female participation.

Figure 2.22 Countries at higher points of the GVC upgrading trajectory exhibit higher legal equality

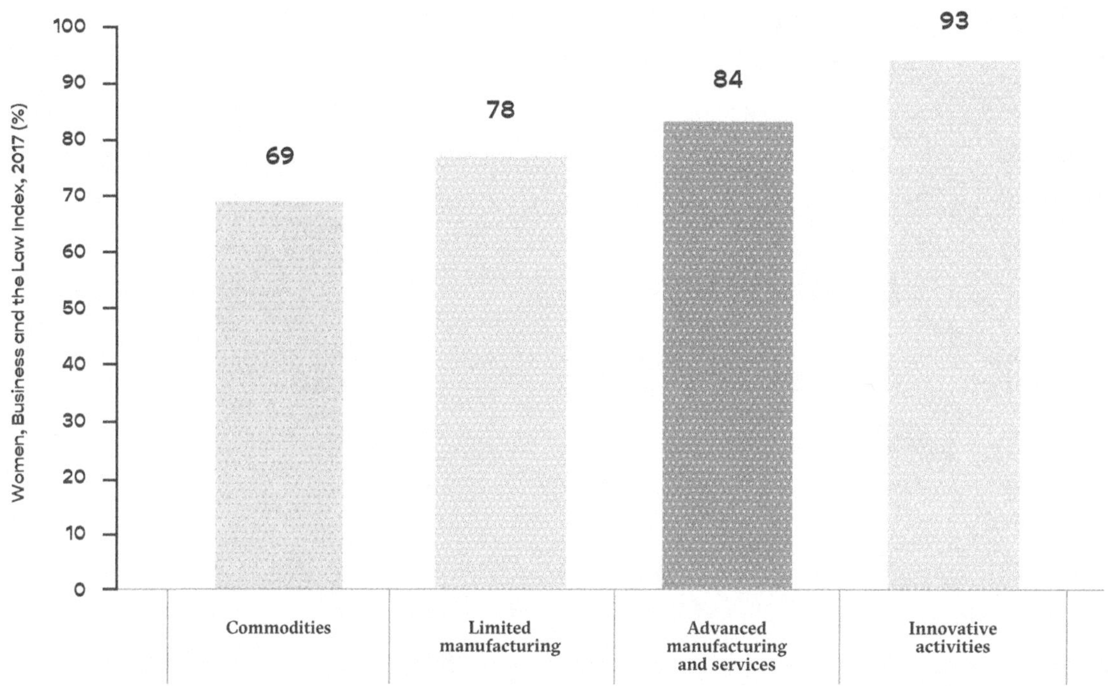

Source: World Bank staff calculations based on definitions of GVC taxonomy groups introduced in World Bank 2019, and Women, Business and the Law data.
Note: GVC = global value chain.

Opportunities for women in trade through digital technology

Digital technology is bringing to global commerce transformative forces that have the potential to benefit women. Digital technologies can empower women socially and economically by creating new employment and entrepreneurial opportunities, removing the trade barriers women face, enhancing access to finance and education, freeing up women's time, and giving women increased voice and agency.

Female business owners face more challenges than male business owners in accessing the support services they need to grow, such as access to networks, training, financing, and markets (ITC 2017; WTO 2018). Digital technologies such as electronic commerce (e-commerce) platforms have the potential to close this gap by bringing female producers and traders closer to markets, offering female consumers a larger variety of products at lower costs, and making it easier for female entrepreneurs to borrow. Digital technologies, such as online platforms, can increase women's education and enable women to leverage their comparative advantages and overcome a range of hurdles in traditional modes of trade. Specifically, technologies enhance women's participation in trade by reducing the cost of trade, opening new opportunities to trade in services, enabling women to better use their skills, and facilitating women's access to finance. New technologies also increase demand for female skills and reduce time and mobility constraints.

Digital technologies empower women business owners

Technology reduces the information and transaction costs associated with cross-border trade. Easier access to market information through simple technology such as mobile phones can decrease regional differences in prices in developing countries, especially in agricultural markets (Aker and Mbiti 2010; Bernard et al. 2007). This increased access is likely to benefit women entrepreneurs because they are often less mobile and thus are more likely to be subject to higher prices in remote markets. More sophisticated technologies such as e-commerce platforms reduce costs dramatically by matching buyers and sellers, and online rating systems and e-payment solutions enhance trust between buyers and sellers (Ba and Pavlou 2002; Resnick and Zeckhauser 2002). Digital solutions that remove the need for face-to-face interactions when trading can help reduce the difficulties women business owners face, such as mobility constraints, discrimination, and even violence. The Internet allows more MSMEs to trade online by lowering initial business costs, which disproportionally benefits women. By allowing women to gain market information in a more timely and cost-effective way, digital methods give women the opportunity to access international opportunities despite mobility constraints due to higher family obligations (Martin and Wright 2005).

Digital technologies are instrumental in gaining international market intelligence and in promoting small venture growth through internationalization, and their effect is even stronger for traditionally disadvantaged groups of entrepreneurs like women (Pergelova et al. 2019). Digital infrastructures have a democratizing effect for female entrepreneurs who pursue international expansion. Online platforms can reduce gender-based discrimination even if they cannot eliminate it. Women sellers on eBay receive on average about 80 cents for every dollar a man receives when selling the identical new product and 97 cents when selling the same used product, which are still significant but smaller gaps than offline (Kricheli-Katz and Regev 2016).

Qualitative evidence also suggests that women use the advantage of anonymity provided by online markets to avoid discrimination. Up to one-third of women work under a gender-neutral pseudonym online (Hyperwallet 2017).

Some evidence shows that women business owners in both trade in goods and trade in services are more present online than they are in traditional businesses in both developed and developing economies. For example, a 2015 survey of Pacific Island exporters showed that firms that are active online have a greater concentration of female executives under 45 years of age than those that are active offline (DiCaprio and Suominen 2015). More generally, the share of women-owned firms active in cross-border e-commerce has been found to be twice as high as the share engaged in offline trade. In the case of Africa, 75 percent of the firms trading exclusively through e-commerce are women-owned (ITC 2017). Etsy (2017), a creative commerce platform, reported that 86 percent of its sellers in the United States are women, and they are more likely to be younger than the typical business owner. On Alibaba, a Chinese e-commerce platform, more than half of all online shops are owned by women (box 2.10). In comparison, only 17.5 percent of small enterprises in China have a female top manager, and the figure globally stands at 18.6 percent.[10] Airbnb (2017), the online marketplace for accommodation, estimates it has more than 1 million women hosts, making up 55 percent of its global host community.

A recent survey conducted by the World Bank in partnership with NexTrade has also shown that differences between men- and women-led e-commerce firms with respect to export participation tend to be smaller than differences across offline firms (box 2.11).[11] In the particular case of surveyed firms in South Asia and Southeast Asia, female-led firms were even more likely to export than male-led firms.

Box 2.10 Online electronic commerce platform offers women new business opportunities

Alibaba Group, based in China, is the largest retail commerce company in the world. More than 7 million small businesses are registered on Alibaba platforms. Among those enterprises active on the platforms, over half (50.79 percent) are led by women.

Some preliminary analysis on women-led enterprises on Alibaba reveals that (i) the share of women-led enterprises is higher on electronic commerce platforms compared with offline businesses; (ii) women-led enterprises are on average smaller in size compared with male-led firms, but the average sales of women-led firms are higher than sales of male-led firms among the larger firms online; (iii) women entrepreneurs are more successful in highly differentiated product sectors such as cosmetics, clothing, grocery, and baby products; and (iv) women are less likely to borrow through microloans but more likely to repay.

The share of female entrepreneurs is higher among small- and micro-size firms and relatively lower among larger firms (table B2.10.1). Conversely, women-led firms have higher average sales among large firms, but lower average sales revenue among smaller firms. This trend may be due to the fact that women are more likely to open an online shop as a part-time job, which prevents them from scaling up the businesses.

Women-led online firms are concentrated in specific sectors and product groups (figure B2.10.1): 66.88 percent of firms selling cosmetic products are led by a woman, and the share of women-led enterprises is 60.44 percent for baby products, 54.29 percent for clothing, 51.97 percent for jewelry and accessories, 51.85 percent for groceries, and 51.19 percent for bags, shoes, and suitcases.

Although women-led firms account for half of all firms selling on Alibaba platforms, their average sales are lower than sales of their male-led counterparts. On average, the sales revenue of women-led firms is 18 percent lower than that of firms led by men. Somewhat surprisingly, in sectors where women are dominant in numbers of firms, women-led enterprises have relatively smaller sales. The median sales are lower for women-led enterprises in all sectors compared with male-led online shops, although the difference is smaller when it comes to sectors such as digital products and services.

Table B2.10.1 How women-led firms compare to men-led firms on Alibaba

Firm size (average annual sales in RMB)	Share of women-led firms among all firms (%)	Average sales revenue per year (compared to men-led firms)	Average age of female entrepreneurs (years)	Average age of male entrepreneurs (years)
> 5 million RMB	45.9	9% higher	37.5	35.4
1 million – 5 million RMB	44.3	5% higher	37.3	35.2
360,000 – 1 million RMB	44.2	Same as men-led firms	37.1	35.1
<360,000 RMB	51.1	21% lower	31.7	31.6

Source: World Trade Organization Secretariat calculations based on Alibaba data for 2018.
Note: Online firms are divided into four groups according to their annual revenue: (i) an online shop with over 5 million RMB in annual revenue is considered a large-sized online firm; (ii) an online shop with annual revenue between 1 million and 5 million RMB is considered a medium-sized firm; (iii) an online shop with an annual revenue of less than 1 million is considered a small firm, and (iv) an online shop with less than 360,000 RMB annual sales is considered a micro-sized firm.

Box 2.10, continued

Figure B2.10.1 Share and average sales of women-led enterprises, by sector

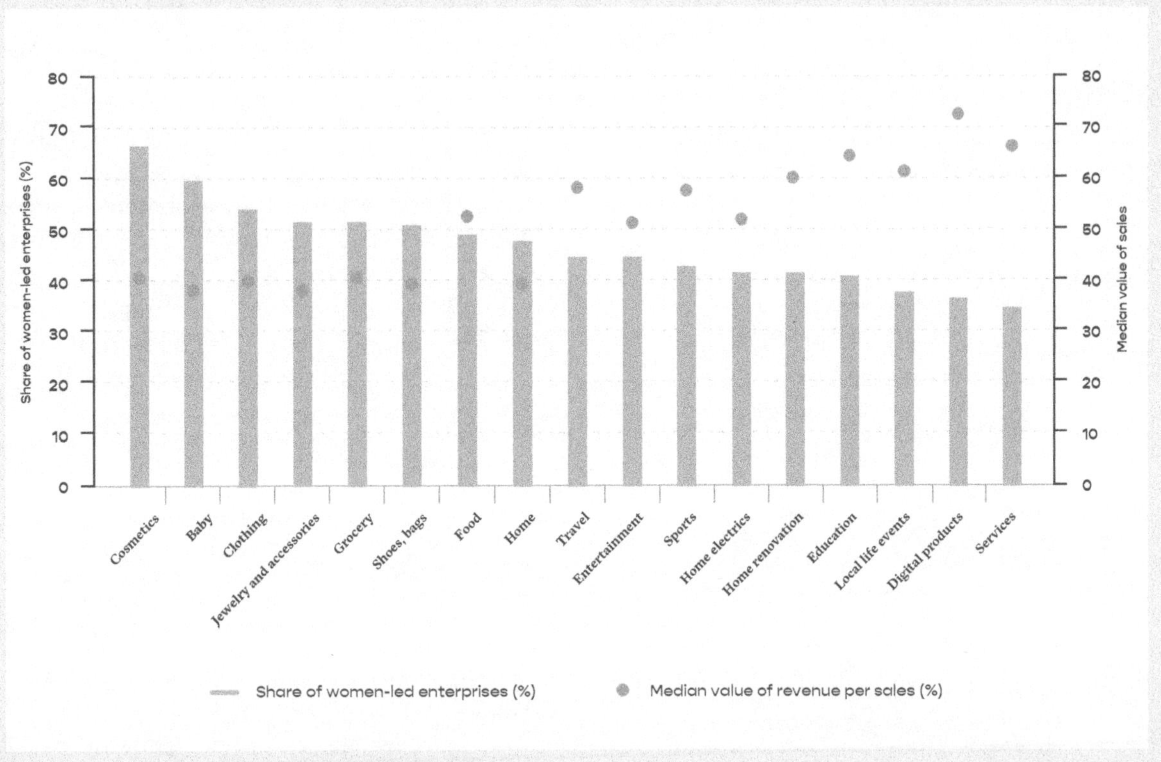

Source: China Women's University and AliResearch 2019.
Note: The bars represent the share of women-led firms in all Alibaba platforms in each sector. The dots show the median sales of women-led firms as a share of median-sales of men-led firms.

Financial services such as loans, savings, and money transfers help businesses build assets and increase their income and make them less vulnerable to economic stress. Data from Ant Credit, a microcredit business that provides loans to small businesses and individual entrepreneurs over the Internet, indicate that women are less likely to borrow online but have higher rates of repayment. On average, only 36 percent of all women-led enterprises operating on Alibaba borrow through Ant Credit. The amount of loans women apply for is on average 6 percent higher than loan requests filed by men, and the average amount of approved loans for women is slightly higher for women than for men (2 percent). Remarkably, the ratio of default is significantly lower for women who borrow. The default rate within 90 days is 27 percent lower for female than for male borrowers, and the financial nonperforming rate is 28 percent lower for women than for men. This evidence echoes findings in similar studies conducted in developed countries, where women business owners are found to receive significantly less early-stage capital than men but ultimately deliver higher revenue (Abouzahr et al. 2018).

Technology can ease women's trade-related constraints

Constraints in the area of access to finance and education as well as legal constraints hold back women in trade as shown in the first section of this chapter. New technologies can help close the gender gaps in finance and education and address legal barriers in various ways and thus benefit women as workers, consumers, and decision makers.

Technology advancements, such as mobile money, digital platforms that match start-ups and providers of financial services, and emerging technologies such as blockchain, may help women overcome barriers they face in accessing finance. In developing countries, for example, mobile phones can dramatically reduce the costs of sending and receiving money, an important issue for rural farmers and traders (Aker et al. 2016). In this context, a study on Kenya estimated that the expansion of a mobile money system helped about 185,000 women to shift their occupations from subsistence farming to business or retail sales (Suri and Jack 2016).

Online crowd-sourcing platforms can reduce discrimination against women in access to finance (Barasinska and Schäfer 2014). Some studies show that peer-to-peer crowdfunding platforms allow women to access trade finance at much lower costs, even if women tend to ask for less money than men. Data from the crowdfunding platform Kickstarter showed that women are 35 percent of the project

Box 2.11 Gender analysis of electronic commerce and online trading in South Asia and Southeast Asia

In South Asia and Southeast Asia, the share of women-led firms engaged in electronic commerce (e-commerce) remains small, which reflects the minimal share of women-led firms in the overall economy. A study examining the depth of e-commerce engagement in the region has identified the main challenges to e-commerce faced by men and women in different types of companies such as small versus large companies or nonexporter versus exporter.

Male-led and female-led e-commerce firms differ in their views on the impediments to trading. On average, interviewed firms with female chief executive officers (CEOs) are 18.6 percentage points more active than their male counterparts in selling and purchasing online. An analysis of responses from traders, however, found no meaningful differences between women- and male-led firms in terms of their e-commerce performance and found that women-led firms face the same barriers as their male counterparts.

Key impediments to engaging in e-commerce within the country and across the border reported by all respondents were a poor regulatory environment for doing business, low access to trade finance, low technical capacity, lack of access to online payment mechanisms, difficulties in e-commerce-related logistics, lack of or unclear digital regulations, and a poor degree of connectivity and information technology (IT) infrastructure. The data showed that firms with female CEOs generally had a more optimistic view of these areas (figure B2.11.1). On average, they rated the existing conditions at 7.65/10 whereas their male counterparts rated them at 6.64/10.

Small firms (fewer than 50 employees) with female CEOs tended to suffer more from inefficiencies in IT connectivity and infrastructure and digital regulations. For cross-border e-commerce, medium firms (51–500 employees) with female CEOs reported gaps in connectivity and

Box 2.11, continued

Figure B2.11.1 Impediments to e-commerce, by gender of firm CEO in South Asia

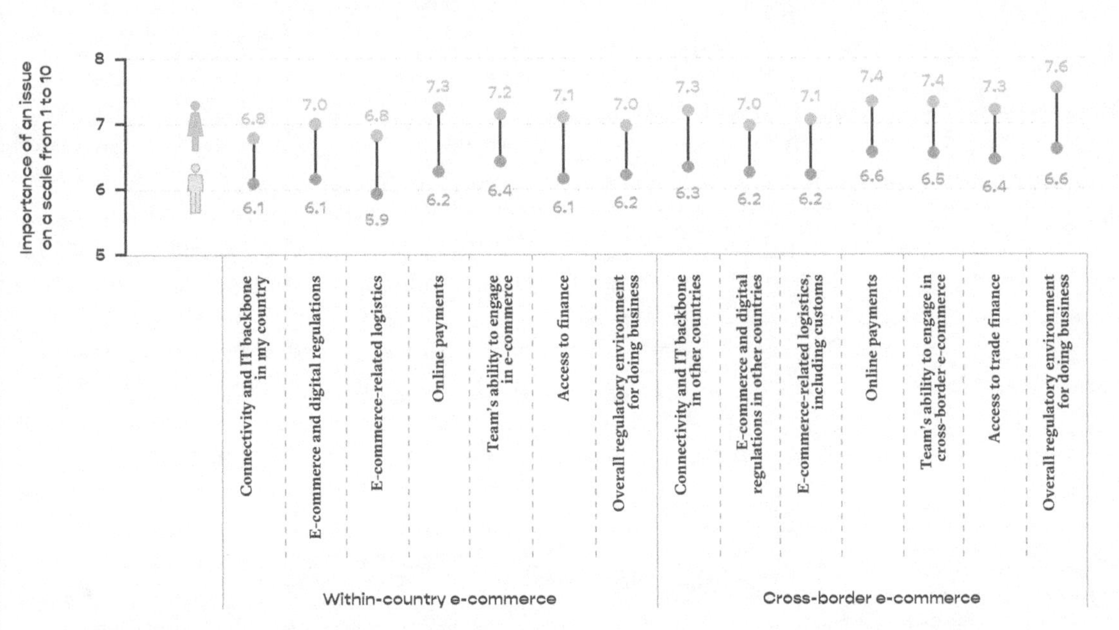

Source: World Bank and World Trade Organization calculations based on survey data produced by the World Bank in partnership with NexTrade.
Note: CEO = chief executive officer; e-commerce = electronic commerce; IT = information technology.

IT infrastructure, e-commerce related logistics, online payments, and shortages in the team's capacity to engage in e-commerce as the major constraints.

Female-led firms reported a 4.5–6.0 percent higher number of export sales over total sales by these firms in 2016–17 than firms of their male counterparts. Additionally, firms with female CEOs in South Asia reported that they were 11 percent more likely to export to foreign markets in 2016–17 than firms with male CEOs. These statistics highlight the potential of e-commerce to spread the gains more equally across genders.

leaders and 44 percent of the investors on the platform (Marom, Robb, and Sade 2016). On average, men seek significantly higher levels of capital and raise more than women. Women enjoy higher rates of success, however, even after controlling for category and goal.

Digital educational platforms can similarly benefit women in trade. Women tend to be more time-constrained (see also chapter 1 and the earlier section in this chapter titled "Social, cultural, and behavioral constraints to women's participation in trade"). Online courses reduce the time requirements for education and are thus likely to benefit women more—particularly because safety concerns on the way to school are one reason for women's lower enrollment rates, as discussed previously. Moreover, online courses can reduce discrimination in STEM subjects because online courses facilitate anonymous grading and participation. Recent empirical evidence shows no gender gap in the completion rates of STEM massive open online courses (MOOCs), although there is still an enrollment gap (Jiang et al. 2018). The probability of enrolling in STEM MOOCs has been found to be higher and the gender gaps in STEM MOOC enrollment and completion rates smaller in less gender-equal and less developed countries.

Digital technology can also be deployed to detect discrimination in hiring, procurement, or similar settings. Supervised machine learning that controls for all job seeker characteristics visible to recruiters has been able to detect that women face a penalty of up to 40 percent in male-dominated professions and vice versa (Kopp, Hangartner, and Siegenthaler 2019). This type of discriminatory behavior might be more prevalent in trading firms because of subconscious or explicit biases toward women's flexibility, so technological supervision of recruiters could help to reduce the gender pay gap of traders. Digital technologies might also inadvertently strengthen discrimination linked to gender stereotypes. In particular, the use of algorithms to parse data and automate the allocation of resources and decision making may lead to discriminatory outcomes for innocent reasons. For instance, even gender-neutral advertisements for STEM education are disproportionately shown to men by online algorithms because advertising to men is less expensive overall than advertising to women; therefore, advertisers who are indifferent to gender end up showing their ads to men more often (Lambrecht and Tucker 2019). This means that algorithms need to be tested to eliminate unintended biases before they are deployed.

Digital technologies emphasize women's networking and social strengths

Women are positioned to gain from a shift in employment toward nonroutine occupations, and away from physical work. Digital technologies encourage the use of communication and collaboration skills, increasing opportunities for women in many services jobs. Recent exploratory research finds that women entrepreneurs perform better when it comes to researching information and connecting with potential partners and customers internationally using digital technologies (Rosenbaum 2017). Women entrepreneurs feel constrained by rigid traditional network structures and prefer ICT as a resource to help them expand internationally.

Women's social skills may represent a comparative advantage in the age of digitalization (Krieger-Boden and Sorgner 2018). Women have been found to enjoy a higher average reputation than men in auction transactions of private sellers on eBay (Kricheli-Katz and Regev 2016). In Upwork, an online marketplace for freelancers to provide services, 44 percent of the workers are women, compared to an offline average of 25 percent of nonagricultural economy globally (World Bank 2016). Alibaba also reports that women-led enterprises receive higher ratings in customer service and logistical service and that they give more accurate descriptions of their products (China Women's University and AliResearch 2019). In particular, the advantages of women are more prominent in markets of highly differentiated consumer products and services such as cosmetics, clothing, jewelry, and baby products (see also box 2.10).

Since 1980 the probability of working in a cognitive/high-wage occupation has risen for college-educated women in the United States (Cortes, Jaimovich, and Siu 2018). This rise is attributed to a greater increase in the demand for female-oriented skills—in particular social skills, which have gained importance in cognitive/high-wage occupations relative to other occupations. A similar trend has been observed for Germany where women have witnessed relative increases in nonroutine analytic and interactive tasks, which are also associated with higher social skill levels. These documented demand shifts in favor of skilled women are positively correlated with technological change and occurred mainly in sectors where social skills are important, such as education and health (Black and Spitz-Oener 2010; Lindley 2012).

Some evidence shows that women workers benefit disproportionally from technological upgrades induced by access to foreign markets. Increased access to the U.S. market after the entry into force of the North American Free Trade Agreement (NAFTA) induced more-productive firms in Mexico to modernize their technology in order to enter the export market (Juhn, Ujhelyi, and Villegas-Sanchez 2013).

Figure 2.23 Women spend more time on household and less on working activities

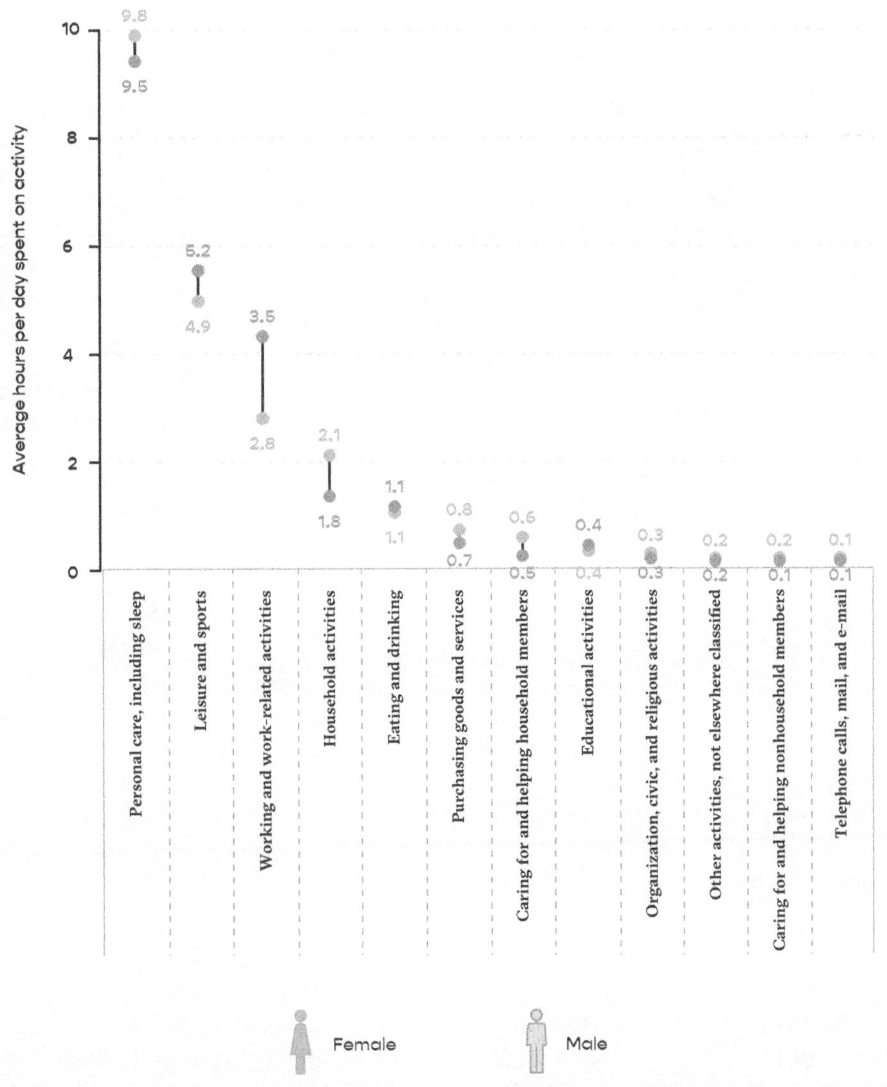

Source: U.S. Bureau of Labor Statistics American Time Use Survey for 2017.

These new technologies involved computerized production processes, which disproportionally benefitted female workers by lowering the need for physically demanding skills. As a result, the relative wage and employment of women improved, especially in blue-collar tasks.

Women as workers benefit from the flexibility of digital work

Digital technologies can flip the demand for flexibility in favor of the worker, rather than the business, providing opportunities that can help women balance other obligations. Chapter 1 and the first section of this chapter have shown that women are less flexible to working long hours because of their responsibilities as primary caregivers. This limited flexibility is particularly detrimental to their employment

Figure 2.24 The probability of job loss due to automation is higher for female workers

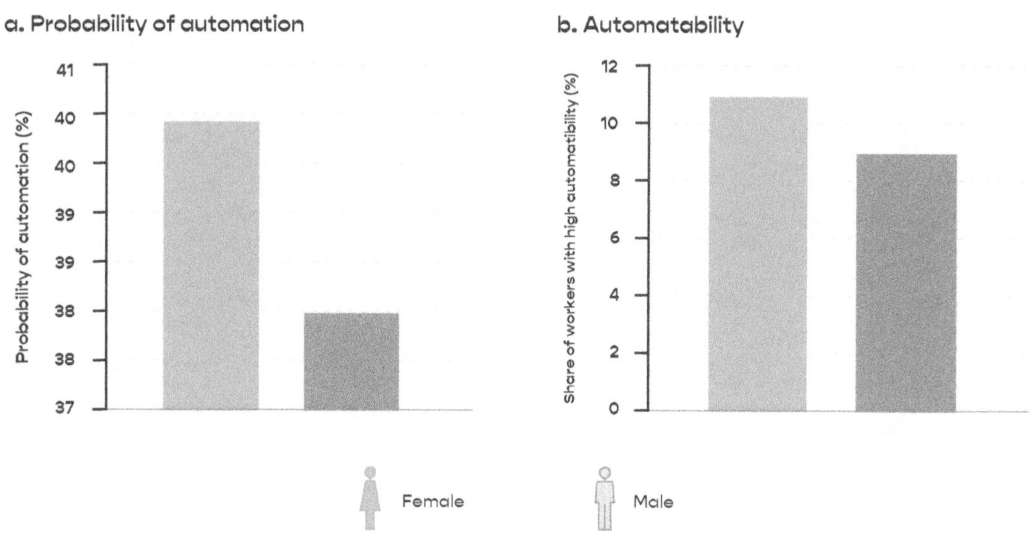

Source: Brussevich et al. 2018; Frey and Osbourne 2017 (panel a).
Note: The probability of automation is estimated using an expectation-maximization (EM) algorithm that relates individual characteristics (age, education, training, among others) and job task characteristics to occupational-level risk of automation. Differences in probability of automation and share of workers with high automatability across gender are statistically significant at 1 percent level. High automatability is defined as having probability of automation greater than or equal to 0.7.

prospects in trading firms. In particular, women spend on average more time than men on household activities, purchasing goods and services, and caring for and helping household members and others (figure 2.23).

Digital technologies can help break down barriers of time and distance between buyers and sellers, while reducing market lag through the real-time exchange of information (Alarcón-del-Amo, Rialp, and Rialp 2016). The flexibility provided by digital technologies can help women participate in the workforce while balancing their work and family obligations. Research has argued that the gender gap in pay could be considerably reduced if firms did not have an incentive to disproportionately reward individuals who worked long hours and worked particular hours. It finds that women working in science and technology have been found to have a higher labor force participation rate and lower gender wage gap. This pattern is attributed to the fact that technology appears to enable women to work part-time or to work more flexibly (Goldin 2014).

Technology creates opportunities for women producers in services

Women's employment shares are high in many services industries that are not trade-intensive—such as hospitality, education, or health (figure 2.3). New technologies enable services that traditionally could not be traded across borders to be traded online. These sectors' trade flows have documented record growth in recent years (WTO 2019), which presents a large opportunity for women workers and producers not only because they are well represented in these sectors but also because online trade reduces the need for mobility traditionally associated with such services. In addition, new technologies lower the entry costs to these sectors because they allow for the provision of services without high up-front capital investments, which alleviates some of the constraints, such as low access to capital, faced by women.

Airbnb (2017) has, for instance, lowered the entry and trade costs for entrepreneurs in the hospitality industry and serves as an intermediary for more than 1 million female hosts. Online courses or video platforms like YouTube can increase the demand and income sources for teachers with early research showing that the number of female instructors online had increased dramatically over a few years to 53 percent of the total (Kim and Bonk 2006). Creative platforms like Etsy allow users to turn unpaid domestic work into paid market work. The health industry is another example where digital technology rapidly removes face-to-face constraints. In 2006 a study documented in an analysis of therapy services the already rising number of female counselors online relative to male counselors (Chester and Glass 2006).

Some technologies could introduce new challenges for women workers

Whereas most digital technologies promise to improve the situation for women in trade, some might have negative effects. Automation caused by digital technologies could, for example, make many jobs in low-skill sectors obsolete, particularly in relation to routine tasks where women make up a higher share of the labor force. Many jobs in manufacturing, office, and administrative support occupations are predicted to be at risk of being automated (Frey and Osborne 2017; Goos, Manning, and Salomons 2014). Automation could cause more female jobs to become obsolete because women perform, on average, more routine tasks than men across all sectors and occupations (figure 2.24) (Brussevich et al. 2018). Although the exact impact of automation on the labor market currently remains elusive, new digital technologies will continue to have an effect on skills development through changes in labor demand, work organization, and skills requirement. In that context, women with access to higher education and digital literacy have been found to have some of the responsive, flexible, and complementary skills needed to adapt, at least in part, to the current and future challenges of the labor market (WTO 2017).

Technology can benefit women as consumers

Technology benefits consumers by saving them time, providing access to information, reducing transaction costs, and giving them more control over the purchasing process (Elliott and Meng 2009). E-commerce technologies can lower consumers' expenditure by reducing travel and other transaction costs (Burinskiene and Burinskas 2012). Women spend on average more time shopping than men. In the United States, women spend an average of 0.82 hours per day on purchasing goods and services, whereas men spend only 0.61 hours. By reducing the amount of time women need to spend shopping, e-commerce can enable women to replace unpaid household work hours with paid hours of work (see figure 2.24).

E-commerce can also benefit female consumers by reducing discrimination they might face when purchasing offline. Comparing traditional markets with e-commerce, the Internet has been found to enable consumers to obtain higher levels of market transparency (Rezabakhsh et al. 2006). In that context, Internet car purchasing is associated with lower gender-based price discrimination (Morton, Zettelmeyer, and Silva-Risso 2003).

Technology can dramatically reduce the costs of sending and receiving money, enabling women to smooth consumption over time and allocate their labor more efficiently. A study in Kenya estimates that access to the Kenyan mobile money system M-Pesa increased per capita consumption levels and lifted 2 percent of Kenyan households out of poverty. The impacts were more pronounced for female-headed households. Mobile money has increased the efficiency of the allocation of consumption over time while allowing a more efficient allocation of labor, resulting in a meaningful reduction of poverty in Kenya (Suri and Jack 2016). In Niger, evidence from the social cash transfer program demonstrates that the greater privacy and control of mobile transfers compared to manual cash transfers shifts intrahousehold decision making in favor of women (Aker, Ghosh, and Burrell 2016).

Notes

1 See WTO (2019) and chapter 3 of this report for an explanation of the various modes of trading services internationally.

2 This relationship is significantly weaker within the services sector, suggesting that barriers in STEM become less relevant as the role of services in trade increases.

3 Of course, trade can also be part of the solution. As discussed in "Trade and women as decision makers" in chapter 1, higher demand for skills by trading firms can act as a signal and induce individuals to obtain more education.

4 Based also on a focus group discussion in Vietnam as part of a Global Survey on Barriers to Trade within the Trade Facilitation Support Program on May 3, 2019.

5 The Great Lakes Region refers to the Democratic Republic of Congo, Rwanda, and Uganda.

6 For more information on the U.S. Bureau of Labor Statistics' Occupational Outlook Handbook, see https://www.bls.gov/ooh/healthcare/home.htm.

7 An exception in this regard are least-developed countries where agriculture is still the dominant source of employment for women. As these countries grow, however, they will likely start to exhibit the same pattern as middle- and high-income countries.

8 Economic upgrading strategies include, among others, improving efficiencies via technology and production advancements (process upgrading); producing higher value or more sophisticated products (product upgrading); and expansion or shifting into new stages of the value chain (functional upgrading) (Humphrey and Schmitz 2002). Many countries see moving into the services segments of GVCs as upgrading strategies for better jobs, where services are becoming increasingly used in the production of goods in value chains and make up important value-added components of GVCs (see "Opportunities for women in trade through servicification" in this chapter). Social upgrading strategies focus on creating more and better jobs with good working conditions and opportunities for advancement (ILO 2016).

9 Prominent scholars contributing to this theory include Caraway (2007) and Jomo (2009) for East Asia, Kucera and Tejani (2014) for a sample of 36 countries, Fussell (2000) in Mexico, and Berik (2000) in the Separate Customs Territory of Taiwan, Penghu, Kinmen, and Matsu.

10 According to data from the World Bank Enterprise Surveys.

11 This survey complements the World Bank's efforts on building fundamental e-commerce diagnostic tools such as the Enterprise Surveys and the Doing Business platform which, among others, provide an overview of the effects of customs procedures and trade regulations. The survey was done in partnership with NexTrade Group to systematically collect data on issues critical to e-commerce players. It is important to note that the response rate of firms in the survey with male CEOs was approximately 70 percent higher than that of firms with female CEOs. Given the small sample size of female respondents/firms with female CEOs, it is difficult to make representative inferences.

References

Abouzahr, K., F. Brooks Taplett, M. Krentz, and J. Harthorne. 2018. "Why Women-Owned Startups Are a Better Bet." Boston Consulting Group, June 6. https://www.bcg.com/en-ch/publications/2018/why-women-owned-startups-are-better-bet.aspx.

Adams-Prassl, Abi, Teodora Boneva, Marta Golin, and Christopher Rauh. 2020. "Inequality in the Impact of the Coronavirus Shock: Evidence from Real Time Surveys." CESifo Working Paper 8265, Munich Society for the Promotion of Economic Research - CESifo GmbH, Munich.

ADB (Asian Development Bank). 2016. "2016 Trade Finance Gaps, Growth, and Jobs Survey." ADB Briefs No. 64, ADB, Manila.

———. 2017. "2017 Trade Finance Gaps, Growth, and Jobs Survey." ADB Briefs No. 83. ADB, Manila.

———. 2019. *Aid for Trade in Asia and the Pacific: Promoting Connectivity for Inclusive Development.* Manila: ADB.

Ahmed, G. 2013. "Global Value Chains, Economic Upgrading and Gender in the Call Center Industry." In *Global Value Chains, Economic Upgrading and Gender: Case Studies of the Horticulture, Tourism, and Call Center Industries*, edited by C. Staritz and J. G. Reis. Washington, DC: World Bank.

Airbnb. 2017. Women Hosts and Airbnb: Building a Global Community. https://www.airbnbcitizen.com/wp-content/uploads/2017/03/Women-Hosts-and-Airbnb_Building-a-Global-Community.pdf.

Aker, J. C., R. Boumnijel, A. McClelland, and N. Tierney. 2016. "Payment Mechanisms and Antipoverty Programs: Evidence from a Mobile Money Cash Transfer Experiment in Niger." *Economic Development and Cultural Change* 65 (1): 1–37.

Aker, J. C., I. Ghosh, and J. Burrell. 2016. "The Promise (and Pitfalls) of ICT for Agriculture Initiatives." *Agricultural Economics* 47 (S1): 35–48.

Aker, J. C., and I. M. Mbiti. 2010. "Mobile Phones and Economic Development in Africa." *Journal of Economic Perspectives* 24 (3): 207–32.

Alarcón-del-Amo, M.C., A. Rialp, and J. Rialp. 2016. "Social Media Adoption by Exporters: The Export-Dependence Moderating Role." *Spanish Journal of Marketing – ESIC* 20 (2): 81–92.

Alesina, A., P. Giuliano, and N. Nunn. 2013. "On the Origins of Gender Roles: Women and the Plough." *Quarterly Journal of Economics* 128 (2): 469–530.

Alon, Titan, Matthias Doepke, Jane Olmstead-Rumsey, and Michèle Tertilt. 2020. "The Impact of COVID-19 on Gender Equality." CRC TR 224 Discussion Paper Series crctr224_2020_163, University of Bonn and University of Mannheim, Germany.

APWINC (Asia Pacific Women's Information Network Center). 2018. "Case Studies of Successful Women Entrepreneurs in the ICT Industry in 21 APEC Economies." APEC Secretariat, Singapore.

Aterido, R., T. Beck, and L. Iacovone. 2013. "Access to Finance in Sub-Saharan Africa: Is There a Gender Gap?" *World Development* 47 (July): 102–20.

Atkin, D., B. Faber, and M. Gonzalez-Navarro. 2018. "Retail Globalization and Household Welfare: Evidence from Mexico." *Journal of Political Economy* 126 (1): 1–73.

Avdiu, Besart, and Gaurav Nayyar. 2020. "When Face-to-Face Interactions Become an Occupational Hazard: Jobs in the Time of COVID-19." Policy Research Working Paper 9240, World Bank, Washington, DC.

Ba, S., and P. A. Pavlou. 2002. "Evidence of the Effect of Trust Building Technology in Electronic Markets: Price Premiums and Buyer Behavior." *MIS Quarterly* 26 (3): 243–68.

Bamber, P., and K. Fernandez-Stark. 2013. "Global Value Chains, Economic Upgrading, and Gender in the Horticulture Industry." In *Global Value Chains, Economic Upgrading, and Gender: Case Studies of the Horticulture, Tourism, and Call Center Industries*, edited by C. Staritz and J. G. Reis, 11–42. Washington D.C.: World Bank Group.

Bamber, P., and D. Hamrick. 2019. "Gender Dynamics and Upgrading in Global Value Chains: The Case of Medical Devices." Background Report for WBG-WTO Global Report on Trade and Gender: How Can 21st Century Trade Help to Close the Gender Gap? Duke Global Value Chains Center.

Barasinska, N., and D. Schäfer. 2014. "Is Crowdfunding Different? Evidence on the Relation between Gender and Funding Success from a German Peer-to-Peer Lending Platform." *German Economic Review* 15 (4): 436–52.

Barber, B. M., and T. Odean. 2001. "Boys Will Be Boys: Gender, Overconfidence, and Common Stock Investment." *Quarterly Journal of Economics* 116 (1): 261–92.

Barrientos, S. 2014. "Gender and Global Value Chains: Challenges of Economic and Social Upgrading in Agri-Food." RSCAS Research Paper No. 2014/96, Robert Schuman Centre for Advanced Studies, European University Institute, San Domenico di Fiesole, Italy.

Beaman, L., K. Niall, and J. Magruder. 2017. "Do Job Networks Disadvantage Women? Evidence from a Recruitment Experiment in Malawi." *Journal of Labor Economics* 36 (1): 121–57.

Beck, T., P. Behr, and A. Madestam. 2011. "Sex and Credit: Is There a Gender Bias in Microfinance?" European Banking Center Discussion Paper No. 2011-027, Tilburg University, Netherlands.

Beck, T., A. Demirgüç-Kunt, and R. Levine. 2007. "Finance, Inequality, and the Poor." *Journal of Economic Growth* 12 (1): 27–49.

Berik, G. 2000. "Mature Export-Led Growth and Gender Wage Inequality in Taiwan." *Feminist Economics* 6 (3): 1–26.

Bernard, A. B., J. B. Jensen, S. J. Redding, and P. K. Schott. 2007. "Firms in International Trade." *Journal of Economic Perspectives* 21 (3): 105–30.

Bianconi, M., F. Esposito, and M. Sammon. 2019. "Trade Policy Uncertainty and Stock Returns." Discussion Papers Series No. 830, Department of Economics, Tufts University, Medford, MA.

Black, S. E., and A. Spitz-Oener. 2010. "Explaining Women's Success: Technological Change and the Skill Content of Women's Work." *Review of Economics and Statistics* 92 (1): 187–94.

Bøler, E. A., B. Javorcik, and K. H. Ulltveit-Moe. 2018. "Working across Time Zones: Exporters and the Gender Wage Gap." *Journal of International Economics* 111 (March): 122–33.

Booth, A. L. 2009. "Gender and Competition." *Labour Economics* 16 (6): 599–606.

Bordalo, P. M., K. Coffman, N. Gennaioli, and A. Shleifer. 2019. "Beliefs about Gender." *American Economic Review* 109 (3): 739–73.

Brana, S. 2013. "Microcredit: An Answer to the Gender Problem in Funding?" *Small Business Economics* 40 (1): 1–14.

Brenton, P., C. Bashinge Bucekuderhwa, C. Hossein, S. Nagaki, and J.-B. Ntagoma. 2011. "Risky Business: Poor Women Cross-Border Traders in the Great Lakes Region of Africa." Africa Trade Policy Note 11, World Bank, Washington DC.

Brenton P., N. Dihel, M. Hoppe, and C. Soprano. 2014. "Improving Behavior at Borders to Promote Trade Formalization: The Charter for Cross-Border Traders." Africa Trade Policy Note 41, World Bank, Washington DC.

Brock, J. M., and R. De Haas. 2019. "Gender Discrimination in Small Business Lending. Evidence from a Lab-in-the-Field Experiment in Turkey." EBRD Working Paper No. 232, European Bank for Reconstruction and Development, London.

Brussevich, M. 2018. "Does Trade Liberalization Narrow the Gender Wage Gap? The Role of Sectoral Mobility." *European Economic Review* 109 (March): 305–33.

Brussevich M., E. Dabla-Norris, C. Kamunge, P. Karnane S. Khalid, and K. Kochhar. 2018. "Gender, Technology, and the Future of Work." IMF Staff Discussion Note 18/07, International Monetary Fund, Washington, DC.

Burinskiene, A., and A. Burinskas. 2012. "Consumer Demand: E-commerce or Traditional Technologies." *Economics and Management* 17 (3): 963–70.

Burstein, A., and J. Vogel. 2017. "International Trade, Technology, and the Skill Premium." *Journal of Political Economy* 125 (5): 1356–412.

Bustos, P. 2011. "Trade Liberalization, Exports, and Technology Upgrading: Evidence on the Impact of MERCOSUR on Argentinian Firms." *American Economic Review* 101 (1):304–40.

Caraway, Teri. 2007. *Assembling Women: The Feminization of Global Manufacturing.* Ithaca, NY: Cornell University Press.

Carlsson, F., D. Daruvala, and O. Johansson-Stenman. 2005. "Are People Inequality-Averse, or Just Risk-Averse?" *Economica* 72 (287): 375–96.

Carranza, E., C. Dhakal, and I. Love. 2018. "Female Entrepreneurs: How and Why Are They Different?" Jobs Working Paper, Issue No. 20, World Bank Group, Washington, DC.

Carter, N., C. Brush, P. Greene, E. Gatewood, and M. Hart. 2003. "Women Entrepreneurs Who Break through to Equity Financing: The Influence of Human, Social and Financial Capital." *Venture Capital* 5 (1): 1–28.

Chester, A., and C. A. Glass. 2006. "Online Counselling: A Descriptive Analysis of Therapy Services on the Internet." *British Journal of Guidance & Counselling* 34 (2): 145–60.

China Women's University and AliResearch. 2019. "2019 Global Research Report of Female Entrepreneurship & Employment." Alibaba Group.

Christian, M., B. Evers, and S. Barrientos. 2013. "Women in Value Chains: Making a Difference." Revised Summit Briefing 6.3 from the Capturing the Gains in Value Chains Summit, Cape Town, South Africa, December 3–5, 2012.

Cortes, G. M., N. Jaimovich, and H. E. Siu. 2018. "The 'End of Men' and Rise of Women in the High-Skilled Labor Market." NBER Working Paper No. 24274, National Bureau of Economic Research, Cambridge, MA.

Coste, A., and N. Dihel. 2013. "Services Trade and Gender." In *Women and Trade in Africa: Realizing the Potential*, edited by P. Brenton, E. Gamberoni, and C. Sear, 97–114. Washington, DC: World Bank.

Croson, R., and U. Gneezy. 2009. "Gender Differences in Preferences." *Journal of Economic Literature* 47 (2): 448–74.

de Vries, G., M. Timmer, and K. de Vries. 2015. "Structural Transformation in Africa: Static Gains, Dynamic Losses." *Journal of Development Studies* 51 (6): 674–88.

Demirgüç-Kunt, A., L. Klapper, D. Singer, S. Ansar, and J. Hess. 2017. *The Global Findex Database 2017: Measuring Financial Inclusion and the Fintech Revolution.* Washington, DC: World Bank.

Depetris-Chauvin, N. D., and G. Porto. Forthcoming. "The Gender Bias of Trade Policy in Developing Countries." Working Paper, World Bank, Washington, DC.

DiCaprio, A., and K. Suominen. 2015. "Aid for Trade in Asia and the Pacific: Thinking Forward about Trade Costs and the Digital Economy." Report for the Asian Development Bank for the Global Aid for Trade Review, July.

Dolan, C., and K. Sorby. 2003. "Gender and Employment in High-Value Agriculture Industries." Agriculture & Rural Development Working Paper 7, World Bank, Washington, DC.

Eckel, C. C., and P. J. Grossman. 1998. "Are Women Less Selfish Than Men? Evidence from Dictator Experiments." *The Economic Journal* 108 (448): 726–35.

———. 2008. "Differences in the Economic Decisions of Men and Women: Experimental Evidence." In *Handbook of Experimental Economics Results*, Volume 1, edited by C. R. Plott and V. L. Smith, 509-519. Amsterdam: North-Holland.

Edmonds, E. V., N. Pavcnik, and P. Topalova. 2010. "Trade Adjustment and Human Capital Investments: Evidence from Indian Tariff Reform." *American Economic Journal: Applied Economics* 2 (4): 42–75.

Egger, P., M. Larch, S. Nigai, and Y. Yotov. 2018. "Trade Costs in the Global Economy: Measurement, Aggregation and Decomposition." Unpublished manuscript, World Trade Organization, Geneva.

Elliott, K. M., and J. Meng. 2009. "Assessing Chinese Consumers' Likelihood to Adopt Self-Service Technologies." *International Business & Economics Research Journal* 8 (2): 27–40.

Etsy. 2017. "Crafting the Future of Work: The Big Impact of Microbusinesses." 2017 Seller Census Report, Etsy, Brooklyn, NY. https://extfiles.etsy.com/advocacy/Etsy_US_2017_SellerCensus.pdf.

Fagan, C. 2001. "Time, Money and the Gender Order: Work Orientations and Working-Time Preferences in Britain." *Gender, Work & Organization* 8 (3): 239–66.

FAO (Food and Agriculture Organization of the United Nations). 2017. "Evidence on Internal and International Migration Patterns in Selected African Countries." Rural Employment Knowledge Materials, FAO, Rome.

Feenstra, R. C., and G. H. Hanson. 1995. "Foreign Investment, Outsourcing and Relative Wages." NBER Working Paper No. 5121, National Bureau of Economic Research, Cambridge, MA.

Fellner, G., and B. Maciejovsky. 2007. "Risk Attitude and Market Behavior: Evidence from Experimental Asset Markets." *Journal of Economic Psychology* 28 (3): 338–50.

Felton, J., B. Gibson, and D. M. Sanbonmatsu. 2003. "Preference for Risk in Investing as a Function of Trait Optimism and Gender." *Journal of Behavioral Finance* 4 (1): 33–40.

Fiszbein, A., N. Schady, F. H. G. Ferreira, M. Grosh, N. Keleher, P. Olinto, and E. Skoufias. 2009. *Conditional Cash Transfers: Reducing Present and Future Poverty.* Washington DC: World Bank.

Fletschner, D., and L. Kenney. 2014. "Rural Women's Access to Financial Services: Credit, Savings, and Insurance." In *Gender in Agriculture: Closing the Knowledge Gap*, edited by A. R. Quisumbing, R. Meinzer-Dick, T. L. Raney, A. Croppenstedt, J. A. Behrman, and A. Peterman, 187–208. Rome: Food and Agriculture Organization of the United Nations.

Francois, J., and B. Hoekman. 2010. "Services Trade and Policy." *Journal of Economic Literature* 48 (September): 642–92.

Frey, C. B., and M. A. Osborne. 2017. "The Future of Employment: How Susceptible Are Jobs to Computerisation?" *Technological Forecasting and Social Change* 114 (January): 254–80.

Fussell, E. 2000. "Making Labor Flexible: The Recomposition of Tijuana's Maquiladora Female Labor Force." *Feminist Economics* 6 (3): 59–79.

Gailes, A., T. Gurevich, S. Shikher, and M. Tsigas. 2018. "Gender and Income Inequality in United States Tariff Burden." Economics Working Paper No. 2018-08-B, U.S. International Trade Commission, Washington, DC.

Gaskell J. C., J. C. Keyser, G. Boc, C. Cangiano, C. Soprano, R. Nkendah, D. Arias Carballo, and B. S. Rabarijohn. 2018. "Breaking Down the Barriers to Regional Agricultural Trade in Central Africa." World Bank, Washington DC.

Gaucher, D., J. Friesen, and A. C. Kay. 2011. "Evidence That Gendered Wording in Job Advertisements Exists and Sustains Gender Inequality." *Journal of Personality and Social Psychology* 101 (1): 109.

Ghani, E., and S. D. O'Connell. 2014. "Can Service Be a Growth Escalator in Low Income Countries?" Policy Research Working Paper 6971, World Bank, Washington, DC.

Goldin, C. 2014. "A Grand Gender Convergence: Its Last Chapter." *American Economic Review* 104 (4): 1091–119.

Goos, M., A. Manning, and A. Salomons. 2014. "Explaining Job Polarization: Routine-Biased Technological Change and Offshoring." *American Economic Review* 104 (8): 2509–26.

GSMA. 2018. "Connected Women—The Mobile Gender Gap Report 2018." GSM Association. https://www.gsma.com/mobilefordevelopment/wp-content/uploads/2018/04/GSMA_The_Mobile_Gender_Gap_Report_2018_32pp_WEBv7.pdf.

Guiso, L., F. Monte, P. Sapienza, and L. Zingales. 2008. "Culture, Gender, and Math." *Science* 320 (5880): 1164–65.

Heath, R., and A. M. Mobarak. 2015. "Manufacturing Growth and the Lives of Bangladeshi Women." *Journal of Development Economics* 115 (C): 1–15.

Hollweg, C. 2017. "The Labor Content of Vietnam's Exports." Unpublished manuscript, World Bank, Washington, DC.

Homewood, K., P. Chenevix Trench, and P. Kristjanson. 2009. "Staying Maasai? Pastoral Livelihoods, Diversification and the Role of Wildlife in Development." In *Staying Maasai? Livelihoods, Conservation and Development in East African Rangelands*, edited by K. Homewood, P. Chevenix Trench, and P. Kristjanson, New York: Springer

Huang, J., and D. J. Kisgen. 2013. "Gender and Corporate Finance: Are Male Executives Overconfident Relative to Female Executives?" *Journal of Financial Economics* 108 (3): 822–39.

Humphrey, J., and H. Schmitz. 2002. "How Does Insertion in Global Value Chains Affect Upgrading in Industry Clusters?" *Regional Studies* 36 (9): 1017–27.

Hyperwallet. 2017. "The Future of Gig Work Is Female: A Study on the Behaviour and Aspirations of Women in the Gig Economy." Hyperwallet. https://www.hyperwallet.com/app/uploads/HW_The_Future_of_Gig_Work_is_Female.pdf.

IFC (International Finance Corporation). 2014. "Striving for Business Success: Voices of Liberian Women Entrepreneurs." Project report, IFC, Washington DC.

ILO (International Labour Office). 2016. *Report IV: Decent Work in Global Supply Chains.* International Labour Conference, 105th Session. Geneva: International Labour Organization.

ITC (International Trade Centre). 2017. "New Pathways to E-Commerce: A Global MSME Competitiveness Survey." ITC, Geneva.

ITC (International Trade Centre) and World Bank Group. 2020. *Pakistan: Company Perspectives. An ITC Series on Non-tariff Measures.* Geneva: ITC.

ITU (International Telecommunications Union). 2016. "How Can We Close the Digital Gender Gap?" ITU News Magazine, Issue No. 04/2016. https://www.itu.int/dms_pub/itu-s/opb/gen/S-GEN-NEWS-2016-P4-PDF-E.pdf.

Jackson, S. M., A. L. Hillard, and T. R. Schneider. 2014. "Using Implicit Bias Training to Improve Attitudes toward Women in STEM." *Social Psychology of Education* 17 (3): 419–38.

Janse van Rensburg, C., C. Bezuidenhout, M. Matthee, and V. Stolzenburg. Forthcoming. "Globalization and Gender Inequality: Evidence from South Africa." WIDER Working Paper, United Nations University World Institute for Development Economics Research, Helsinki.

Jensen, R. T. 2012. "Do Labor Market Opportunities Affect Young Women's Work and Family Decisions? Experimental Evidence from India." *Quarterly Journal of Economics* 127 (2): 753–92.

Jiang, S., K. Schenke, J. S. Eccles, D. Xu, and M. Warschauer. 2018. "Cross-National Comparison of Gender Differences in the Enrollment in and Completion of Science, Technology, Engineering, and Mathematics Massive Open Online Courses." *PLOS ONE* 13 (9): e0202463.

Jomo, K. S. 2009. "Export-Oriented Industrialisation, Female Employment and Gender Wage Equity in East Asia." *Economic and Political Weekly* 44 (1): 41–49.

Juhn, C., G. Ujhelyi, and C. Villegas-Sanchez. 2013. "Trade Liberalization and Gender Inequality." *American Economic Review* 103 (3): 269–73.

Jürges, H. 2006. "Gender Ideology, Division of Housework, and the Geographic Mobility of Families." *Review of Economics of the Household* 4 (4): 299–323.

Kanze, D., L. Huang, M. A. Conley, and E. T. Higgins. 2017. "Male and Female Entrepreneurs Get Asked Different Questions by VC's and It Affects How Much Funding They Get." *Harvard Business Review,* June 27, 2017.

Kiefer, A. K., and D. Sekaquaptewa. 2007. "Implicit Stereotypes, Gender Identification, and Math-Related Outcomes: A Prospective Study of Female College Students." *Psychological Science* 18 (1): 13–18.

Kim, K-J., and C. J. Bonk. 2006. "The Future of Online Teaching and Learning in Higher Education: The Survey Says...." *Educause Quarterly,* No. 4. http://faculty.weber.edu/eamsel/Research%20Groups/On-line%20Learning/Bonk%20(2006).pdf.

Kimelberg, S. M., and L. A. Nicoll. 2012. "Business Location Decisions in the Medical Device Industry: Evidence from Massachusetts." *Economic Development Quarterly* 26 (1): 34–49.

Kleinjans, K. J. 2009. "Do Gender Differences in Preferences for Competition Matter for Occupational Expectations?" *Journal of Economic Psychology* 30 (5): 701–10.

Kodama, N., B. S. Javorcik, and Y. Abe. 2018. "Transplanting Corporate Culture across International Borders: Foreign Direct Investment and Female Employment in Japan." *The World Economy* 41 (5): 1148–65.

Kopp, D., D. Hangartner, and M. Siegenthaler. 2019. "Monitoring Hiring Discrimination through Online Recruitment Platforms." Unpublished manuscript, ETH Zurich.

Kricheli-Katz, T., and T. Regev. 2016. "How Many Cents on the Dollar? Women and Men in Product Markets." *Science Advances* 2 (2): e1500599.

Krieger-Boden, C., and A. Sorgner. 2018. "Labor Market Opportunities for Women in the Digital Age." *Economics: The Open-Access, Open-Assessment E-Journal* 12 (28): 1–8.

Kucera, D., and S. Tejani. 2014. "Feminizations, Defeminization, and Structural Change in Manufacturing." *World Development* 64 (December): 569–82.

Lambrecht, A., and C. Tucker. 2019. "Algorithmic Bias? An Empirical Study of Apparent Gender-Based Discrimination in the Display of STEM Career Ads." *Management Science* 65 (7): 2966–81.

Lan, J., and B. Shepherd. 2018. "Gender, Structural Transformation and Deindustrialization." Working Paper DTC-2018-5, Developing Trade Consultants, New York.

Lavy, V. 2008. "Do Gender Stereotypes Reduce Girls' or Boys' Human Capital Outcomes? Evidence from a Natural Experiment." *Journal of Public Economics* 92 (10): 2083–105.

Lavy, V., and E. Sand. 2018. "On the Origins of Gender Gaps in Human Capital: Short- and Long-Term Consequences of Teachers' Biases." *Journal of Public Economics* 167 (November): 263–79.

Lejárraga, I., H. L. Rizzo, H. Oberhofer, S. Stone, and B. Shepherd. 2014. "Small and Medium-Sized Enterprises in Global Markets: A Differential Approach for Services?" OECD Trade Policy Paper No. 165, OECD Publishing, Paris.

Lindley, J. 2012. "The Gender Dimension of Technical Change and the Role of Task Inputs." *Labour Economics* 19 (4): 516–26.

Lopez-Acevedo, G., and R. Robertson, eds. 2016. *Stitches to Riches? Apparel Employment, Trade, and Economic Development in South Asia.* Directions in Development. Washington DC: World Bank.

Maertens, M., and J. Swinnen. 2009. "Are African High-Value Horticulture Supply Chains Bearers of Gender Inequality?" Paper presented at the FAO-IFAD-ILO Workshop on Gaps, Trends and Current Research in Gender Dimensions of Agricultural and Rural Employment: Differentiated Pathways out of Poverty.

Marom, D., A. Robb, and O. Sade. 2016. "Gender Dynamics in Crowdfunding (Kickstarter): Evidence on Entrepreneurs, Investors, Deals and Taste-Based Discrimination." Working Paper. https://papers.ssrn.com/sol3/papers.cfm?abstract_id=2442954.

Martin, L. M., and L. T. Wright. 2005. "No Gender in Cyberspace? Empowering Entrepreneurship and Innovation in Female-Run ICT Small Firms." *International Journal of Entrepreneurial Behaviour and Research* 11 (2): 162–78.

Mendoza, A., G. Nayyar, and R. Piermartini. 2018. "Are the 'Poor' Getting Globalised?" Policy Research Working Paper 8609, World Bank, Washington, DC.

Microsoft. 2017. "Why Europe's Girls Aren't Studying STEM." Microsoft Publishing, Paris.

Milkman, K. L., M. Akinola, and D. Chugh. 2015. "What Happens Before? A Field Experiment Exploring How Pay and Representation Differentially Shape Bias on the Pathway into Organizations." *Journal of Applied Psychology* 100 (6): 1678.

Minetti, R., P. Murro, Z. Rotondi, and S. C. Zhu. 2019. "Financial Constraints, Firms' Supply Chains, and Internationalization." *Journal of the European Economic Association* 17 (2): 327–75.

Morton, F. S., F. Zettelmeyer, and J. Silva-Risso. 2003. "Consumer Information and Discrimination: Does the Internet Affect the Pricing of New Cars to Women and Minorities?" *Quantitative Marketing and Economics* 1 (1): 65–92.

Moss-Racusin, C. A., J. F. Dovidio, V. L. Brescoll, M. J. Graham, and J. Handelsman. 2012. "Science Faculty's Subtle Gender Biases Favor Male Students." *Proceedings of the National Academy of Sciences* 109 (41), 16474–79.

Muellbauer, J. 2020. "The Coronavirus Pandemic and US Consumption." VOX CEPR Policy Portal, April 11, 2020. https://voxeu.org/article/coronavirus-pandemic-and-us-consumption.

Muralidharan, K., and N. Prakash. 2017. "Cycling to School: Increasing Secondary School Enrollment for Girls in India." *American Economic Journal: Applied Economics* 9 (3): 321–50.

Muravyev, A., D. Schäfer, and O. Talavera. 2009. "Entrepreneurs' Gender and Financial Constraints: Evidence from International Data." *Journal of Comparative Economics* 37 (2): 270–86.

Nano, E., G. Nayyar, S. Rubinova, and V. Stolzenburg. 2019. "Services Liberalization and Educational Attainment: Evidence from India." Unpublished manuscript, World Trade Organization, Geneva.

Nelson, J. A. 2018. *Gender and Risk-Taking: Economics, Evidence, and Why the Answer Matters*. London: Routledge.

Ngai, L. R., and B. Petrongolo. 2017. "Gender Gaps and the Rise of the Service Economy." *American Economic Journal: Macroeconomics* 9 (4): 1–44.

Niederle, M., and L. Vesterlund. 2011. "Gender and Competition." *Annual Review of Economics* 3 (1): 601–30.

Nielsen. 2020. "Nielsen Investigates: 'Pandemic Pantries' Pressure Supply Chain amid COVID-19 Fears." Nielsen Insights, March 2, 2020. https://www.nielsen.com/us/en/insights/article/2020/nielsen-investigation-pandemic-pantries-pressure-supply-chain-amidst-covid-19-fears.

Nilsson, Patricia, and Emiko Terazono. 2020. "Can Fast Fashion's $2.5tn Supply Chain Be Stitched Back Together?" Financial Times, May 17, 2020. https://www.ft.com/content/62dc687e-d15f-46e7-96df-ed7d00f8ca55.

OECD (Organisation for Economic Co-operation and Development). 2015. "What Lies Behind Gender Inequality in Education?" PISA in Focus No. 49, OECD Publishing, Paris.

———. 2017. *The Pursuit of Gender Equality: An Uphill Battle*. Paris: OECD Publishing.

OECD and World Bank Group. 2015. "Inclusive Global Value Chains." Report prepared for submission to the G-20 Trade Ministers Meeting, Istanbul, October 6, OECD and World Bank Group.

OECD and WTO (World Trade Organization). 2013. *Aid for Trade at a Glance: Connecting to Value Chains*. Paris and Geneva: OECD and WTO.

Orkoh, E., and V. Stolzenburg. 2020. "Gender-Specific Differences in Geographical Mobility: Evidence from Ghana."

Staff Working Paper ERSD-2020-01, World Trade Organization, Geneva.

Paton, Elizabeth. 2020. "'Our Situation is Apocalyptic': Bangladesh Garment Workers Face Ruin." New York Times, March 31, 2020. https://www.nytimes.com/2020/03/31/fashion/coronavirus-bangladesh.html.

Pergelova, A., T. Manolova, R. Simeonova-Ganeva, and D. Yordanova. 2019. "Democratizing Entrepreneurship? Digital Technologies and the Internationalization of Female-Led SMEs." *Journal of Small Business Management* 57 (1): 14–39.

Petro, Greg. 2020. "Coronavirus and Shopping Behavior: Men And Women React Differently." *Forbes,* March 13, 2020. https://www.forbes.com/sites/gregpetro/2020/03/13/coronavirus-and-shopping-behavior-men-and-women-react-differently.

Pickles, J., and S. Godfrey. 2012. "Economic and Social Upgrading in Global Apparel Production Networks." Revised Summit Briefing 6.2 from the Capturing the Gains in Value Chains Summit, Cape Town, South Africa, December 3–5, 2012.

Pope, D. G., and J. R. Sydnor. 2010. "Geographic Variation in the Gender Differences in Test Scores." *Journal of Economic Perspectives* 24 (2): 95–108.

Resnick, P., and R. Zeckhauser. 2002. "Trust among Strangers in Internet Transactions: Empirical Analysis of e-Bay's Reputation System." In *The Economics of the Internet and E-Commerce,* Volume 11, edited by M. R. Baye, 127–57. Emerald Group Publishing Ltd.

Rezabakhsh, B., D. Bornemann, U. Hansen, and U. Schrader. 2006. "Consumer Power: A Comparison of the Old Economy and the Internet Economy." *Journal of Consumer Policy* 29 (1): 3–36.

Rocha, N., and D. Winkler. 2019. "Trade and Female Labor Participation: Stylized Facts Using a Global Dataset." Policy Research Working Paper 9098, World Bank, Washington, DC.

Rodrik, D. 2016. "Premature Deindustrialization." *Journal of Economic Growth* 21 (1): 1–33.

Rosenbaum, G. O. 2017. "Female Entrepreneurial Networks and Foreign Market Entry." *Journal of Small Business and Enterprise Development* 24 (1): 119–35.

Rubiano-Matulevich, E., and M. Viollaz. 2019. "Gender Differences in Time Use: Allocating Time between the Market and the Household." Policy Research Working Paper 8981, World Bank, Washington, DC.

Ruppert Bulmer, E. N., C. H. Hollweg, D. Lederman, and L. D. Rojas Alvarado. 2014. *Sticky Feet: How Labor Market Frictions Shape the Impact of International Trade on Jobs and Wages.* Directions in Development. Washington, DC: World Bank Group.

Sachetti, F. C., A. Hunt, C. Currie, F. Filgueira, G. D. Langou, M. Beneke de Sanfeliu, S. Gammage, R. Hayashi, and M. Thomas. 2019. "A Gendered Perspective on Changing Demographics: Implications for Labor, Financial and Digital Equity." Paper prepared for Think 20 Japan 2019, March 30, Tokyo.

Seguino, S. 2000. "The Effects of Structural Change and Economic Liberalization on Gender Wage Differentials in South Korea and Taiwan." *Cambridge Journal of Economics* 24 (4): 437–59.

Seric, Adnan, and Deborah Winkler. 2020. "COVID-19 Could Spur Automation and Reverse Globalisation—to Some Extent." VOX CEPR Policy Portal, April 28, 2020. https://voxeu.org/article/covid-19-could-spur-automation-and-reverse-globalisation-some-extent.

Seror, M., R. Record, and J. Clarke. 2018. "Glass Barriers: Constraints to Women's Small-Scale, Cross-Border Trade in Cambodia and Lao PDR." In *Trade and Poverty Reduction: New Evidence of Impacts in Developing Countries*, edited by World Bank Group and World Trade Organization, 148–173. Geneva: World Trade Organization.

Shepherd, B., and S. Stone. 2012. "Global Production Networks and Employment: A Developing Country Perspective." OECD Trade Policy Papers, Organisation for Economic Co-operation and Development, Paris.

Slaughter, M. J. 2013. "American Companies and Global Supply Networks: Driving US Economic Growth and Jobs by Connecting the World." U.S. Council for International Business and the United States Council Federation, New York.

Song, L., S. Appleton, and J. Knight. 2006. "Why Do Girls in Rural China Have Lower School Enrollment?" *World Development* 34 (9): 1639–53.

Staritz, C., and J. G. Reis. 2013. *Global Value Chains, Economic Upgrading and Gender: Case Studies of the Horticulture, Tourism, and Call Center Industries*. Washington, DC: World Bank.

Steffens, M. C., P. Jelenec, and P. Noack. 2010. "On the Leaky Math Pipeline: Comparing Implicit Math-Gender Stereotypes and Math Withdrawal in Female and Male Children and Adolescents." *Journal of Educational Psychology* 102 (4): 947.

Suri, T., and W. Jack. 2016. "The Long-Run Poverty and Gender Impacts of Mobile Money." *Science* 354 (6317): 1288–92.

Tang, H., and Y. Zhang. 2017. "Do Multinationals Transfer Culture? Evidence on Female Employment in China." CESifo Working Paper 6295, CESifo, Munich.

Twining-Ward, L. 2019. "World Bank We-Fi WeTour Women in Tourism Enterprise Survey for Sierra Leone and Ghana." Unpublished manuscript.

UNWTO (United Nations World Tourism Organization). 2020. "International Tourist Arrivals Could Fall by 20–30% in 2020." UNWTO, Madrid. https://www.unwto.org/news/international-tourism-arrivals-could-fall-in-2020.

USITC (United States International Trade Commission). 2010. "Small and Medium-Sized Enterprises: Characteristics and Performance." Investigation No. 332-510, USITC Publication 4189, USITC, Washington, DC.

Vahter, P., and J. Masso. 2019. "The Contribution of Multinationals to Wage Inequality: Foreign Ownership and the Gender Pay Gap." *Review of World Economics* 155 (1): 105–48.

van der Vleuten, M., S. Steinmetz, and H. van de Werfhorst. 2019. "Gender Norms and STEM: The Importance of Friends for Stopping Leakage from the STEM Pipeline." *Educational Research and Evaluation* 24 (6–7): 1–20.

WHO (World Health Organization). 2013. *Global and Regional Estimates of Violence against Women: Prevalence and Health Effects of Intimate Partner Violence and Non-partner Sexual Violence*. Geneva: WHO.

World Bank. 2011. "Facilitating Cross-Border Trade between the DRC and Neighbors in the Great Lakes Region of Africa: Improving Conditions for Poor Traders." Report No. 62992-AFR, World Bank, Washington, DC.

———. 2012. *World Development Report 2012: Gender Equality and Development*. Washington DC: World Bank.

———. 2014a. "World–Global Financial Inclusion (Global Findex) Database 2014." Report, World Bank, Washington,

DC. https://microdata.worldbank.org/index.php/catalog/2512.

———. 2014b. "The Fruit of Her Labor: Promoting Gender-Equitable Agribusiness in Papua New Guinea." Policy Note, World Bank, Washington, DC.

———. 2015. "Great Lakes Trade Facilitation Project. Project Appraisal Document." World Bank, Washington, DC.

———. 2016. *World Development Report 2016: Digital Dividends Overview.* Washington, DC: World Bank.

———. 2019. *World Development Report 2020: Trading for Development in the Age of Global Value Chains.* Washington, DC: World Bank.

World Bank Group. 2016. "Integrating Sierra Leone's Small-Scale Traders into the Formal Economy." World Bank Group, Washington DC, May.

———. 2017. "South Caucasus Gender Assessment Technical Assistance Report: Tourism and Hospitality Value Chain Analysis—Georgia." World Bank Group, Washington, DC.

———. 2018a. *Women, Business, and the Law 2018.* Washington DC: World Bank Group.

———. 2018b. "Issues of Inclusivity: Ensuring Inclusive Growth from Trade and RVC Integration." Background paper to ASA Support to SADC Industrialization, World Bank, Washington, DC.

———. 2019. "Profiting from Parity: Unlocking the Potential of Women's Businesses in Africa." World Bank Group, Washington, DC.

World Bank Group and World Trade Organization. 2015. "The Role of Trade in Ending Poverty." World Trade Organization, Geneva.

———. 2018. *Trade and Poverty Reduction: New Evidence of Impacts in Developing Countries.* Geneva: World Trade Organization.

WTO (World Trade Organization). 2016. *World Trade Report 2016: Levelling the Trading Field for SMEs.* Geneva: WTO.

———. 2017. *World Trade Report 2017: Trade, Technology and Jobs.* Geneva: WTO.

———. 2018. *World Trade Report 2018: The Future of World Trade—How Digital Technologies Are Transforming Global Commerce.* Geneva: WTO.

———. 2019. *World Trade Report 2019: The Future of Services Trade.* Geneva: World Trade Organization.

———. 2020a. "The Economic Impact of COVID-19 on Women in Vulnerable Sectors and Economies."WTO Information Note, WTO, Geneva. https://www.wto.org/english/tratop_e/covid19_e/covid19_e.htm.

———. 2020b. "Trade in Services in the Context of COVID-19." WTO Information Note, WTO, Geneva, May 28. https://www.wto.org/english/tratop_e/covid19_e/services_report_e.pdf.

Chapter 3

POLICY RESPONSES TO PROMOTE *WOMEN'S* BENEFITS FROM TRADE

Key messages

- Removing trade barriers that impede women's access to international markets can contribute to enhancing women's participation in trade and benefits from trade. Women would benefit from lowered tariffs and nontariff barriers and improved trade facilitation and access to trade finance.

- Women's participation in and benefit from trade is enhanced by maintaining a predictable trading environment underpinned by World Trade Organization rules. Ongoing World Trade Organization negotiations and initiatives related to services, agriculture, electronic commerce, and micro, small, and medium enterprises could further empower women in the world economy.

- Trade policies alone cannot always increase women's participation in trade. Complementary policies are essential to improve women's capacity to engage in trade by improving their access to education, financial resources, digital technologies, information, and infrastructure.

- Well-targeted and adequately financed labor market adjustment policies can help women maximize the benefits of trade-opening and mitigate the potential risks associated with trade openness.

- Ultimately, well-designed and well-implemented strategies to enhance women's benefits from trade hinge on the availability of relevant gender-related data. The lack of sex-disaggregated data, however, has hindered the ability of policy makers to identify the differential impacts trade policy may have on women and men. Both the World Bank and the World Trade Organization are now leading efforts to address shortcomings in data. This joint report will enable future research and policy making to consider the impact of trade on gender equality.

This chapter looks at efforts by governments, civil society, the private sector, and multilateral institutions to address trade and women's economic empowerment. It prioritizes actions that could be most effective in opening markets for women and building their capacity to trade. It also identifies risks that trade poses to women as workers and proposes mitigating policies. The chapter concludes with a discussion of efforts by the World Bank and the World Trade Organization (WTO) to address trade and gender.

Priorities to increase market access for *women*

Trade policy itself is a critical determinant in lowering the trade costs faced by women and improving women's access to international markets. Discriminatory trade policies that make women-dominated industries less competitive and productive than their male counterparts are widespread. Such trade barriers should be removed if trade benefits to women are to be achieved. In that context, policy makers need to address tariffs and nontariff measures (NTMs) that hurt women traders, workers, and consumers; trade facilitation measures that enable women to trade as safely and easily as men; and access to trade finance that empowers women to access international markets.

Lowering tariff and nontariff barriers on trade in goods

Tariffs and NTMs impede women's participation in trade. Better trade policies on tariffs and NTMs would enhance women's access to new opportunities in international markets, including services trade, digital trade, and participation in global value chains (GVCs). With more affordable production inputs and everyday consumer goods, women will be able to compete on a more equal footing with men.

Although most applied tariffs are relatively low, particularly in high-income countries, tariffs on some products that governments consider to be sensitive remain high. Female workers, particularly in developing economies, are affected by stubbornly high tariffs on agricultural goods. Regions such as Sub-Saharan Africa still have high tariffs on most goods. Tariffs on textiles, which are subject to higher tariffs than similar manufactured goods, strike a double blow against women as both the biggest consumers and the most frequent workers in the sector (Taylor and Dar 2015).

Eliminating the gender-related tariff differentials (for the same products) or reducing or removing altogether the relevant applied tariffs would help women business owners to access more and bigger markets. Lower tariffs would also allow women entrepreneurs or women suppliers to GVCs to have access to higher-quality inputs at world prices and therefore would increase their productivity. In the agricultural sector, lower tariffs may help resolve existing discrimination by helping women to access inputs, such as seeds, pesticides, and fertilizers, thereby improving the quality of their crops, enabling them to diversify into alternative crops or activities, and mitigating the gender gap in productivity.

Unjustified, discriminatory, and nontransparent NTMs also hurt women traders, particularly small traders. NTMs raise the compliance costs associated with regulations and standards. Technical regulations and standards that are well-designed and less trade-restrictive improve firm competitiveness and mitigate trade costs.[1]

NTMs are rarely designed with any gender consideration, and widespread disparities exist in how NTMs affect women and men (UNECE 2018). At their most extreme, NTMs can exclude from workplaces women who cannot adequately use specific protective equipment designed for men's body types.[2] For instance, most protective equipment, including goggles and full body suits, is based on the size and characteristics of male individuals. Failure to reflect physical differences can adversely affect the safety of women workers.

Several measures that can alleviate these biases have been identified and adopted by some economies and standardizing bodies. Promoting the participation of women in standard setting and more actively consulting women in the implementation of standards can improve how those standards reflect women's interests and needs. This includes developing and sharing best practices on how to account for biological and cultural differences in standards development and implementation, developing gender indicators and criteria that can be used in standards development, and identifying and undertaking actions to ensure that standards contribute to gender equality.

Reducing barriers to services trade

The services trade faces higher costs compared to trade in goods, and these higher costs disproportionately affect women. The need to be close to customers and the existence of complex policy regimes raise costs for suppliers and consumers of services (WTO 2019). Lowering trade costs in services can accelerate development and create opportunities for women as traders, workers, and consumers in both traditional and digital trade.

Services trade policies aimed at protecting domestic markets reduce competition, hinder foreign direct investment, and reduce firm competitiveness. A lack of competition in services decreases the productivity of services firms and increases costs. Services play a key role as production inputs for farmers, manufacturing firms, and other services firms. When services such as transport, finance, and energy are protected from competition, the productivity growth (and thus income) of an entire economy can be negatively affected. This effect has serious consequences for women, because services employ more women than manufacturing does. Efficient services can also help address some of the constraints that women face. More efficient and less costly transport services and financial services, for example, help with women's mobility and financial constraints, respectively.

The types of policies that remove trade barriers differ depending on the mode of supplying services (Sauvé 2019). Policies promoting traditional cross-border supply of services are of particular importance for enhancing women's economic opportunities. Services sectors, such as education, health, and social care services, are experiencing a rapid expansion thanks to digitalization and medical tourism. In developing countries, women who are constrained financially and who are less time-flexible than men could benefit from improved access to foreign educational services without having to leave home. In that context, policies establishing a clear domestic legal digital framework can promote services delivered online by accelerating firms' and consumers' access to secure, interoperable, and digitized services and payments. Electronic commerce (e-commerce) is particularly important for women because selling goods through digital channels can overcome some of the constraints that women face when exporting, including their time and mobility constraints.

Lifting restrictions on the ability to consume services abroad can also benefit women as consumers. Women would gain through increased access, quality, and diversity of available services, including medical and educational services. The removal of certain legal restrictions, such as the ban on traveling abroad without a legal male guardian, nonrecognition of foreign diploma requirements, or nonreimbursement of health services obtained abroad, could further contribute to women's economic empowerment in the country providing the services because women tend to work in the services, such as tourism or health services, typically consumed abroad.

Policies facilitating, among others, the establishment of affiliate, subsidiary, or representative offices of a foreign-owned company can benefit female workers. Foreign firms (through foreign direct investment) are more likely to employ, pay higher wages to, and enhance career development prospects for women.

The temporary movement of people to supply services in another country could increase opportunities for women to supply their services abroad. Bilateral agreements can promote the international recruitment of personnel in specific sectors, including those in which women might be predominantly employed, such as health care and social work.[3] Although most of these arrangements are limited and cover only a very small proportion of doctors and nurses, they may provide women in both developed and developing economies with new work opportunities abroad, higher wages, and greater knowledge, skills, and experience. The effectiveness of labor arrangements ultimately depends on whether they are able to avoid gender-based discrimination in recruitment and employment, overcome cultural barriers, and not leave countries of origin facing a shortage of skilled professionals (that is, brain drain).

Enhancing cross-border trade through trade facilitation and trade finance

Women engaged in moving goods across borders face a number of challenges, including time and skill constraints, limited access to trade finance, and higher exposure to extortion and physical harassment. These challenges are particularly pronounced for small-scale women traders in developing and least-developed economies. Reducing constraints and challenges for women engaged in cross-border trade can strengthen their trading opportunities, including participation in GVCs; expand their income source; and enable them to engage in larger-scale formal trade.

The design and implementation of effective trade facilitation measures hinge on identifying the specific challenges and barriers faced by cross-border traders, including women (WTO 2015). The adoption and implementation of domestic policies in compliance with commitments established under the WTO Trade Facilitation Agreement (TFA) can be a catalyst for women traders by creating predictable and efficient customs processes, reducing clearance times and trade costs, reducing the opportunity for fraudulent practices at the border, and increasing the involvement of women in trade facilitation decision mechanisms.[4]

Transparent, nondiscriminatory, and easy-to-access information on tariffs, taxes, rules, and procedures is a critical determinant of export competitiveness, and even more so for female traders for whom time and access to trade networks are more limited. The establishment of a National Trade Facilitation Committee in charge of facilitating both domestic coordination and implementation of the TFA provisions can ensure that women participate in the design, implementation, monitoring, and evaluation of trade facilitation measures by providing comments on proposed rules related to the movement of goods. In Zambia, where over 70 percent of small cross-border traders are women, the cross-border traders association is involved in various consultation meetings within the National Trade Facilitation Committee. The guarantee of a right to appeal customs administrative decisions provided in the TFA can also benefit women traders, who can be confronted in some cases with an unbalanced amount of discretionary power from customs authorities at the border.

In parallel, reducing bureaucratic and cumbersome border procedures using digital technologies, as supported by the TFA, can enable some women to work from an office or home instead of having to use intermediaries. Electronic payment also reduces face-to-face interaction with customs officials, which could reduce the level of harassment and bribes paid, a particular concern of women traders. Women traders without access to information and communications technology (ICT) can still benefit from harmonized

Box 3.1 The beneficial effects of trade facilitation for women

In the Great Lakes Region of Africa, small-scale cross-border trade plays a major role, providing goods, services, jobs, and incomes. Women constitute a very large proportion of this cross-border trade, which is often a critical source of livelihoods for women and their families (ILO 2013; Lesser and Moisé-Leeman 2009). Yet the potential of small-scale cross-border trade to increase women's income and job creation, while simultaneously reducing poverty, is not being fully realized because of the unpredictable and insecure trading environment.

With support from the World Bank, the governments of the Democratic Republic of Congo, Rwanda, and Uganda, in cooperation with the Common Market for Eastern and Southern Africa, are implementing the Great Lakes Trade Facilitation Project to reduce the risks at the border, facilitate cross-border trade, and increase the capacity for commerce, especially for small-scale and women traders.

The project provides support to improve border infrastructure to cater to the needs of small-scale traders (such as pedestrian lanes, lighting, and fencing), construct border markets, simplify policies and procedures for small-scale traders, and provide extensive training and capacity building of traders and customs officials. The project also supports the implementation of a Charter for Cross-Border Traders, which establishes a basic set of rights and obligations for traders and officials to enable traders to safely use the official border post and avoid unwarranted prosecution and goods confiscation. These rules are expected to encourage behavioral change, enhance processing times, facilitate trade, and ultimately make the border a friendly environment.

In December 2018, the World Bank conducted a pilot study to collect information from traders on the challenges to trading across borders in the Great Lakes Region and the impacts such trading can have on a household's access to nutrition, health, and education. Focus group discussions with small-scale traders and interviews with female small-scale traders, border officials, and trade information desk officers revealed that harassment is lower at border crossings subject to project interventions compared to a border crossing where the project has not been active. The presence of a trade information desk officer also helped mitigate harassment by border officials. Most traders reported that their trading activities have increased their quality of life, allowing them to increase the nutritional intake for themselves and their families as well as allowing improved access to health care and to education for their children.

and streamlined customs procedures (box 3.1). These trade facilitation measures can be complemented by capacity-building activities for traders, customized for different gender needs, such as awareness programs on traders' rights and obligations and digital training. More generally, trade facilitation measures can be complemented by other policies, including those aimed at improving border infrastructure—such as pedestrian lanes, safe and affordable accommodation, childcare facilities, storage, and proper sanitation facilities—to cater to the needs of women small-scale traders.[5]

Limited financial inclusion, including access to trade finance, is a global problem that affects women disproportionately and can limit opportunities for women traders. Improving women's access to trade finance can contribute to empowering women-owned and managed firms. Trade finance is an important source of short-term credit typically used by companies that export or import goods. Smaller traders, in particular women, often have very limited access to loans to cover the cost of goods they plan to buy or sell, which can prevent them from trading. Even with a confirmed order, banks often do not provide loans for these types of transactions. In order to receive such loans, smaller traders must have a strong trading record and be in a position to pay relatively high interest (Sachetti et al. 2019; WTO 2014, 2016).

In this context, programs that build up traders' credit histories can help women traders overcome some of the disadvantages they face because of a lack of access to credit. The harmonization of financial regulations within a region can further support the comparability of credit information and histories in the regional financial market and expand women traders' potential financing sources (von Hagen 2015). In parallel, the rise of financial technologies (fintech) is seen by some experts as a potential solution to the finance gap for micro, small, and medium enterprises (MSMEs), including women-owned companies, provided they have access to and knowledge about ICT (DiCaprio, Yao, and Simms 2017; Jenik 2017). Fintech encompasses a wide variety of financial instruments, including peer-to-peer lending and crowdfunding, that could enhance digital performance and alleviate some of the challenges to cross-border e-commerce faced by MSMEs, including women-owned firms (Suominen 2018).

Priorities to increase *women's* capacity to engage in international trade

The extent to which women can take advantage of trade opportunities, including in trade in services, digital trade, and GVCs, depends on more than trade policies. Investments in education, health systems, and infrastructure can provide women the human capital they require to benefit from trade, particularly as workers and traders. On a macro level, functioning capital and labor markets, macroeconomic stability, and effective governance, including the reduction of gender imbalances, are preconditions for the development of trade.

For women to fully benefit from trade, changes in sociocultural attitudes are often necessary. Trade policies cannot overcome discriminatory legal and sociocultural barriers that prevent women from opening a bank account, running their own businesses, working in certain sectors, or crossing borders. Such discriminatory legal and sociocultural barriers often raise the costs of formalization for women traders and female entrepreneurs, forcing them to earn a living through the informal sector. Informality reduces job security and access to resources, including training and financial support.

Targeted policies can help women overcome these challenges; maximize the benefits of trade opening, including services trade, digital trade, and GVC participation; and access productive resources. Most of these policies are designed to reduce domestic market inefficiencies and beyond-the-border constraints affecting women, such as access to education, financial resources, digital technologies, and information (table 3.1). A well-designed set of complementary policies hinges on the extent to which these measures are coordinated and cohesive, or at least not contradictory.

Some policies most relevant to women are not gender-specific. For instance, programs establishing national identity systems can also facilitate access to finance because in most countries opening a financial account requires a legal proof of identity. This challenge is particularly relevant for women in low-income countries because they tend not to have a formal identity document as men do. Other policies might be designed specifically to target women. For instance, some education initiatives support the construction of all-women public engineering colleges in less developed areas to address the fact that in some regions women often cannot continue education because of social taboos related to studying in mixed-gender colleges (Ghose 2019). Depending on the issue at hand, gender-specific policies may complement existing non-gender-specific policies. Similarly, some policies may target women in general, whereas other policies may focus on a subpopulation of women based on specific socioeconomic or geographical criteria. The choice to cover some women and not others is intended to acknowledge that women are not a homogeneous group.

Some complementary policies, such as education policies, have been extensively analyzed through a gender lens to maximize their economic impact on women. For many other policies, however, such as access to digital technology, no or limited information exists about their gender impacts. Part of this lack of information is due to the absence of relevant sex-disaggregated data, which prevents impact assessments for women and men. Despite this lack of information, table 3.1 provides insights on the specific issues and measures that some governments have considered in order to target women.

Table 3.1 Building women's capacity to trade—some examples of policies

Capacity improvement area	Policies and actions
• **Developing human capital:** Promoting women's access to basic and higher education enhances women's role in trade and contributes to the economy's success in competitive international markets.	• Basic and targeted training, such as capacity-building activities to adopt, develop, and spread new technology. • Training focused on trade issues, such as implementation and development of customs procedures, technical barriers to trade, sanitary and phytosanitary measures, and enforcement of intellectual property rights (Coche, Kotschwar, and Salazar-Xirinachs 2006). • In-kind conditional cash transfers as an incentive to make students stay enrolled in secondary school (Muralidharan and Prakash 2013). • Grants to families who send their girls to school; provision of textbooks, meals, and health care combined with scholarships and awareness campaigns (Khandker, Pitt, and Fuwa 2013; Schultz 2004). • Flexible school schedules to accommodate girls' responsibilities for taking care of their younger siblings or attending to household chores. • Building and staffing convenient and locally located schools to reduce commuting time (Herz and Sperling 2004). • Promotion of science, technology, engineering, and mathematics (STEM) curricula and teaching girls computing skills, such as programming, robotics, and web designs. • Mentoring courses for women to boost their self-confidence (Bekh 2014), especially female mentors in STEM fields (Dasgupta and Dennehy 2017; Dasgupta and Stout 2014).
• **Improving access to digital technology:** Developing and expanding digital infrastructure, including high-speed broadband networks in both cities and rural areas can often be a precondition for women entrepreneurs, workers, and consumers to gain from new trading opportunities.	• Equipping women with digital devices (mobile phones or computers), in particular in rural areas. • Information and communication technology training courses to improve women's ability to understand, use, modify, and create digital content and services (Omiunu 2019; WTO 2018).

Table 3.1, continued

• **Better access to finance:** Improving women's access to finance, including by addressing disparities in access to financing and legal rights between men and women, can bring significant improvements for female traders and consumers.	• Abrogation of discriminatory legal provisions, including laws discriminating against women in relation to opening a bank account and registering their businesses. • Specific loan programs with preferential terms regarding collateral requirements, loan maturity, and interest rate to make more financial funds available to women operating in the informal sector. • Loan programs complemented with tailored business, financial, and marketing training. • Gender-responsive budget in national financial sector plans based on data on women's financial inclusion. • Simplified procedure to open a deposit account and reform of credit reporting systems to recognize alternative forms of collateral, such as reputation based on repayment histories. • National identity systems facilitating the establishment and provision of legal proof of identity required to open a financial account.
• **Enhancing access to trade-related information:** Gathering and disseminating trade-related information on market conditions, prices, and the quality of goods can reduce trade costs and help women access new trade opportunities.	• Publicly accessible website containing information and explanations of key trade provisions of trade agreements of particular relevance to micro, small, and medium enterprises. • Appointment of "gender focal points" at various levels of government and state institutions in charge of dealing with their respective institution's gender mainstreaming strategy. • Trade fairs and workshops bringing together business owners and buyers operating in specific sectors. • Trade promotion programs targeted at women exporters providing training as well as contact with international buyers and access to international business platforms (Frohmann 2017).
• **Improving access to infrastructure:** Investment in infrastructure and measures promoting nondiscriminatory access to infrastructure can help ensure a level playing field for companies and reduce the barriers facing small firms.	• Improved transport and logistical infrastructure, including in remote and rural areas. • Setting up a globally recognized conformity assessment infrastructure to enhance capability and resources to meet technical and sanitary and phytosanitary requirements.

Mitigating the risks from trade faced by *women*

Economic openness, increased trade and investment, and technological change create greater wealth and opportunities. They also result in job contraction in sectors that become less competitive. Trade helps improve economic efficiency by enhancing the productivity of certain firms, by allowing for more specialization, or by providing access to a broader range of inputs. For those benefits to materialize, however, labor and capital need to be reallocated from less productive to more productive activities, firms, or sectors in each country. For some workers, this may mean losing their jobs, possibly going through a spell of unemployment, and often training to get a new job in a different field.

The more smoothly this adjustment process takes place, the lower the costs for displaced workers and the greater the net gains to society. But workers who do not necessarily have the right skills or live in the expanding regions may not be able to transition quickly or at all. These frictions are a drag on the economy, and particularly the labor market, and can lead to social or political unrest. Even if on average the effects of trade are positive, workers with inadequate and outdated skills in affected regions or sectors can suffer important and persistent losses.

A broad range of tailored and coordinated measures targeted primarily, but not exclusively, at the labor market can make economies more responsive to change and support women workers and entrepreneurs in adjusting to new economic conditions (Bacchetta, Milet, and Monteiro 2019). These are known as adjustment policies, which refers broadly to measures taken to make the labor market and the economy in general more efficient and responsive to economic and technological changes by lowering the cost of reallocating resources.

Although no trade adjustment program targeted specifically toward women workers is currently in place, trade adjustment programs can still be relevant to maximize women workers' gains from trade. Well-targeted and adequately financed adjustment assistance through a mix of labor, competitiveness, and compensation policies can help workers manage the cost of adjusting to trade, while making sure that the economy captures as much as possible the benefits from these changes (IMF, World Bank Group, and WTO 2017). Beyond improving economic efficiency, adjustment policies offer a way to compensate those who lose out from the dislocation or to maintain political support for innovation and trade openness.

Adjustment policies may be general and designed to help workers adjust to economic change, no matter its initial cause, or may be designed to address a specific economic change, such as trade openness (WTO 2017). Adjustment policies may involve active or passive labor market policies. Active labor market policies, on the one hand, aim to increase the likelihood that unemployed workers will find new jobs, through training or job-search assistance, for example. Access to education provides women not only with the skills to seize existing trading opportunities but also with the skills to adjust to new economic conditions. Passive labor market policies, on the other hand, help by providing financial support to workers who have lost their jobs. Views diverge somewhat about the effectiveness of the latter, but training programs in both developed and developing economies tend to have stronger effects on women (Card, Kluve, and Weber 2018; Escudero et al. 2019). The provision of career counseling and caregiving activities to help balance family and work life can be particularly relevant for women workers.

Compared to industrialized countries, a larger share of the workforce in developing countries is employed in the informal sector, in agriculture, and in state-owned enterprises. Adjustment programs in developing countries need to take into

Credit: © AYA images/ Shutterstock.com. Used with permission; further permission required for reuse.

account the particular challenges that arise from those sectors. Self-employment and the informal sector can provide an important buffer for workers who lose their jobs in formal employment (Goldberg and Pavcnik 2003; Lima, Ponczek, and Ulyssea 2019).

Although formally gender-neutral, adjustment programs may include de facto biases against women. Women may be adversely affected if the adjustment programs exclude some sectors in which female employment is concentrated. Because women might not be well-equipped or might not have received prior training to take up jobs in a different sector, this exclusion may make them prone to look for jobs in the same sector in which they were initially working and thus they may remain out of the program's reach. Similarly, a limited allocation of funds for training purposes may be a constraint for women who are displaced from female-dominated industries and who do not have access to the training that would help them secure jobs in male-dominated sectors (Vijaya 2007).

Because most female-dominated sectors are made up of micro and small firms, a de facto gender bias may also arise if the adjustment program covers only large or medium firms or requires a large number of workers in the same sector in one or more neighboring regions to be eligible for support. Similarly, an adjustment program that sets the number of weekly working hours required to qualify for the program higher than women's average number of hours may be biased against women—who make up a larger share of part-time workers. Programs that consider re-entrant workers as new entrants and require the completion of a large minimum number of annual work hours might also be problematic for women, who often have to leave their jobs temporarily to fulfill care responsibilities and want to reenter the labor force later (Townson and Hayes 2007).

Programs that propose classroom and on-the-job training but require the participants to pay the cost (based on their average pay) could be considered more costly for women, because they may have to pay for childcare while they attend the training (Attanasio, Kugler, and Meghir 2011). Training programs may promote gender stereotypes if they provide training only for female-dominated occupations—such as care activities, hairdressing, and cooking—preventing women from acquiring the necessary technical skills to enter male-dominated industries (Sansonetti 2016). Designing effective, nonbiased programs therefore requires analyzing the labor market situation, including the characteristics of participating women and the reasons behind gender gaps in employment outcomes (see chapter 1) (CEPAL 2016; Cho and Kwon 2010; Del Boca 2015; World Bank 2012).

Collective efforts to promote *women's* economic empowerment

Over time, governments, international organizations, and some private sector companies have incorporated a gender-trade perspective into their activities. This practice has been spurred in part by pressure from civil society—particularly women's organizations, which have been active in raising their concerns related to gender and trade at the national, regional, and international levels. These initiatives demonstrate the importance of incorporating a gender perspective into the promotion of inclusive economic growth.

Gender and trade policy formulation

Several governments have used unilateral and bilateral trade policy to promote women's empowerment. In preparation for trade negotiations, some countries have chosen to conduct or are required to undertake impact assessments of potential trade agreements. In some cases, a gender dimension is added to the analysis.[6] Most sustainability impact assessments undertaken by the European Union include some gender aspects, although the gender analysis has not always been carried out in a systematic way (Viilup 2015). More generally, some national, regional, and local governments use a gender impact assessment system to determine whether any new law, policy, or program is likely to have an impact on the state of equality between women and men.

In a few economies, ministries and governmental agencies responsible for gender equity and women's empowerment are involved in trade policy formulation and implementation. Ensuring the equal representation of women and men in political and decision-making structures can better reflect and address the concerns of women as producers, workers, and consumers. Some governments, such as those of Canada and the European Union, have also set up transparency mechanisms to collect stakeholders' views, including from women's organizations, about ongoing trade negotiations. In the case of Canada, all new programs, policies, and initiatives, including trade policies, include a gender-based analysis (Department of Finance, Canada 2019). The information collected along with the results of ex ante impact assessments can be used to identify products and market segments with positive implications for women. This information can also be used to elaborate complementary policies, such as adjustment assistance, to mitigate adverse impacts some women might experience because of trade policy.

Governments have also used trade relationships to provide incentives for their suppliers to improve gender standards. Several countries have adopted trading schemes that impose lower tariffs to imports from certain developing and least-developed economies. These nonreciprocal preferential access schemes cover goods produced, exported, and consumed prominently by women, such as clothing. Although most of these schemes do not include any provisions explicitly related to women, the African Growth Opportunity Act (AGOA) adopted by the United States and the Generalized System of Preferences (GSP) scheme established by the European Union include explicit gender-related provisions.

The AGOA, signed into law in 2000, grants duty-free tariffs on all goods manufactured in eligible African countries and imported into the United States. Section 106 of the AGOA further requires the "promotion of the role of women in social and economic development in Sub-Saharan Africa." Many African women workers have benefitted from the scheme, with the creation of about 300,000 jobs between 2000 and 2009, most of which were in labor-intensive industries that employ a large number of women (Paez et al. 2010). In addition, section 123 of the AGOA requires Overseas Private Investment Corporation initiatives to provide support to women entrepreneurs by expanding opportunities for women and maximizing employment opportunities for poor individuals.

The GSP provides a set of unilateral trade measures under which exporters in developing countries are either exempted from tariffs or subject to lower tariffs. The European Union GSP has three components: (i) the standard GSP agreement for all beneficiary nations, (ii) the GSP+ scheme that grants zero tariffs, and (iii) the Everything but Arms (EBA) arrangement specifically for least-developed economies. Both standard GSP and EBA provide for the withdrawal of preferences for the beneficiary developing countries in case of violations of international conventions, some of which address women's conditions.[7] The GSP+ defines stricter obligations and monitoring by providing for a deeper market access conditioned upon ratification of and compliance with several international conventions in human rights, labor rights, the environment, and good governance. Overall, the monitoring mechanism of the GSP+ suggests that, although some challenges persist in addressing discrimination and domestic violence against women, some countries have seen improvements with the creation of a large number of job opportunities for women along with the adoption of guidelines on gender equality, the launch of a gender equality council, the establishment of social networks connecting the relevant stakeholders, and the implementation of laws fighting violence against women (European Commission 2018).

Some governments have established government procurement schemes that award contracts for services only to companies guaranteeing compliance with the principle of equal pay for men and women (Harris Rimmer 2017). Other countries have adopted specific declarations, directives, resolutions, or agreements on trade and gender (box 3.2) (Monteiro 2018).

Gender-related provisions in preferential trade agreements

Preferential trade agreements (PTAs) are sometimes viewed as laboratories in which new types of provisions are negotiated to address pressing trade-related issues and challenges. As of July 2020, 80 PTAs, of which 69 are notified to the WTO and in force, refer explicitly to women and to gender-related issues. More than 250 agreements refer implicitly to gender issues, such as human rights, vulnerable groups, corporate social responsibility,[8] and social dimensions of sustainable development, including labor discrimination (Monteiro 2018). Despite increased explicit and implicit references to gender in PTAs, more effort is needed to gauge the effectiveness of these provisions in advancing women's economic empowerment.

Like most other types of provisions in PTAs, gender-related provisions vary greatly in terms of structure, location, language, and scope. Most gender-related provisions are couched in language that requires best efforts to be made. The most common type of gender-related provision in PTAs addresses cooperation on gender and gender-related issues, including labor discrimination and access to health and social policy. Some gender-related provisions are found in an increasing number of PTAs, but other provisions are included in only a single or a couple of, often recent, PTAs.

Although the number of PTAs with gender-related provisions has increased at a relatively slow pace, the last three years have witnessed a significant increase in the number of PTAs with gender-related provisions and in the average number of gender-related provisions included in a given agreement. The PTAs to which Chile is a party with Argentina, Brazil, and Uruguay and the amended PTAs negotiated by Canada with Chile and Israel include a chapter dedicated to trade and gender with the most detailed and comprehensive gender-related provisions to date (figure 3.1).

Gender provisions range from references to gender-related principles and international agreements to specific commitments on

Box 3.2 East African Community's Gender Equality, Equity, and Development Bill

The East African Legislative Assembly (EALA), established under the Treaty for the Establishment of the East African Community (EAC), passed in 2017 the EAC Gender Equality, Equity, and Development Bill. The legislation derives its mandate from Articles 121 and 122 of the EAC Treaty, which specify detailed commitments to promote women's empowerment, integration, and participation, including through appropriate legislation and other measures.

The main objective of the legislation is to advance gender equality and equity through the development, harmonization, implementation, and monitoring of gender-responsive legislation, policies, programs, and projects at national and regional levels as well as the elimination of all provisions, laws, and practices hindering or compromising the achievement of gender equality and equity. Besides provisions establishing principles of gender equality, it addresses 13 themes: legal and state obligations to protect human rights; media; education; health; power and decision making; economic empowerment; agriculture and food security; land rights; trade; peace and security; environmental management; extractive industries; and marginalized groups.

The trade-related provisions of the bill commit the parties to promote the equal participation of women and men in regional trade, taking into consideration gender dimensions and the right to personal safety when engaging in cross-border trade. The parties are further required to take all appropriate measures to enhance trade in the EAC, including by eliminating the gender and nontariff trade barriers through the adoption of appropriate regulations or guidelines and administrative practices that secure the rights of men and women engaged in cross-border trade and investment ventures.

The parties also have the obligation to review their trade policies to make them gender responsive and take steps to minimize the negative impacts of trade agreements. In addition, the parties made the commitments to ensure that women and men in the informal sector have equal access to financial resources, legal aid, and other resources on terms commensurate with their financial circumstances, and that women have equal access and rights to credit, capital, mortgages, and security.

domestic gender-related policy, corporate social responsibility, and cooperation (figure 3.2). A few of these provisions call for or require the adoption and effective implementation of gender-related policies. A few other provisions promote transparency and public awareness of domestic gender-related laws and policies. Some provisions specify that domestic programs aimed at supporting women, including support for women-owned firms or indigenous women, are exempted from the obligations related to government procurement or trade in services.

A couple of recent PTAs include a gender-related provision in the investment chapter explicitly specifying that a targeted discriminatory measure based on manifestly wrongful grounds, such as gender, breaches the obligation of fair and equitable treatment and full protection and security to the other party's investments and investors. A similar provision is found in a few recent bilateral investment treaties.[9]

A number of gender-related provisions, typically found in a chapter dedicated to trade and gender, establish institutional arrangements, such as the designation of a national contact point and establishment of a committee on trade and gender to discuss the agreement's commitments related to

Figure 3.1 Inclusion of gender-related provisions in PTAs is not recent

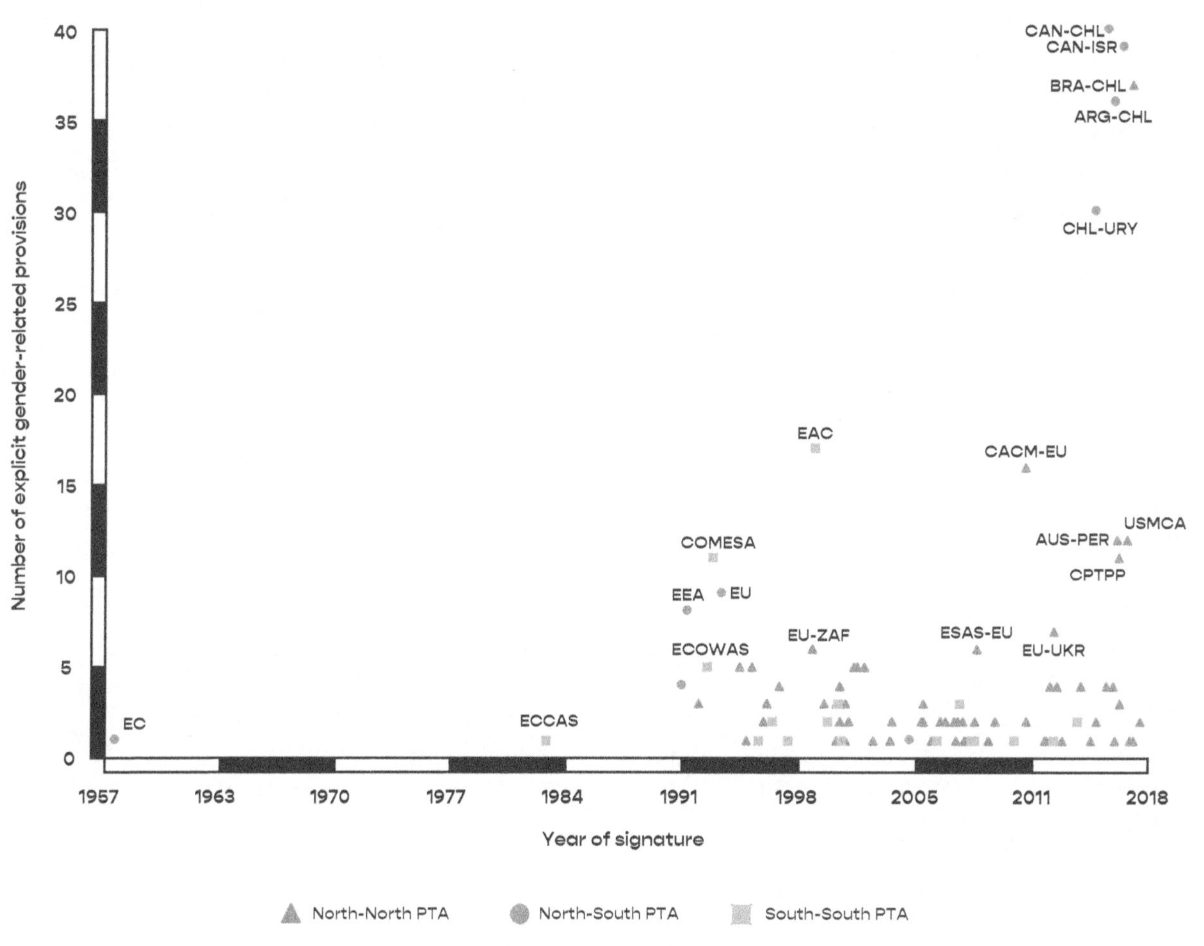

Source: Updated from Monteiro 2018.

Note: Analysis based on 572 preferential trade agreements (PTAs), including 305 agreements currently in force and notified to the World Trade Organization. Original and amended PTAs are analyzed separately. "North" is defined as high-income countries, whereas "South" is defined as middle- and low-income countries according to the World Bank's country classification. CACM = Central American Common Market; COMESA = Common Market for Eastern and Southern Africa; CPTPP = Comprehensive and Progressive Agreement for Trans-Pacific Partnership; EAC = East African Community; EC = European Communities; ECCAS = Economic Community of Central African States; ECOWAS = Economic Community of West African States; EEA = European Economic Area; ESAS = Eastern and Southern African States; EU = European Union; USMCA = United States-Mexico-Canada.

gender, including exchanging information on cooperation activities. Some PTAs establish consultation procedures to address any issue arising under the gender chapter. Most gender chapters are excluded from the PTA's dispute settlement chapter.

One important issue is to what extent gender-related provisions, in particular the most recent and comprehensive ones, are implemented. Although most PTAs with more comprehensive provisions have yet to enter into force (as of December 2019), one of the institutional arrangements foreseen is the review of the implementation of their respective gender chapter. For the time being, the effectiveness of gender-related provisions remains to be investigated, even though some anecdotal evidence suggests that some provisions are being effectively implemented.[10]

Figure 3.2 Main broad types of gender-related provisions in PTAs

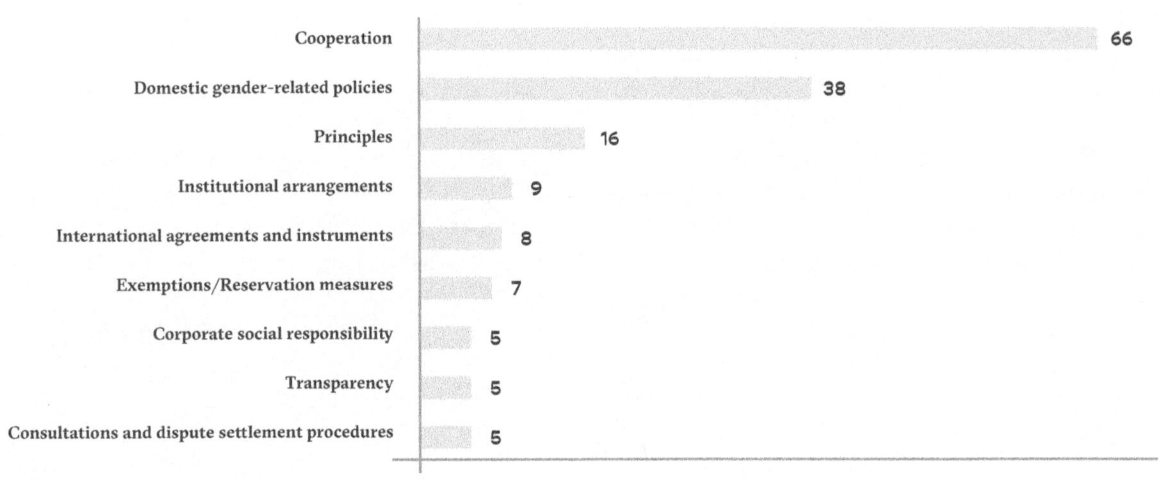

Source: Updated from Monteiro 2018.
Note: Analysis based on 572 preferential trade agreements (PTAs), including 305 agreements currently notified to the World Trade Organization.

Private sector gender initiatives

Women's economic empowerment cannot fully materialize without the engagement of the private sector. Some private sector companies, in particular some retailers, brands, and suppliers, have adopted voluntary gender-related initiatives. Although some initiatives incorporate women as an important target group, such as in the context of corporate social responsibility programs, others are specifically gender-focused.

Some initiatives promote women's access to training for skills development, health services, maternity benefits, education, leadership, and financial management. Other initiatives aim at awareness raising and policy development to address gender-based violence. Certain initiatives aim to enhance value captured by women working in smallholder productions. Some companies have also established lists of potential certified women-owned business suppliers with a view to diversifying their suppliers base (Schott 2017).

Some of these private sector–led initiatives are part of government partnerships or international initiatives.[11] For instance, the Women's Empowerment Principles, launched in 2013 by UN Women (the United Nations Entity for Gender Equality and the Empowerment of Women), encourage firms of all size to promote gender equality in the workplace, marketplace, and community. This international initiative complements other initiatives and instruments related to corporate social responsibility, such as the Organisation for Economic Co-operation and Development Guidelines for Multinational Enterprises providing multilaterally agreed nonbinding principles and standards for responsible business conduct, including the principle of gender nondiscrimination in the workplace. More recently, the International Trade Centre's "She Trades" initiative provides, among other things, business-to-business services for women with an online platform and application to connect potential buyers, investors, suppliers, and business support organizations. The initiative also fosters collaboration between business-support organizations, cooperatives, alliances, and private sector companies.

Gender, the World Bank, and the WTO

Both the World Bank and the WTO, through their different functions and activities, promote trade as a means to improve women's lives as traders, workers, and consumers. The WTO has been instrumental in promoting trade and development by keeping markets open for all, including women (Handley and Limão 2017; Larch et al. 2019). WTO agreements provide a rule-based, transparent, and predictable environment in which international trade can operate and expand. By creating a stable and predictable trading environment, the WTO protects women from the risks and uncertainty created by opaque and unpredictable trade policies. Although gender equality is not explicitly mentioned in WTO agreements, WTO rules help ensure that members interested in adopting policies to promote women's economic empowerment do so in a nondiscriminatory, open, and predictable trading environment (Acharya et al. 2019).

Several ongoing negotiations and joint initiatives on agriculture, trade in services, investment facilitation, e-commerce, and MSMEs established by WTO members are particularly relevant to women even though they are not specifically targeted toward women. The relevance of these discussions and negotiations for women stems from the fact that women are highly represented as workers and traders in specific sectors, types of firms, or modes of transaction.

Although work opportunities for women in manufacturing and especially services have increased, women continue to be the main workforce in agriculture in many developing countries. Yet agricultural goods, where female consumers or traders tend to be overrepresented, continue to be subject to high tariffs and other trade restrictions. WTO members committed in the Nairobi Decision on Export Competition to phase out agricultural export subsidies and restrict agricultural export credits that distort the markets. This was an important step toward better-functioning international and domestic markets. In an effort to take further steps in this direction, WTO members are currently negotiating commitments on domestic support with a view to reduce trade distortions in agricultural trade that can inhibit investment in productivity and resilience.

Because women entrepreneurs in services are overwhelmingly small business owners and many women are employed in service activities, the prospect of reduced regulatory compliance costs can be an especially important determinant of the competitiveness and growth prospects of female-led firms. Under the Joint Ministerial Statement Initiative on Domestic Services Regulation, participating WTO members have been holding discussions aimed at strengthening General Agreement on Trade in Services disciplines on domestic regulation relating to licensing, qualification requirements and procedures, and technical standards. Some of the proposals put forward cover how to ensure that domestic regulations do not discriminate on the basis of gender.[12]

Multinational enterprises can be instrumental in creating expanded job opportunities for women, particularly in labor-intensive, export-oriented sectors. Under the Joint Ministerial Statement Initiative on Investment Facilitation for Development, some WTO members are pursuing discussions to enhance understanding of the growing links between trade and investment and how investment serves as a catalyst for trade.

Although women still tend to have less access to digital technologies than men, the rise of these technologies promises to help women traders and consumers improve their access to trade. The WTO Work Program on Electronic Commerce has established a framework to examine all trade-related issues relating to global e-commerce, including those relating to the development of the infrastructure for e-commerce. More recently, under the Joint Statement Initiative on Electronic Commerce, some WTO members are discussing textual proposals on customs duties on electronic transmissions, flow of information, privacy, cybersecurity, and telecommunications.

Because women traders tend to be predominantly owners or managers of MSMEs, connecting small and medium-sized firms to international markets can help support economic transformation of an economy in a way that is gender inclusive. Under the Joint Statement Initiative on MSMEs, some WTO members committed to discuss and identify "horizontal and nondiscriminatory solutions" to improve the participation of MSMEs in international trade. The Informal Dialogue on MSMEs seeks to develop solutions that would apply to all companies (but would benefit MSMEs the most) while taking into account the specific needs of developing countries.

Although the issue of women and trade is not formally in the WTO agenda, in December 2017, on the margins of the 11th WTO Ministerial Conference, 118 WTO members and observers launched the Buenos Aires Declaration on Trade and Women's Economic Empowerment. As of December 2019, 123 governments, representing more than 75 percent of world trade, have signed the Declaration. The Buenos Aires Declaration provides a platform to better understand the links between trade and women's economic empowerment to make trade more inclusive. The Declaration specifically identifies two existing WTO instruments that can be used to make trade more inclusive for this purpose—the Trade Policy Review mechanism (box 3.3) and the Aid for Trade initiative (box 3.4).

The 2017–19 WTO Trade and Gender Action Plan was adopted to focus on four main objectives: raising awareness of the links between trade and gender, supporting WTO members' activities in this area, analyzing and collecting new data on the impact of trade measures on gender issues, and providing training for government officials and WTO Secretariat staff. As part of the WTO Trade and Gender Action Plan, the WTO also launched a training program on the nexus between trade and women's economic empowerment in the context of WTO rules and the different perspectives of members as to how they can be translated into trade policies.[13]

The World Bank engagement in trade and gender ranges from global and country-specific analytical work, technical assistance, and capacity building aiming at strengthening the existing knowledge on the links between trade and gender equality to more practically assisting developing countries in their efforts to support women traders and to ensure that women gain from trade. A critical component of the World Bank's work is collecting and analyzing new data from a gender perspective, which will help to reveal how men and women are differently affected by trade policies and their implementation. The World Bank is also integrating gender into a variety of operational trade-related projects such as supporting small-scale female traders in East and West Africa, increasing trade finance to women-owned SMEs, and supporting women's trade networks in Pakistan.

Credit: © SmartPhotoLab/ Shutterstock.com. Used with permission; further permission required for reuse.

Under the World Trade Organization (WTO) Trade Policy Review (TPR) mechanism, WTO members conduct periodic collective assessments of each member's trade policies. These transparency exercises promote greater understanding of members' trade policies, including some measures that explicitly promote women's economic empowerment. An increasing number of TPR reports refers to trade policies, practices, or measures targeting women's economic empowerment. In particular, 77 TPRs carried out between 2014 and 2018, representing almost 70 percent of all TPRs undertaken in that period, reported at least one trade policy supporting women's economic empowerment (figure B3.3.1). The analysis of these TPRs reveals three main areas of support: (i) private sector, including micro, small, and medium enterprises (MSMEs); (ii) agriculture and fisheries; and (iii) government procurement.

Figure B3.3.1 The number of Trade Policy Review reports with gender policy has increased

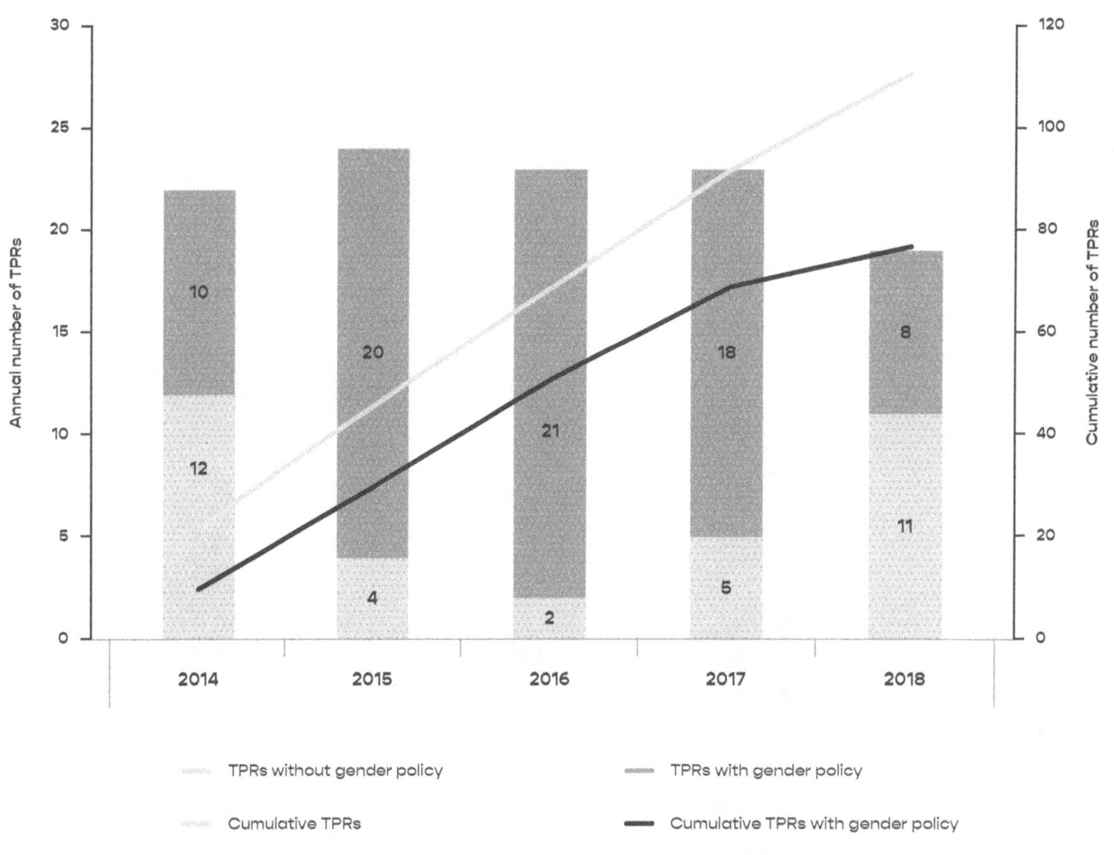

Source: der Boghossian 2019b.
Note: The number of Trade Policy Reviews (TPRs) corresponds to the number of World Trade Organization members under review that included trade policies supporting women's empowerment in their respective World Trade Organization Secretariat reports, government reports, and question-and-answer sessions.

Private sector

Several governments have established financial and nonfinancial incentives to promote women-owned MSMEs in particular, and more generally the private sector. Whereas some governments have set up support programs for MSMEs with specific funding quotas for female-owned firms, others have launched funds dedicated only to women-owned companies, mostly start-ups. These financial schemes are often complemented by other types of assistance schemes for women-owned MSMEs, such as marketing assistance and training on business and financial management. In parallel, some governments have created financial incentives for firms, including export-oriented ones, to hire unemployed women or recruit and retain women who have been on career breaks.

Agriculture and fisheries

Some governments have put in place measures to support women's economic empowerment in the agricultural and fisheries sector. Some programs establish financial support schemes for women operating in the agricultural sector, including the agri-food business, and the small-scale fisheries sector. Other programs provide technical assistance and training for women farmers and fisherwomen with the objective of increasing productivity and production, and in some cases complying with sanitary and phytosanitary requirements. Some programs foresee the provision of inputs, such as fertilizer, to women farmers in case of emergency.

Government procurement

Government procurement policies are used by some governments to promote women-owned MSMEs and gender equality. Some government procurement schemes establish a certain percentage of designated government procurement contracts or total spending for women-owned small businesses, in some cases targeted only at rural women. Other government procurement policies explicitly prohibit gender-based discrimination in the allocation of procurement contracts and have put in place schemes that give preference to companies implementing gender equality or wage equality policies.

Box 3.4 Women's economic empowerment in Aid for Trade

The Aid for Trade initiative, led by the World Trade Organization (WTO) and of which the World Bank is a partner, supports developing and least-developed countries in building their trade capacity and increasing their exports by addressing four key areas: (i) trade policy and regulations, (ii) economic infrastructure, (iii) building productive capacity, and (iv) trade-related adjustment.

Gender equality has been an intrinsic part of the Aid for Trade initiative since its inception in 2006. At its launch, the WTO Aid for Trade Task Force established the principle of incorporating the gender perspective into Aid for Trade, along with the commitment to harmonize efforts on cross-cutting issues, such as gender equality. Over the years, donors and partner countries have gradually and increasingly integrated gender into their Aid for Trade objectives (figure B3.4.1). The 2019 Aid for Trade monitoring and evaluation exercise reveals that most donors' Aid for Trade strategies and partner countries' national or regional development strategies seek to promote women's economic empowerment.

Box 3.4, continued

Figure B3.4.1 Promotion of women's economic empowerment is increasingly part of Aid for Trade objectives

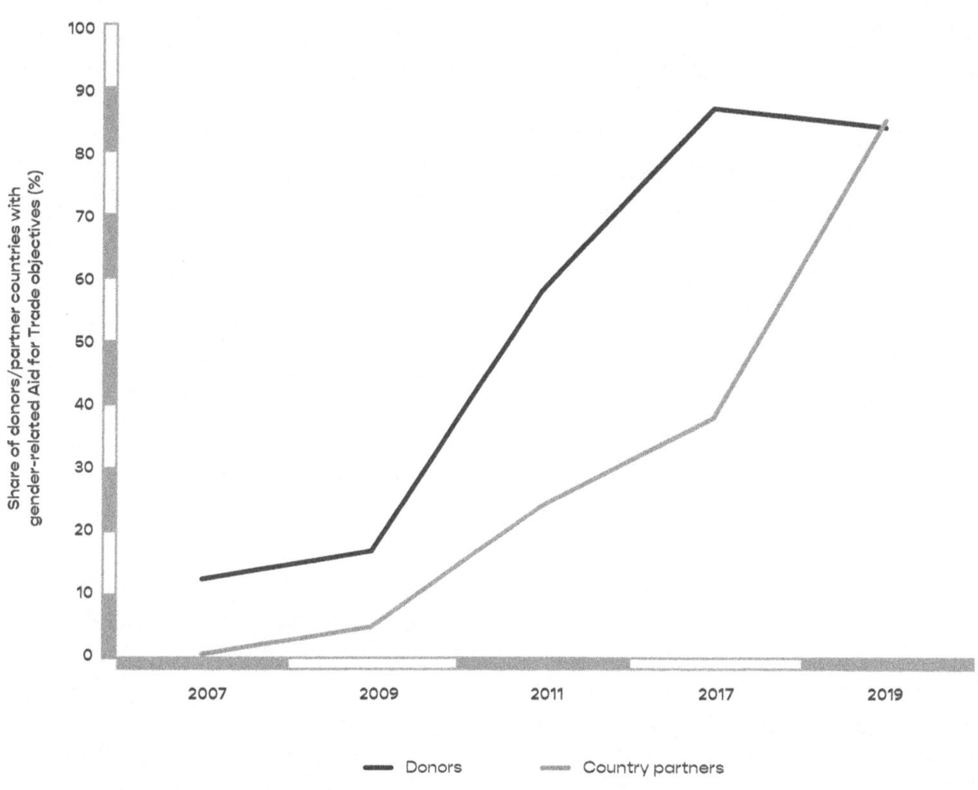

Source: der Boghossian 2019a, based on Aid for Trade monitoring exercises by the Organisation for Economic Co-operation and Development and the World Trade Organization.

Although the objectives and strategies formulated by donors and partner countries have evolved over the 12 years of existence of the Aid for Trade initiative, the main target group of gender-related Aid for Trade strategies remains women entrepreneurs, with a particular focus on women traders and farmers. According to the 2019 Aid for Trade monitoring and evaluation exercise, donors and partner countries consider that Aid for Trade programs can contribute to women's economic empowerment by providing access to finance, improving access to information for women, and supporting the growth and economic development of women, among other things (figure B3.4.2). In that context, both donors and country partners consider that education and training, building productive capacity, and developing business support services and banking and financial services are some of the Aid for Trade financing forms that can best support women's economic empowerment.

Box 3.4, continued

Figure B3.4.2 Donors and partner countries consider Aid for Trade's contribution to women's economic empowerment through different channels

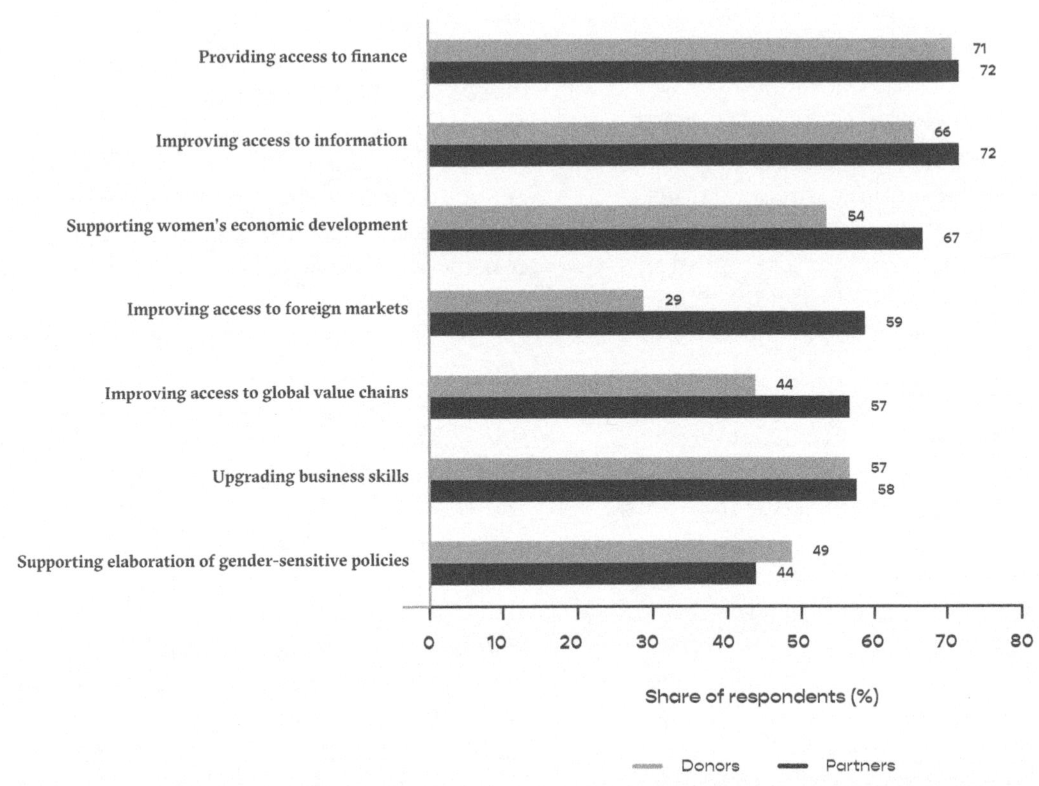

Source: der Boghossian 2019a, based on Aid for Trade monitoring exercises by the Organisation for Economic Co-operation and Development and the World Trade Organization.
Note: The survey question reads as follows: "How best can Aid for Trade make a contribution to women's economic empowerment?"

Although gender equality is reflected in the objective of many Aid for Trade strategies, it has yet to be fully integrated in the donors' and partner countries' Aid for Trade priorities. As a result, most gender-related Aid for Trade financial flows are allocated to programs and projects in which gender equality is only one of the cooperation areas being addressed.

The assessment of the impact of Aid for Trade on women's economic empowerment remains particularly challenging for non-gender-specific Aid for Trade projects. So far, only case studies provide information on the tangible results delivered by gender-related Aid for Trade projects. For instance, the Kalangala Infrastructure Services and Renewables Project was found to have a positive impact on women's livelihoods in Uganda by providing women with electricity and creating job opportunities. Similarly, a capacity-building and standards-compliance project on litchi food safety was found to have increased litchi exports to the European market from Madagascar, where women represent a large segment of the workforce in that industry.

Although these case studies provide important insights, several donors have recognized the need for a more systemic approach in evaluating the impact of Aid for Trade on women's economic empowerment. In that context, and more recently, major donors are in the process of developing tools and indicators to assess quantitatively and qualitatively the impact of their gender-related Aid for Trade activities on women's economic empowerment.

Steps to further inclusiveness

There is increasing awareness that trade can help gender equality and that governments, business, and international organizations can collectively advance a gender-inclusive trade agenda. This volume is a recognition that more effort is needed to address the relationship between trade and gender.

Policies and initiatives that allow women to tap into the benefits from trade require an examination of the actions taken to date and whether they have been effective in addressing these inequalities. The absence of gender-related trade data has hindered the ability of policy makers to identify the differential impacts trade policy may have on women and men. Both the World Bank and WTO now lead efforts to address shortcomings in data.

A critical component of the World Bank's work is collecting and analyzing data from a gender perspective, which will help to clarify how men and women are differently affected by trade policies and their implementation. In preparation for this joint report, the World Bank launched the Gender Disaggregated Labor Database (GDLD) with information at the individual level on employment and wages by skill, age, and other individual characteristics. Other relevant sex-disaggregated data and gender statistics covering demography, education, health, economic opportunities, public life and decision making, and agency are available at the World Bank's Gender Data Portal.[14]

One of the functions of the WTO is to collect, assess, and disseminate information about members' trade policies, including those related to women. The Trade Policy Review mechanism and the notifications that members are required to make about their own laws and policies, including PTAs, are important sources of information on gender-related trade policies.[15] In the context of this report, a database mapping all gender-related provisions in PTAs has been created and analyzed.

More generally, the development of gender-related trade statistics is done in collaboration with statistical agencies and other government offices as well as other international organizations, including the World Bank and the WTO.[16] Efforts to collect and publish gender data are of utmost importance and will enable future research and policy making to consider the impact of trade on gender equality.

Going forward, international institutions can support trade and gender equality through the maintenance and strengthening of open, rules-based, and transparent trade. Ongoing negotiations and initiatives by the World Bank and WTO related to services, agriculture, e-commerce, and MSMEs could further empower women in the world economy. In addition, impact evaluations of international assistance can provide feedback on the kinds of interventions that are most effective in promoting gender equality in trade. Further analysis and technical assistance should continue to take advantage of increasing access to sex-disaggregated data to identify priority sectors, skills, and markets in which women have a comparative advantage.

Notes

1 These measures include harmonization, equivalence, and mutual recognition of technical regulations and standards; establishment or improvement of testing, certification, and accreditation facilities; transparency and information dissemination of the technical requirements; public-private partnerships as well as cooperation between importers and producers/exporters.

2 Other standards might reflect a workplace culture not adapted to the needs of women. Other standards may also be based on insufficient data on the different reactions between women and men (UNECE 2018).

3 The World Health Organization Global Code of Practice on the International Recruitment of Health Personnel calls on the organization's member states to put in place bilateral, regional, or multilateral arrangements to promote cooperation and coordination in the area of international recruitment. For instance, in Finland, the Recruitment of Foreign Health and Social Care Professionals to Finland (Mediko), launched in 2008, has provided counseling to more than 80 doctors, mainly from the Russian Federation, wishing to practice in Finland. Mediko has also recruited more than 150 Spanish nurses who attended Finnish language courses in Spain. Cooperation between Finnish training institutions and those in Estonia, Russia, and Spain also plays an important role (Dumont and Lafortune 2017).

4 The TFA, which entered into effect in 2017, aims to promote trade facilitation through improved transparency, simplified and automated procedures, coordinated border management, and consultative mechanisms (WTO 2015).

5 The World Bank has, under the Trade Facilitation Support Program (TFSP), initiated a global survey to identify specific challenges faced by women cross-border traders at the firm level with the aim of minimizing the global data gap on the nature of barriers that women cross-border traders face.

6 The United Nations Industrial Development Organization (UNIDO) has developed a Trade and Gender Toolbox that provides a systematic framework to assess the potential impact of trade reforms on women and gender equality.

7 These international conventions include the United Nations Convention on the Elimination of All Forms of Discrimination Against Women (CEDAW), the International Covenant on Economic, Social, and Cultural Rights (ICESCR), and the International Labour Organization Conventions 100 and 111 (Equal Remuneration Convention and Anti-discrimination Convention).

8 Corporate social responsibility refers to the responsibility of companies for the effects of their activities on society and the environment at large.

9 The analysis is based on the review of 2,824 bilateral investment treaties, whose text is available in the United Nations Conference on Trade and Development (UNCTAD) International Investment Agreements-Investment Policy Hub (https://investmentpolicy.unctad.org/international-investment-agreements). A gender provision is found only in the agreements between Belarus and India, Brazil and Guyana, Moldova and the United Arab Emirates, and Rwanda and the United Arab Emirates. As with PTAs, several bilateral investment treaties also include provisions, often in the preamble, referring potentially and implicitly to gender-related issues, such as the protection of human rights, (internationally recognized) labor rights and vulnerable groups, and the promotion of corporate social responsibility, which often encompass the principles of gender equality and nondiscrimination on gender grounds.

10 For instance, in the context of the PTA between Canada and Colombia, a research project entitled "Improving the Capacity to Act on Gender Equality in Colombia: A Fresh Look at the Coffee Export Sector," was funded by the government of Canada (Canada-Americas Trade-Related Technical Assistance Fund/CATRA).

11 More recently, some private sector companies have been promoting the adoption of a plurilateral initiative to combat gender discrimination (Insider Interview 2019).

12 For more information, see https://www.wto.org/english/news_e/news17_e/serv_11jul17_e.html.

13 Several training programs on women and trade have been developed and complement WTO's activities. For instance, UNCTAD provides online training on the relationship between trade and trade policy and gender equality. In collaboration with the International Trade Centre, UNCTAD also set up a "Gender and Trade Executive Training Seminar" examining the interplay of trade, gender, and sustainable development. Other relevant international and regional cooperation initiatives are aimed at developing production capacity, upgrading

the technology of small firms, improving market access, enhancing trade facilitation, and promoting access to trade finance. Many international and regional organizations, including the International Trade Centre and UNCTAD, provide trade capacity building to enhance the ability of developing and least-developed countries to participate in international trade. More recently, the World Bank and UPS Corporate announced a new partnership to provide e-learning modules on different e-commerce topics to help women-owned and women-led SMEs in Middle East and North African countries seeking to expand their businesses across borders.

14 For more information on the Gender Data Portal, see http://datatopics.worldbank.org/gender/home.

15 For more information on the Integrated Trade Intelligence Portal, see http://i-tip.wto.org and https://www.wto.org/tpr.

16 For instance, many international organizations, such as the International Labour Organization, the Food and Agriculture Organization of the United Nations, the Organisation for Economic Co-operation and Development, the United Nations Economic and Social Commission for Asia and the Pacific, and the World Intellectual Property Organization, are collecting and publishing gender-related data.

References

Acharya R., O. Falgueras Alamo, S. Mohamed Thabit Al-Battashi, A. der Boghossian, N. Ghei, T. Parcero Herrera, L. A. Jackson, U. Kask, C. Locatelli, G. Marceau, I.-V. Motoc, A. C. Müller, N. Neufeld, S. Padilla, J. Pardo de Léon, S. Perantakou, N. Sporysheva, and C. Wolff. 2019. "Trade and Women—Opportunities for Women in the Framework of the World Trade Organization." *Journal of International Economic Law* 22 (3): 323–54.

Attanasio, O., A. Kugler, and C. Meghir. 2011. "Subsidizing Vocational Training for Disadvantaged Youth in Colombia: Evidence from a Randomized Trial." *American Economic Journal: Applied Economics* 3 (3): 188–220.

Bacchetta, M., E. Milet, and J.-A. Monteiro, eds. 2019. *Making Globalization More Inclusive: Lessons from Experience with Adjustment Policies*. Geneva: World Trade Organization.

Bekh, O. 2014. "Training and Support for Women's Entrepreneurship." ETF Working Paper, European Training Foundation, Turin.

Card, D., J. Kluve, and A. Weber. 2018. "What Works? A Meta Analysis of Recent Active Labor Market Program Evaluations." *Journal of the European Economic Association* 16 (3): 894–931.

CEPAL (Comisión Económica para América Latina y el Caribe). 2016. "Women's Participation in Chile's Mining Sector Increases Steadily." *Notes for Equality* No. 19, CEPAL, Santiago de Chile. https://oig.cepal.org/sites/default/files/nota_de_igualdad_19_mujeres_en_la_mineria_ing_revised.pdf.

Cho, J., and T. Kwon. 2010. "Affirmative Action and Corporate Compliance in South Korea." *Feminist Economics* 16 (2): 111–39.

Coche I., B. Kotschwar, and J. M. Salazar-Xirinachs. 2006. "Gender Issues in Trade Policy-Making." OAS Trade Series, Organization of American States, Washington DC.

Dasgupta, N., and T. C. Dennehy. 2017. "Female Peer Mentors Early in College Increase Women's Positive Academic Experiences and Retention in Engineering." *Proceedings of the National Academy of Sciences* 114 (23): 5964–69.

Dasgupta, N., and J. G. Stout. 2014. "Girls and Women in Science, Technology, Engineering, and Mathematics: STEMing the Tide and Broadening Participation in STEM Careers." *Policy Insights from the Behavioral and Brain Sciences* 1 (1): 21–29.

Del Boca, D. 2015. "The Impact of Child Care Costs and Availability on Mothers' Labor Supply." ImPRovE Working Paper No. 15/04, Herman Deleeck Centre for Social Policy, University of Antwerp.

Department of Finance, Canada. 2019. *Gender Report Budget 2019*. Ottawa: Government of Canada.

der Boghossian, A. 2019a. "Women's Economic Empowerment: An Inherent Part of Aid for Trade." WTO Staff Working Paper No. ERSD-2019-08, World Trade Organization, Geneva.

———. 2019b. "Trade Policies Supporting Women's Economic Empowerment: Trends in WTO Members." WTO Staff Working Paper No. ERSD-2019-07, World Trade Organization, Geneva.

DiCaprio, A. Y. Yao, and R. Simms. 2017. "Women and Trade: Gender's Impact on Trade Finance and Fintech." ADBI Working Paper Series No. 797, Asian Development Bank, Manila.

Dumont, J.-C., and G. Lafortune. 2017. "International Migration of Doctors and Nurses to OECD Countries: Recent Trends and Policy Implications." In *Health Employment and Economic Growth: An Evidence Base*, edited by J. Buchan, I. S. Dhillon, and J. Campbell, 81–118. Geneva: World Health Organization.

Escudero, V., J. Kluve, E. López Mourelo, and C. Pignatti. 2019. "Active Labour Market Programmes in Latin America and the Caribbean: Evidence from a Meta-analysis." *Journal of Development Studies* 55 (12): 2644–61.

European Commission. 2018. "Report on the Generalised Scheme of Preferences Covering the Period 2016–2017." Report from the Commission to the European Parliament and the Council, European Commission, Brussels.

Frohmann, A. 2017. "Gender Equality and Trade Policy." Working Paper No. 24/2017, World Trade Institute, Bern.

Ghose, D. 2019. "Higher Education Response to India's IT Boom: Did State Governments Play a Role?" In *Making Globalization More Inclusive: Lessons from Experience with Adjustment Policies*, edited by M. Bacchetta, E. Milet, and J.-A. Monteiro, 139–61. Geneva: World Trade Organization.

Goldberg, P. K., and N. Pavcnik. 2003. "The Response of the Informal Sector to Trade Liberalization." *Journal of Development Economics* 72 (2): 463–96.

Handley, K., and N. Limão. 2017. "Policy Uncertainty, Trade, and Welfare: Theory and Evidence for China and the United States." *American Economic Review* 107 (9): 2731–83.

Harris Rimmer, S. 2017. *Gender-Smart Procurement Policies for Driving Change*. London: Chatham House.

Herz, B. K., and G. B. Sperling. 2004. *What Works in Girls' Education: Evidence and Policies from the Developing World*. New York: Council on Foreign Relations.

ILO (International Labour Organization) 2013. *Women and Men in the Informal Economy: A Statistical Picture*. Geneva: ILO.

IMF (International Monetary Fund), World Bank, and WTO (World Trade Organization). 2017. "Making Trade an Engine of Growth for All: The Case for Trade and for Policies to Facilitate Adjustment." Prepared for discussion at the G20 Sherpas, March 23–24, Frankfurt.

Insider Interview. 2019. "UPS Pushes WTO Plurilateral Initiative to Combat Gender Discrimination." *World Trade Online*, August 28, 2019, https://insidetrade.com/daily-news/ups-pushes-wto-plurilateral-initiative-combat-gender-discrimination.

Jenik, I. 2017. "Regulatory Sandboxes: Potential for Financial Inclusion?" *CGAP* (blog), August 17, 2017, https://www.cgap.org/blog/regulatory-sandboxes-potential-financial-inclusion.

Khandker, S., M. Pitt, and N. Fuwa. 2013. "Subsidy to Promote Girls Secondary Education: The Female Stipend Program in Bangladesh." MPRA Paper 23688, University Library of Munich, Munich. https://mpra.ub.uni-muenchen.de/23688/1/MPRA_paper_23688.pdf.

Larch, M., J.-A. Monteiro, R. Piermartini, and Y. Yotov. 2019. "On the Effects of GATT/WTO Membership on Trade: They Are Positive and Large after All." CESifo Working Paper No. 7721, Center for Economic Studies, Munich.

Lesser, C., and E. Moisé-Leeman. 2009. "Informal Cross-Border Trade and Trade Facilitation Reform in Sub-Saharan

Africa." OECD Trade Policy Working Paper No. 86, Organisation for Economic Co-operation and Development.

Lima, V., V. Ponczek, and G. Ulyssea. 2019. "Enforcement of Labour Regulation and the Labour Market Effects of Trade: Evidence from Brazil." In *Making Globalization More Inclusive: Lessons from Experience with Adjustment Policies*, edited by M. Bacchetta, E. Milet, and J.-A. Monteiro, 71–85. Geneva: World Trade Organization.

Monteiro, J.-A. 2018. "Gender-Related Provisions in Regional Trade Agreements." WTO Staff Working Paper No. ERSD-2018-15, World Trade Organization, Geneva.

Muralidharan, K., and N. Prakash. 2013. "Cycling to School: Increasing Secondary School Enrollment for Girls in India." NBER Working Paper No. 19305, National Bureau of Economic Research, Cambridge MA.

Omiunu, O. G. 2019. "E-Literacy-Adoption Model and Performance of Women-Owned SMEs in Southwestern Nigeria." *Journal of Global Entrepreneurship Research* 9 (26): 1–19.

Paez, L., S. Karingi, M. Kimenyi, and M. Paulos. 2010. "A Decade (2000–2010) of African-U.S. Trade under the African Growth Opportunities Act (AGOA): Challenges, Opportunities and a Framework for Post AGOA Engagement." African Economic Conference Article, African Development Bank Group, Abidjan.

Sachetti, F. C., G. Diaz Langou, F. Filgueira, M. Thomas, S. Gammage, C. Currie, M. Beneke de Sanfeliú, A. Hunt, and R. Hayashi. 2019. "A Gendered Perspective on Changing Demographics: Implications for Labor, Financial and Digital Equity." Policy Brief Prepared for Think 20 Japan 2019, T20, Tokyo.

Sansonetti, S. 2016. "Assessment of the European Globalisation Adjustment Fund from a Gender Equality Perspective." Study for the FEMM Committee, European Commission, Brussels.

Sauvé, P. 2019. "Gendered Perspectives on Services Trade and Investment." Unpublished manuscript, World Bank Group, Washington, DC.

Schott, L. 2017. *Private Sector Engagement with Women's Economic Empowerment: Lessons Learned from Years of Practice*. Oxford: Saïd Business School, University of Oxford.

Schultz, T. P. 2004. "School Subsidies for the Poor: Evaluating the Mexican Progresa Poverty Program." *Journal of Development Economics* 74 (1): 199–250.

Suominen, K. 2018. "Women-Led Firms on the Web: Challenges and Solutions." ICTSD Issue Paper, International Centre for Trade and Sustainable Development, Geneva.

Taylor, L. L., and J. Dar. 2015. "Fairer Trade, Removing Gender Bias in US Import Taxes." *The Takeaway* 6 (3): 1–4.

Townson, M., and K. Hayes. 2007. *Women and the Employment Insurance Program*. Toronto: Canadian Centre for Policy Alternatives.

UNECE (United Nations Economic Commission for Europe). 2018. *Recommendations on Regulatory Cooperation and Standardization Policies*. Geneva: UNECE.

Viilup, E. 2015. "The EU's Trade Policy: From Gender-Blind to Gender-Sensitive?" Policy Note, European Parliament, Brussels.

Vijaya, R. 2007. "Trade, Job Losses and Gender: A Policy Perspective." *Forum for Social Economics* 36 (2): 73–85.

von Hagen, M. 2015. "Trade and Gender—Exploring a Reciprocal Relationship: Approaches to Mitigate and Measure Gender-Related Trade Impacts." Deutsche Gesellschaft für Internationale Zusammenarbeit, Bonn.

World Bank. 2012. "Soft Skills or Hard Cash? What Works for Female Employment in Jordan?" Working Paper, World Bank Group, Washington, DC.

WTO (World Trade Organization). 2014. "Financial Inclusion and the GATS: Barriers to Financial Inclusion and Trade in Services." Note by the Secretariat—Committee on Trade in Financial Services, S/FIN/W/88, November 14, WTO, Geneva.

———. 2015. *World Trade Report 2015: Speeding Up Trade: Benefits and Challenges of Implementing the WTO Trade Facilitation Agreement*. Geneva: WTO.

———. 2016. "Financial Inclusion and the GATS: Barriers to Financial Inclusion and Trade in Services." Note by the Secretariat—Committee on Trade in Financial Services, S/FIN/W/88/Add.1, June 13, WTO, Geneva.

———. 2017. *World Trade Report 2017: Trade, Technology and Jobs*. Geneva: WTO.

———. 2018. *World Trade Report 2018: The Future of World Trade: How Digital Technologies Are Transforming Global Commerce*. Geneva: WTO.

———. 2019. *World Trade Report 2019: The Future of Services Trade*. Geneva: WTO.

ECO-AUDIT
Environmental Benefits Statement

The World Bank Group is committed to reducing its environmental footprint. In support of this commitment, we leverage electronic publishing options and print-on-demand technology, which is located in regional hubs worldwide. Together, these initiatives enable print runs to be lowered and shipping distances decreased, resulting in reduced paper consumption, chemical use, greenhouse gas emissions, and waste.

We follow the recommended standards for paper use set by the Green Press Initiative. The majority of our books are printed on Forest Stewardship Council (FSC)–certified paper, with nearly all containing 50–100 percent recycled content. The recycled fiber in our book paper is either unbleached or bleached using totally chlorine-free (TCF), processed chlorine–free (PCF), or enhanced elemental chlorine–free (EECF) processes.

More information about the Bank's environmental philosophy can be found at http://www.worldbank.org/corporateresponsibility.